The River That Isn't
A Tale of Survival and Prosperity
River Bourgeois, Cape Breton
1714–1994

Gervais (Garvie) Samson

Claudine (Fougere) Laforce, Editor

Writing , Research and Publishing: Gervais (Garvie) Samson

Editing and Layout: Claudine Laforce Communications, Dartmouth

Cover Design: Napier Graphic Design, Halifax
Cover Photo: The "Tyler" courtesy of Jack and Ida LeVesconte

Canadian Cataloguing in Publication Data
Samson, Garvie, 1937–
The River That Isn't

ISBN 0-9699105-0-9

1. River Bourgeois (N.S.) — History, Pictorial work. I. Title.
FC2349.R58S36 1994 971.6'98'00222 C94-950279-0
F1039.5.R58S36 1994
Reprint 1995

Table of Contents

Forward

Any book about River Bourgeois is bound to be of great interest. This is one of the oldest and most enduring communities in Cape Breton and the present-day inhabitants of it carry with them not only the memories, but the many good, solid attitudes of other times. I am absolutely delighted that Garvie Samson has taken it on himself to write this book and I hope it will get the audience it deserves.

Farley Mowat
October 31, 1994

Preface

This Work is a study of the people and community of River Bourgeois since it was first settled in the early 1700s. It is the result of extensive research, interviews, and the accumulation of documentation and photographs during the last 10 years. Hopefully you will enjoy learning about the people of the River and the surrounding communities who worked together to survive cold, famine and hunger, to leave us with a legacy worth preserving.

You will note that frequently, members of the same family spell their family names differently. For example, my father spelled his surname–Sampson, with a "p", while the "p" is omitted in mine. The reason is that as men sought employment outside the River, their original names–Bourque, Sampson, Paté and LeBlanc–were considered to be degrading. Therefore, before they went for job interviews, they changed their names to an English version. When servicemen enlisted, often the English versions of their names were used. Because of the legalities in changing to their correct name, it was rarely done and the English version was adopted.

River Bourgeois does not have a river, but rather two sheltered harbours which are filled and emptied with the changing tides. The current at these narrow entrances flows so swiftly that a mariner approaching the entrances would assume it was a river; therefore the title,*The River that Isn't*.

As for the name *Bourgeois*, listed in earlier documents as *Bourgoise,* there are two theories. The first is that it was so called because of the many merchants, believed to be middle class, who established here. This does not fit because the name was used before the merchants arrived. The second theory, is that it comes from an Indian word *Nabigwonchek,* meaning a *brig or ship's place*. The latter theory I believe to be more interesting.

I wish to express my sincere appreciation to Claudine (Fougere) Laforce, daughter of Russell and Rita Fougere, who has worked on this project with such diligence, interest and enthusiasm.

Garvie

Garvie Samson

This Work is dedicated to my parents
James and Theresa Sampson

Acknowledgements

During the last ten years, numerous people have provided information and photographs used in this Work. The following list includes most of the contributors and I sincerely apologize for anyone I may have inadvertently omitted. Out of respect, we have placed the names of those who died since this project began in boldface.

Delta Babin, Mary Bona, Joseph and Margaret Bouchard, Robert (Bobbie) Boucher, Colleen Bouchie, Kenneth Bouchie, Margaret Rachel Bouchie, Kate Boudreau, Mary (Mathilda) Boudreau, George and Catherine Boudreau, Lucille and Alfred (Buddie) Boudreau, Ephrem Boudreau, **Kate Boudreau,** Ina and **Marshall Bourinot**, Adrian Bourque, **Claude Bourque,** Ernie and Margaret Bourque, Gilbert and Patricia (Mann) Bourque, Blaise and Deirdre Boyd, Valerie Boyd, Anthony (Delore) and **Hilda Burke**, Alfred and **Maude Burke,** Austin and Gladys Burke, Charlie and Angela Burke, Gerald Burke, Herman Burke, Hilda (à Joe) Burke, Lawrence Burke, Sr. Lola Burke, Marlaine Burke, Peter Burke, Richard J. Burke, Roderick Burke, Sam Burke, Victor and Evelyn Burke, Leona Campbell, **Eva (LeVesconte) Clare,** Ann Clow, Madeline Cook, David R. Cumby, Estwood and Margaret Davidson, George and Martha DeRoche, Mariah Dewolfe, Arthur and Margaret Digout, Francis Digout, Fred and Thérese Digout, Mary Emma Digout, George and Sharon Digout, **Peter Digout,** Sarah Digout, Arthur P. Doary, Fred and Evangeline (Geline) Doary, Mary Ellen Donahoe, Sr. Eugenie Doucett, Howard Doucett, Allen Dunlop, Gertrude Elliott, Mary LaVache Etienne, Robert (Bun) Foley, Carmen Fougere, Evelyn Fougere, Joseph Fougere, Leo Fougere, Hubert and Marguerite Fougere, Mimi Fougere, Rennie Fougere, Russell and Rita Fougere, Laura Gillen, Gordon Gillis, Robert and Lina Gordon, Valerie Goyetche, Genevieve Grimes, Rev. Regis Halloran, Margaret Heidecker, Stella Hinds, **Harriette (Hattie) Johnson,** Vincent Kendall, Walter Kendall, Elmer King, Charlie Kyte, Anthony and Beatrice Landry, Celeste Anne Landry, Douglas and Eva Landry, Rita and **John L. Landry**, Morris and Lucille Landry, Clarence and Elsie LeBlanc, Fred and Charlotte LeBlanc, Peter LeBlanc, Yves Leclerc, John (Jack) and Ada LeVesconte, John LeVesconte, Allen MacDonald, Rev. Bernard MacDonald, Rev. Hugh MacDonald, Muriel MacDonald, Patsy MacKay, John G. (Chink) and Joan MacLean, Sadie MacLean, Francis Martell, Emily Anne (Millie Ann) Mills, Herman and Margaret Morrison, Jim O'Neil, Murray Osborne, Nellie McPhee, Leo and Mae McPhee, Stanley and Monique McPhee, Dr. Robert Morgan, Farley and Claire Mowat, Ned Norwood, Michael Owens,

Cecelia Pace, John Pertus, Sr. Genevieve Pettipas, Fred, Pauline and Ann Marie Pitts, Colin and Claire Pottie, Jean Pottie, Lorenzo and Margaret Pottie, Peter (Milton) Pottie, Robert Reston, Albert Richard, Fabian and Casilda Richard, James, Jean and Judy Richard, Vincent Richards, Maryanne Rissesco, Alfie Romain, Nick Ryan, Cecil Robertson, Gerald Robertson, Elliott and Kay Robertson, Rev. Lloyd Robertson, Maryann Robertson, Raymond Robinson, Trudy Sable, Alfie Sampson, Anselm and Hilda Sampson, Bernard and Lenova Sampson, Billie Sampson, Dorothy Sampson, Edward and Florence Sampson, James Peter and Caroline Sampson, Lawrence (Bucky) and Ann Sampson, Linda and **Laurence Sampson**, Peter Sampson, **Rachel Sampson,** Rita Sampson, Theresa and **James A. Sampson,** Vincent and Vivian Sampson, Sr. Ann Samson, Dr. Jim Smith, Louise and **Steve Smith**, Robert and Patricia Smith, Rufine Swan, Thomas Sweet, Peter Tapper, Jim and Gerald Taylor, Mae and **Amos Thibeau,** Alfred and Anne Touesnard, David and Gladys Touesnard, Cletus and Mary Touesnard, Clifford and Ann Louise Touesnard, Edward and Florence Touesnard, Emile Touesnard, Jr., Gerard and Cecile Touesnard, Tina Touesnard, Maureen Trudeau, Josephine Veo, Neil Wilcox.

I would would be remiss if I did not offer a special word of thanks to my family for their encouragement and support during this undertaking.

Chapter I
Establishment of River Bourgeois

Geography

River Bourgeois is situated in Cape Breton, Nova Scotia along Route 4, 30 miles east of the Canso Causeway and four miles west of St. Peter's, founded in 1650. It is bordered on the south by Lennox Passage and Isle Madame, on the west by Louisdale, and on the north by the County of Inverness.

To facilitate mail delivery, post offices assumed the name of the area in which the community was located. These include (from east to west): River Tillard, River Bourgeois (which includes the Lower End, Church Point and the North Side to Boyd's Lane), Cannes (from Boyd's Lane west to the head of the River) and to the western boundary of the community, Hawker (originally named False Bay), to the north–Thibeauville and Seaview, and to the south–South River Bourgeois. Other areas included: the Brickery in River Tillard bordering St. Peter's Bay, Grand Gulley between the Brickery and River Bourgeois, the Lower End close to the Old School, the Church Point, and in South River Bourgeois–Richard's Pond and Les Etangs which border on Lennox Passage. See **Plate 100.**

Throughout the book, reference is made to the A.F. Church Map. This was a map of River Bourgeois compiled by the province in 1888. See **Plate 101**.

Establishment

In 1714, L'Hermitage, a high-ranking officer in Louisbourg, gave permission to 24 Acadians to settle at River Tillard on the west side of St. Peter's Bay. To protect these settlers and because of the proximity of Port Toulouse (St. Peter's) to the English fishery of Canso and the important Strait of Canso, a small fort was built on the south side of Point Jerome by Couagne in 1715. A garrison of 40 men under Jacques de Pension was installed. The location of the fort is now part of a Provincial Park Campground.

In 1752, Sieur de la Roque compiled a census of Sainte Esprit–Port Toulouse (St. Peter's) and Rivière à Tillard (Tillia River) during his *Tour of Inspection*. He describes the problem of fortifying the harbour at Port Toulouse, mentions the land of l'ancienne (former) Briquerie, and lists the inhabitants as follows:

Settlers in la Briquerie (Brickery)

- **Honore Prejean**, coaster, native of Cadie, aged 40 years. Married to Marie Brossard, native of Port Royal, age 30 years. They had five sons

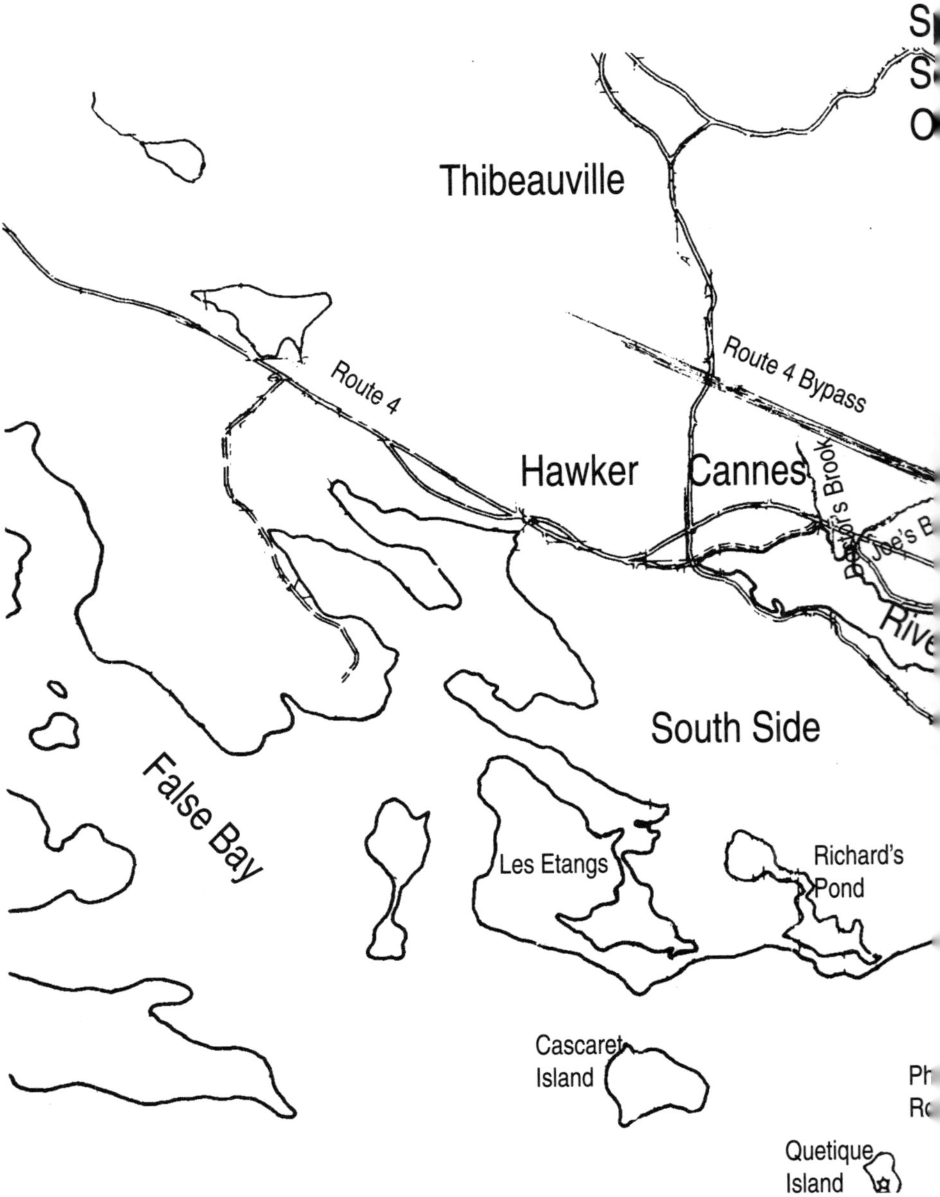
Thibeauville
Route 4
Route 4 Bypass
Hawker
Cannes
South Side
False Bay
Les Etangs
Richard's
Pond
Cascaret
Island
Quetique
Island

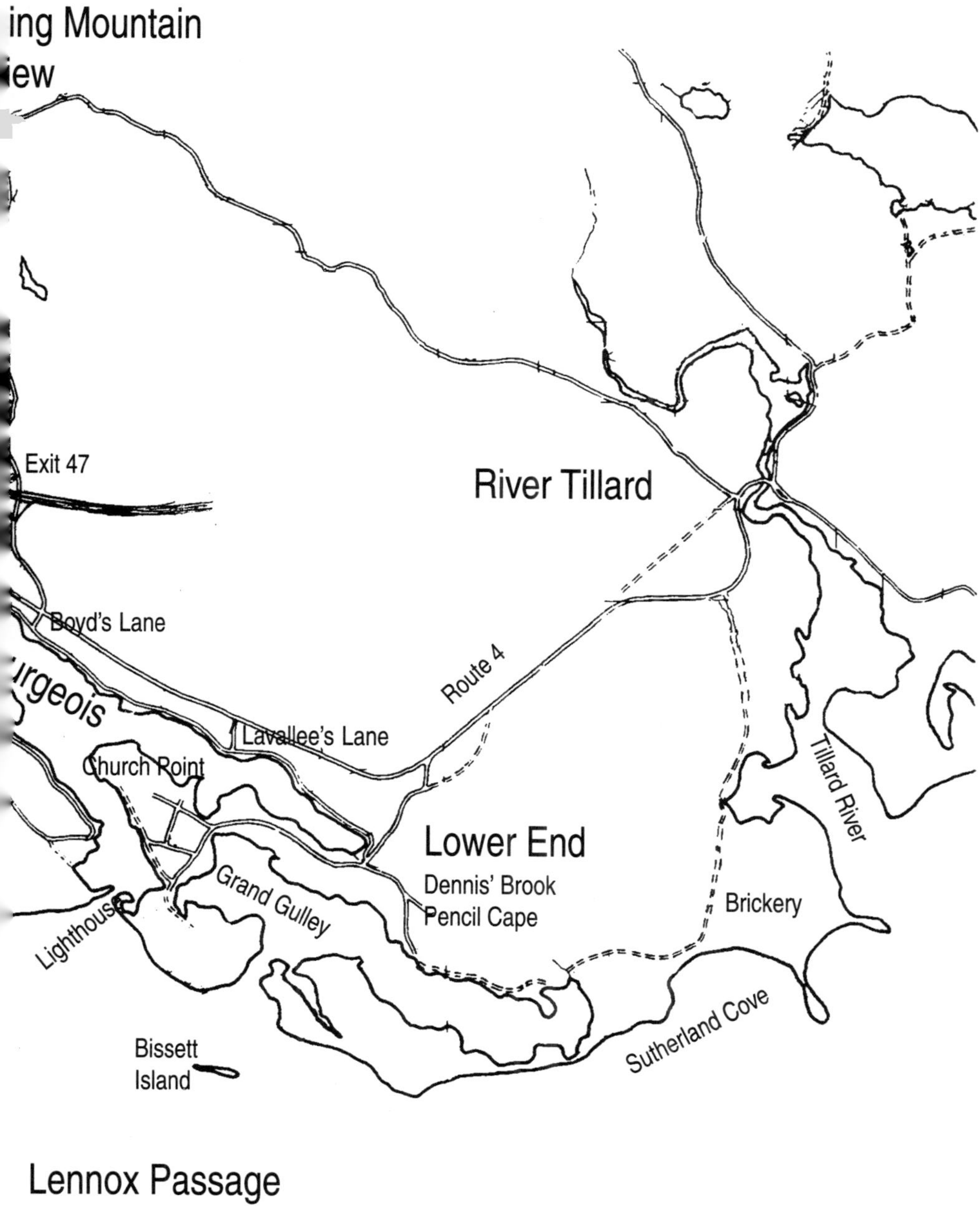

*NOT TO SCALE
Plate 100

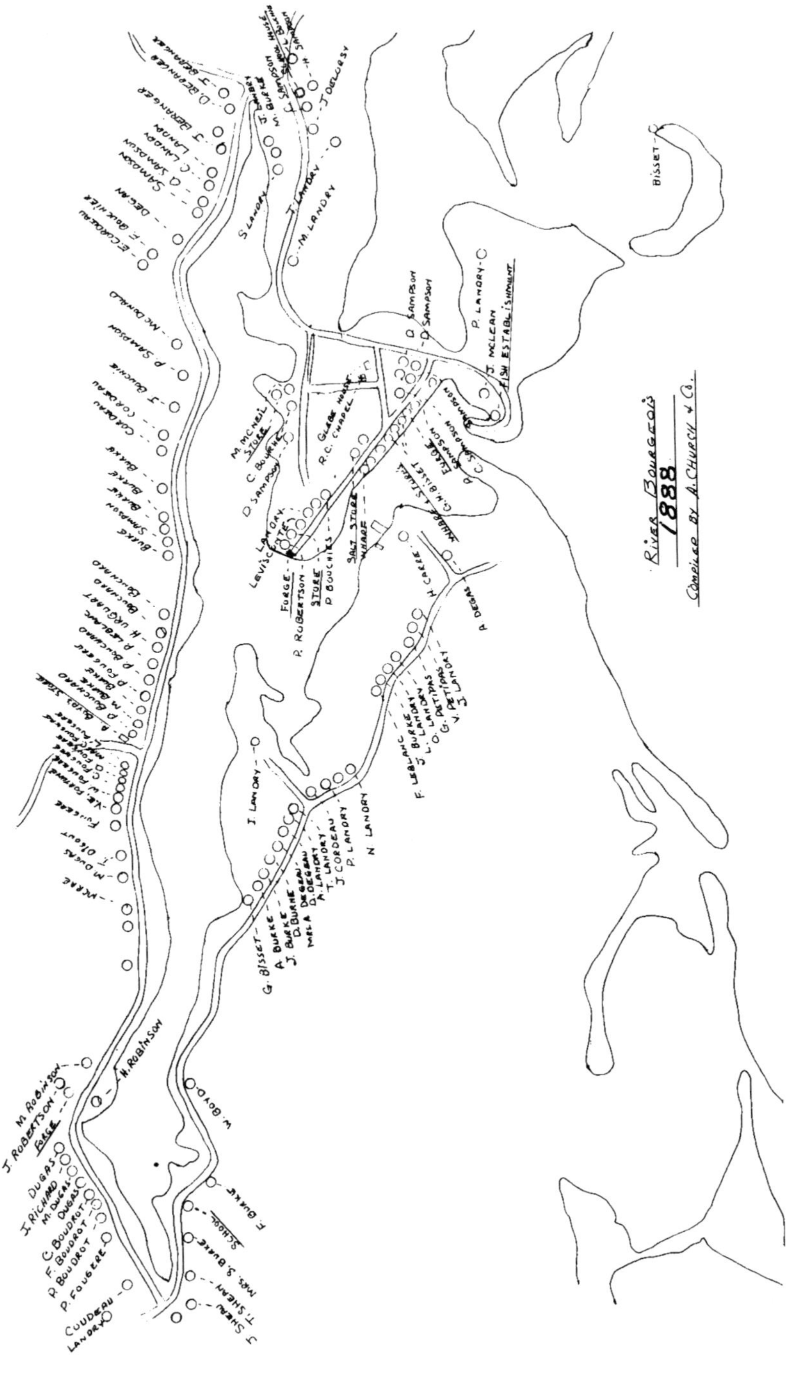

Plate 101

and three daughters: Felix aged 11 years, Ciprien aged 5 years, Julien aged 2 years, two sons each aged 2-1/2 months not yet named, Marie Ann aged 9 years, Felicite aged 7 years, Madeleine aged 2 years. The land on which Prejean has built was sold to him by Charles Boudroit. He has done no clearing.

- **Thomas Nolen**, aged 27, native of Ireland, in the capacity of domestic. Livestock includes one ox, three fowls, one bateau. He is in the colony since 1732.

- **Marguerite Dugas**, widow of the late Joseph Boudroit, native of Port Royal, aged 46 years. She has two sons and one daughter: Louison aged 19 years, Charlie aged 14 years, Marguerite aged 16 years;

- **Joseph Boudroit**, coaster, her son, native of Port Toulouse, aged 30 years. Married to Judith Fougere, native of said place, aged 19 years. They have a daughter, Jeanne, aged 4 months.

- **Pierre Boudroit**, coaster, native of Petit Saint Pierre, aged 25 years. Married to Josette Dugas, aged 19 years. They have two cows, two calves and two fowls.

Other information included in the report:

- The land on which they are located was given them verbally by Messrs. de Saint-Ovide, and Le Normand, and is situated on the coast of Saint Pierre. They have made a clearing for a garden, and the rest of the place is in pasture land. Their meadows are on Barachois à Decoust on the lands of Isle Madame.

- They could cut 100 quintals of hay, if only it could be well-saved, but they only grow and cut grass sufficient for the livestock they have. The lands were granted to them by the late Monsieur La Vallière, Commandant at Porte Toulouse.

- We left Port Toulouse on the 20th of February and arrived at the Rivière à Bourgeois at six o'clock in the evening of the same day.

He describes River Bourgeois as follows:

The Rivière à Bourgeois empties its waters in the little channel a league and a half from Port Toulouse. It takes its source in a large basin situated a quarter of a league from its mouth in the northern part of Isle Royale. It lies east and west, and is estimated as being a half league in length. The breadth of the river is unequal but it's average width is estimated as 150 toises. Its entrance lies north and south. At high tide, there are 15–16 feet of water in the river throughout its whole course of a quarter of league in extent, whilst over the whole area of the basin already mentioned the depth varies from 3–5 feet. Vessels of 100 tons burden can enter and load with the cordwood and dimension timber, which is cut by the settlers of Port Toulouse during the winter. All the shores of the basin, as well as the lands in the interior, are covered with hardwood.

On February the 21st we left Rivière à Bourgeois, and reached the creek à Descoust, situated in the lands of the Isle Madame the same day.

There is no information regarding the inhabitants from 1750–1770 until Léle Cordeau was given a parcel of land in Les Etangs (the ponds) in 1770. Later, land was given to Urbain Cordeau, Richard McPhee, Patrice Paté and Galetan Richard.

The Bourque family, my maternal ancestors were later inhabitants. They included: Aimé, Charles, Damien (Guedou) and Abraham.

From the Etangs area, people moved or were already settled in different parts of the community.

In 1805, a substantial land grant was issued to residents of the community. It is recorded in a document report to Crawley. It names the following as owners: Peter, John, Belony and Thomas Landris (Landry), Lewis Bouché (Boucher) and John and Lewis Sampson. The parcel of land in question ran from the Post Road to the Atlantic and from Sporting Mountain Road to Indian Hill, close to River Tillard. This area of land was subdivided to other inhabitants as time passed.

In a survey of Cape Breton in 1811, the following 19 families are listed as residing in River Bourgeois. (This list may not be complete.)

Name	Occupation	No. in Family
Peter John Landry	Mariner	family of 9
Benoit Landry	fisherman	family of 9
John Landry	fisherman	family of 6
Thomas Landry	fisherman	family of 4
Anselm Landry	fisherman	family of 6
John Samson	fisherman	family of 9
Martin Samson	fisherman	family of 5
Lewis Samson	fisherman	family of 6
Andrew DuGat	fisherman	family of 7
Martial DuGat	fisherman	family of 7
Joseph Bourque	fisherman	family of 6

Pete Bourque	fisherman	family of 4
John Bourque	fisherman	family of 3
Lewis Boucher	fisherman	family of 15
John Boucher	fisherman	family of 1
Simon Fougere Sr.	yeoman	family of 7
Simon Fougere Jr.	fisherman	family of 4
Xavire Pitre	yeoman	family of 6
Mathurin Babin	yeoman	family of 8
		Total of 122 people

* During the same survey, there were only 6 families in St. Peter's with a total population of 37 people.

Throughout the chapter on **Religion**, reference is made to population fluctuation, and the following may be of interest.

Census of Canada, Table 10

1871–964	1881–1,100
1891–1,120	1901–1,129
1911–1,119	1921–1,073
1931–1,073	1941–1,021

Questionable statistics recorded as follows:
1951–896 and 337
1966–437
1968–602
1971–445
1994–300 families, between 850–900 people

Trivia

Until the arrival of the United Empire Loyalists in 1783-84, Nova Scotia was sparsely populated. In 1767, the non-aboriginal population was 11,650. Of these, Americans numbered 5,969; Germans 1,883; Scots 149 and Acadians 921. No statistics are available for English and French.

Chapter II
Industries

Primary Industries

Fishing was a major industry in River Bourgeois until the 1900s, though the community never had its own large processing plant. The Lobster Cannery, which employed 8–10 people, was the largest single employer. So how did this community of almost 1,000 souls, survive? The answer to this question lies in diversification; the employment of small groups of people in small industries and businesses. During the Depression, many family members found employment outside the community and these have been mentioned in this chapter as a matter of interest. The very first industry in River Bourgeois, however, was not fishing; it was the manufacturing of bricks.

Brick Manufacturing

During his *Tour of Inspection* in 1752, Sieur de la Rouque referred to l'ancienne (former) Briquerie in Rivière à Tillard (Tillia River), where bricks had been manufactured 30 years earlier for the Fortress of Louisbourg. The Briquerie, located along the coast 60 miles west of Louisbourg, was selected by the French because of its unique clay deposit. The material, known as *The Kingsville Series Clay*[1], is the most suitable for the manufacturing of brick, and is a rare commodity along the coast of Cape Breton. Interestingly, there were two small deposits located close together, one at St. Peter's and the other at River Tillard.

Michael Mailloux[2], a French soldier who spent his boyhood at Port Toulouse, confirms the existence of the Briqueries in his writings of his sailing trips to Louisbourg with his father between 1740–1758, delivering vegetables, meat and bricks for the big fort. A coastal map, *Le Port Toulouse* **Plate 200**, shows the location of Briqueries at St. Peter's and River Tillard in 1731.

Bricks were manufactured either by soldiers from Louisbourg or by civilians under their supervision. Manufacturing occurred between 1722–1758. In 1990, Charlie Burke and I were kindly received by Claire and Farley Mowat from River Tillard, who showed us one of the pits on their property from which materials were surface-mined. A sample brick made in River Bourgeois is shown in **Plate 201**, on display at the Nicholas Denys Museum in St. Peter's. Herman Morrison, who donated the brick, assured me that this was an original he found at the Briquerie property originally owned by his parents.

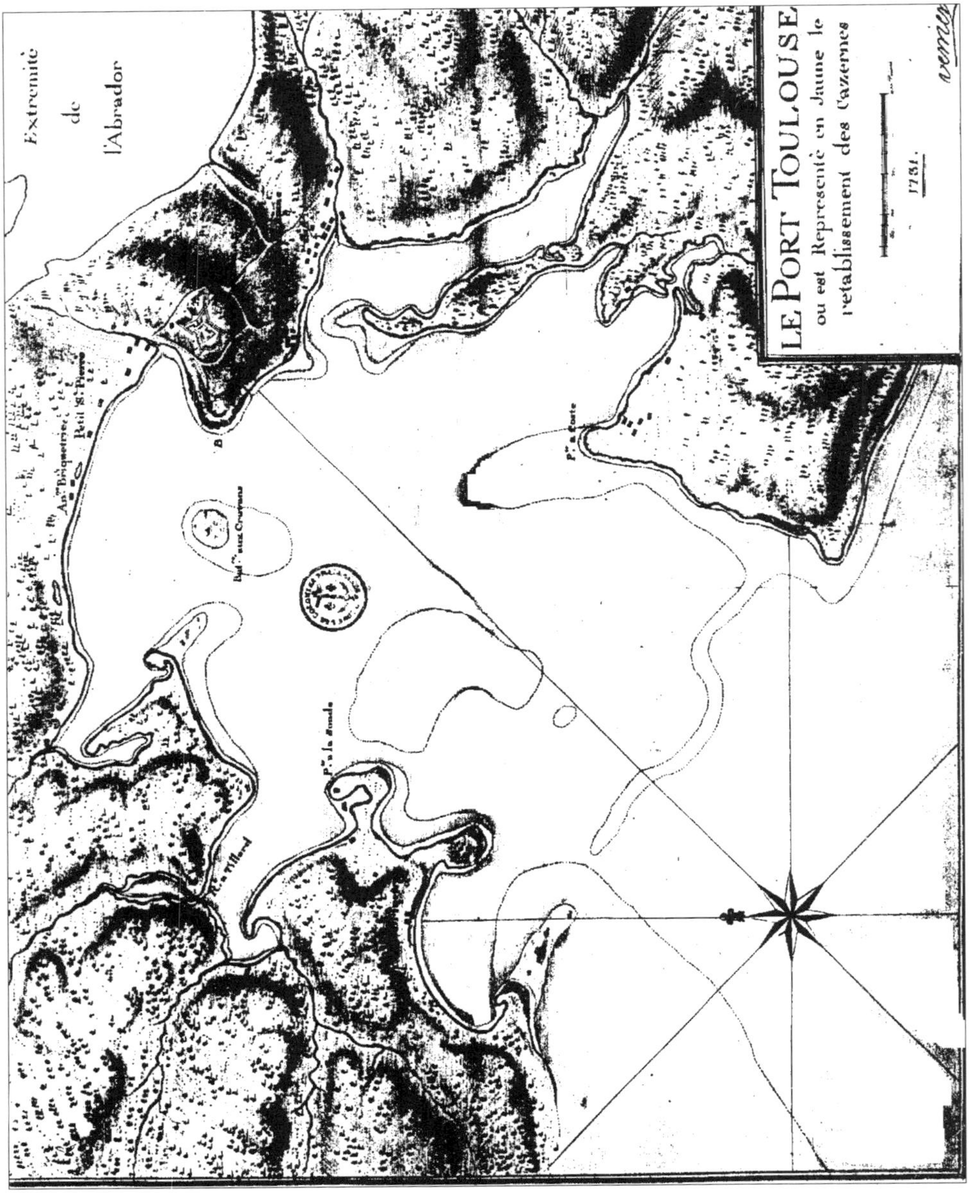

Plate 200—Courtesy of Nicholas Deny's Museum, St. Peter's, Cape Breton

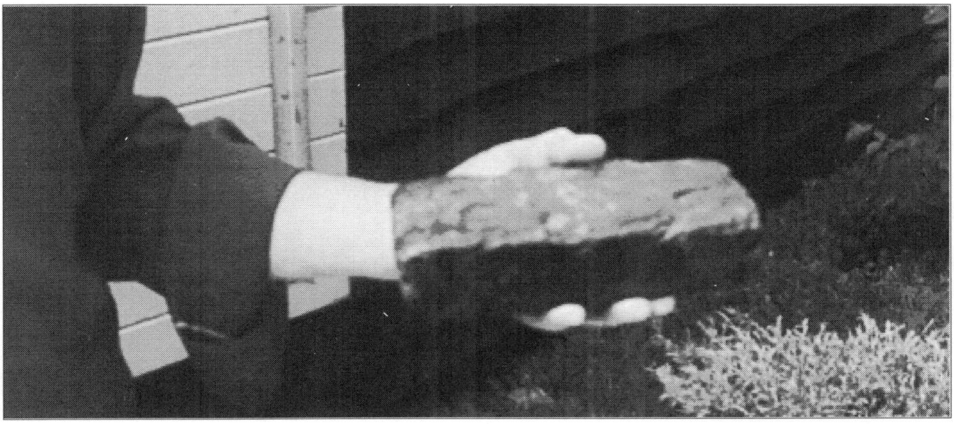

Plate 201—Taken by Garvie Samson

Fishing and Processing

Following its loss of Acadia in 1713, France founded the colony of Ile Royale (Cape Breton) and built the Fortress of Louisbourg to protect it. Fishing became an important industry with the increased demand for food at Louisbourg, the developing local communities, and increasing exports to centres such as Halifax and Boston. Religion also played a significant role in the fishing industry as Catholics were obliged to eat fish during numerous feast days. Codfish was preferred by the foreign markets and local waters abounded with cod and other species such as halibut, herring, mackerel, lobster, eels and smelts.

Unrest in Europe helps industry

Political unrest in Europe encouraged businessmen, especially from the Jersey Islands, to search abroad for new business opportunities. One of the first businessmen to establish in the community was George Edward Bissett[3]. He purchased three parcels of land at the harbour entrance from Queen Victoria on November 16, 1837, for the sum of 12 pounds and 10 shillings. The acquisition included five acres, 23 poles and 46 yards of land, three stores, a wharf, one water lot and a dwelling house. The location and number of buildings suggest there was a well-established fishing business there before 1837.

In later years, George Henry Bissett constructed three large warehouses/ stores, shown in **Plate 202**, at the sea-wall, east of the existing Government wharf. The last of these stores was dismantled in the late 1940s by Firman Bouchie, with some of the material being used to construct a small storage shed which is still in use.

A key businesses which operated until the early 1940s was the LeVesconte family store. Their warehouse/store, shown in **Plate 203,** was located 100

Plate 202–Courtesy of Maurice and Lucille Landry

yards west of the existing Government wharf at Church Point. Their first operation was a very modest store established by Peter LeVesconte on the roadway next to Peter Robertson's forge at La Pointe à Nanonne. William LeVesconte, in his diary[4] of 1879, writes about their business operations in D'Escousse and mentions his frequent meetings with his son Peter and Peter Robertson (the blacksmith) in River Bourgeois.

The LeVesconte business was multi-faceted. They handled the purchase and export of salted and dried fish, the sale of fish supplies, gear and provisions, acted as a depot for incoming and outgoing freight and as a retail store stocking dry goods, household items, wearing apparel and groceries. William Isaac LeVesconte, son of William Sr. from D'Escousse, was the store's first owner and his son, Peter, was the last. Docité Landry, who lived on the South Side, is reported to have been the store clerk for 40 years. The fishing trade began to decline in the early 1930s, and the LeVescontes were subject to the Depression as was every other business. The warehouse/store was closed by 1942.

Plate 203–Courtesy of Clara Dennis, PANS

For many families, the fishery required total family commitment. Nellie McPhee recalls working with Virginia Burke and Marie Susie Landry at their family operation in 1916. Typically upon a vessel's return from the fishing grounds, they would row to the vessel anchored across from their field by Charlie (Tom) Sampson's house where the crew would lower pallets of freshly salted cod into their rowboat. It was Nellie's responsibility to wash the salt from the fish, carry the catch to her father's store and perform the laborious task of drying it on flakes. This involved loading and unloading racks morning and night and turning the fish several times during the day. Fish were dried in the fall when the sun was less intense. Anthony Landry, who also did this work, recalls that the normal pay was 50 cents per quintal (220 lbs) of finished product.

David Sampson, who lived on property presently owned by Cletus and Mary Touesnard, began his fishing career in 1859 and operated fishing vessels into the 1920s. He co-owned the *Morning Star* and *Ajax* with Urban Sampson. His business was continued by his son Anselm who owned and captained the *John Vincent*, the *Alex Fraser*, the *Minnie A.* in 1905, and the *Rosie M.B.* in 1913. The *Rosie M.B.*, a 75-ton schooner shown in **Plate 204,** was one of the last vessels to carry on trade in the River. During her last fishing voyages in the 1920s, she was captained by Simon Goyetche.

Plate 204–Courtesy of Margaret Digout

Front (L to R)–Capt. Anselm G. Samson, Fabian (à Docité) Landry, Murdock Rançon, Andrew ??, Abraham Landry
Back–Paul Samson, Isaac Burke, Joseph Samson

Lobster Industry

The lobster industry was a small scale business in River Bourgeois until the 1870s. The popularity of the species escalated over time which led to uncontrolled fishing and the rapid depletion of lobster stocks. The sale of berried lobsters was prohibited in 1873, however catches continued to decline. In an effort to re-establish the industry between 1911 and 1917, hatcheries were established on Isle Madame. One such hatchery was located in Arichat and the government patrol steamer *Davis* carried the spawns to the fishing grounds. Efforts were unsuccessful, with the loss of spawns at the hatchery and problems with deposition on the fishing grounds rendering the operation fruitless. The Arichat hatchery closed[5] in 1917.

Lobster Cannery

The *Leslie & LeVesconte Cannery*[6] was situated on the South Side, 450 yards from the River Inlet Lighthouse. Thomas Leslie and William LeVesconte opened the factory around 1911 at the site where Henry Carée of Guysborough once operated a small fish establishment and store.

The facilities, shown in the background of **Plate 205**, included a white processing plant on a wharf and a two and one-half story red building called the Cannery, situated south of the plant. The canning operation is described by Fred LeBlanc, who lived in the next field and working there for a short time, in **Appendix 1.**

To make an early start, many of the workers slept in the Cook House during the week and returned to their homes during the weekends. Amos Thibeau enjoyed tending the early morning fires with his fellow workers, Sam McPhee and John Thibeau. They gained a head-start boiling water in the caldron for

Plate 205

the cooking operation. As the fishermen rowed by the plant before day break, Amos remembers hearing their French conversations and the rhythmic sounds of their leather-covered oars rubbing against the tewel pins, echoing off the hills lining the channel. Returning from their lobster pots, usually before noon, the fishermen discharged their catch at the Cannery or at the triangular holding tanks anchored by the lighthouse.

Most cannery workers were from the South Side and Thibeauville. Foremen included: John P. Burke (who lived across from the plant), Peter (Pat) J. Thibeau (a fisheries inspector for some time), Andrew Robertson (Grand Gulley) and John Henry Thibeau (Thibeauville). John Henry was the last foreman at this cannery and worked a few years at the South Bar Cannery under John P. Burke. Other employees included: Minnie Richard, Mary Louise Landry (John Sampson's wife), July Cordeau, Josephine Dugas, Mary and Henry Fougere, Mary Burke, John Burke (Victor Burke's brother), Superior and Damien (Gadeau) Burke, Annie Dugas, Fred LeBlanc, Celeste Anne Landry, Amos Landry, Agnus Landry (Mrs. Alex Bouchie), Charlie and Henry Fougere, Minnie Burke, Catherine Pottie, Millie, Edmond, Robbie and Ned Thibeau (Ned soldered the tops on cans with an iron like in **Plate 206**, held in safekeeping by Leo McPhee).

Cooks included Henrietta Thibeau and Mary Ann (Mrs. Placide Burke). Charlie Burke recalls going to the Cook House to eat some of Mary Anne's molasses cookies. On occasion, she cooked fudge for the children to entice them to stay overnight as company. Louise Smith, (Steve Smith's wife), recalls working at the factory and sleeping in the Cook House. Gladys Touesnard remembers the children calling it the *haunted house* because the floors were terribly shaky and squeaky. Celeste Anne Landry recalls that the Thibeau girls were among the few who spoke English at the factory. Amos Thibeau was responsible for firing the boiler while John Thibeau and Sam McPhee took care of miscellaneous work such as removing lobster shells,

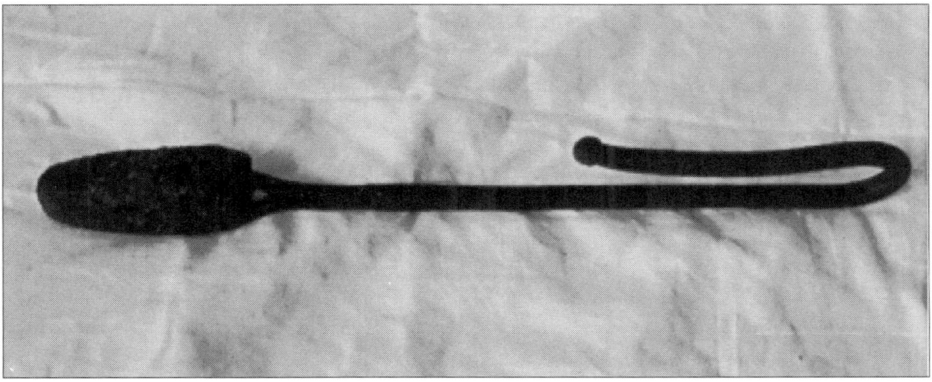

Plate 206–Taken by Garvie Samson

filling the kettle with fresh water and lobster, cleaning work tables and transporting the canned lobsters to storage. Robbie Thibeau was the chief cracker and Minnie Thibeau was the weigher.

Captains who worked directly for Leslie & LeVesconte as smackers included: Alexander (Alex) Bouchie (captain of the *Cibyl*), Beni Samson, Daniel Sampson and Thomas Sampson.

According to Fred LeBlanc, the lobster canning operation closed in 1928 at which time he was transferred to the larger factory in South Bar. Alex Thibeau, Felix Pottie and Leo McPhee also worked there when John P. Burke was the Operations Manager. This plant closed in 1930.

Following closure of the Lobster Factory, the buildings were rented to a business lady from D'Escousse, Maria Susan Ranson. She used the facilities for several years to store fish. Maria purchased codfish from the fisherman, employed local ladies to *make fish* on flakes which were stored in the old lobster factory building. In the fall, the larger vessels, such as the Rosie M.B., would purchase the dried cod and transport it to ports such as Halifax and Boston.

The Cannery building was purchased and dismantled by Peter Landry in 1932; he constructed a hen house with the materials. Peter's wife, Celeste Anne told me they raised 100 hens which produced eggs for their large family and extras were sold to the neighbours.

Associated Canneries

In addition to the Cannery in River Bourgeois, Leslie & LeVesconte had plants at South Bar, Bras d'Or, Port Morien and Pointe Michaud. The company used three smackers to purchase and transport lobster from fisherman in the plant areas. Leo McPhee recalls that on numerous occasions the vessels arrived at the plant loaded to the gunnels. Lobster sources included Point Aconi, Low Point, South Bar and Boulardrie. The South Bar plant alone employed 18 workers.

Canneries were also located in Petit de Grat where firms such as William Duff, A & R Loggie, Nevill Bros, John A. Landry and Richmond Shorefish operated. During the late 1920s and early 1930s, all factories suffered from the new trend of shipping live lobsters to the American markets. This competition, reduction in fish stocks, and a drop in sales because of the Depression, forced plant closures.

Outdoor Hatchery

The failure of conventional indoor hatcheries prompted Leslie & LeVesconte to experiment outdoors where lobsters could propagate as in their natural habitat.

Nature had provided the beginning of a suitable site, close by the lighthouse. The 1837 surveyor drawing confirms that the lagoon was not entirely enclosed and to form a pond it was necessary to construct a dyke 70-feet in length, and a dam to regulate the flow of water to and from the pond. Fresh salt water passed into the pond every nine hours, (assuming the level of the pond was allowed to fluctuate 2-1/2 feet) by the natural rise and fall of the tides.

Construction of the dyke and dredging of the pond was done by horse-drawn equipment and manual labour. The final pond measured 80-feet across at high tide, and had an area of just under one acre. Fertilized lobsters were introduced to their new environment with high expectations. However with winter, the shallow pond froze solid, and so did the lobsters. That was the end of this costly adventure.

The undertaking wasn't a complete failure according to Jack LeVesconte. The pond served as a great skating rink and as a marina where Jack and his brothers and sisters spent many hours skating and sailing their small boats. Jack's boyhood love for vessels never died as he enjoys making model schooners. One of his works, a model of the *The Bluenose*, is on display at Mac Askill's Museum in St. Peter's.

Clam Processing

This small, short-lived business was operated by two entrepreneurs from the United States in 1956. They rented a building from Allan Touesnard, located at the east end of his Church Point farm. The company purchased clams from local diggers then cooked, bottled and exported them to the U.S. It was a small operation, employing only four people on a seasonable basis. Workers including my sister, Marguerite Fougere, recall the business very well as the owners left unannounced, leaving the employees stuck for two weeks wages.

Ship and Boat Building

Although there were a considerable number of vessels constructed over the years in River Bourgeois, there was never an organized shipyard. Vessels were constructed by fishermen for their own use. Although there were a few large vessels built, most were small so fishermen did not have to travel far to obtain their desired catch. Larger vessels were used for extended fishing trips to the Grand Banks, Gulf of St. Lawrence or to North Bay. At these fishing grounds, captains found large fish stocks and crews of 10–12 fished in dories from the mother ship. Large vessels were also used to transport cargo to distant ports such as Halifax, Boston and the West Indies. Upon their return, they brought salt, lumber and food products, and the odd barrel of rum. In October and November, cargo ships transported vegetables from

P.E.I., coal from Sydney, and food supplies from Halifax and Boston.

The earliest boat constructed in River Bourgeois was the *Morning Star* registered in Sydney[7] in 1810 under the name of Lewis Bouchie, builder/ owner. She was a 62-ton schooner measuring 52-feet, 8-inches in length. From that date until the 1920s, there were several schooners built every year. These vessels are listed in **Appendix 2**.

In the early 1920s, motors began to replace sail as the means of propulsion and a new shape of vessel emerged. The *Cape Islander*, designed especially for motor installations, offered many advantages over sail, though it was more costly to operate. It was independent of the wind, faster, had greater manoeuvrability, required a smaller crew, and drew less water. This style of boat continues to be the most popular among coastal fishermen.

Two of the experimenters in constructing the *Cape Islander* in the mid-1930s were Charlie Burke and Leo Digout. Their first adventure was a 30-foot x 9-foot vessel constructed in LeVesconte's workshop, next to the lighthouse. When the vessel was completed, the shop closed and Charlie and Leo purchased the building for $25 to salvage the 2-inch x 6-inch flooring material. At the same time, they constructed the *Sea Sled*, an 18-foot speed boat, on the second floor of G. H. Bissett's last standing warehouse, next to the Government wharf.

The *Whirl*, shown in **Plate 207**, was operated out of River Bourgeois in the mid-1920s as a patrol boat. The crewman were: Ernst Landry (captain), William Robertson (engineer) and Peter Fougere (deck hand).

Jim Bouchie, working away from the River as a diesel mechanic for many years, returned home in the 1960s and began constructing fishing and pleasure boats. He designed and constructed 20 boats, many of which still grace the local waters. He completed renovations on the famed, *Boat Who Wouldn't Float*, owned by Farley Mowat, with my father, Jimmy Sampson, his lifelong friend. **Plates 208 and 209** show a 24-foot boat, one of six designed and built by my father as a hobby.

Plate 207–Courtesy of Delta Babin

Concrete Boat

The use of concrete instead of wood to construct a vessel's hull was not the norm, and it certainly wasn't an industry.

Plate 208–Taken by Garvie Samson

Plate 209–Taken by Garvie Samson

However, such interest was shown in the boats constructed by Walter Kendall that they have been included.

The construction method, known as *ferrocement*, is known throughout the world. The manufacturers define it as *a special type of reinforced concrete compound of closely spaced layers of continuous nonmetallic mesh embedded in cement-sand mortar.* It combines the strength of wire mesh and concrete. To form a ship's hull, a light wooden frame is constructed to the desired shape and size. Layers of mesh are attached to the framework then thin layers of cement and sand are applied from the exterior using a sponge trowel, and finished with a steel trowel. Inserts are imbedded in the concrete to attach the floor, engine bed and bulkheads, similar to wood construction.

Kendall constructed two boats in a field, measuring 36-feet, 9-inches x 14-feet; a considerable undertaking for one man under the conditions. Upon the successful completion of his second vessel, he sailed to P.E.I. for a load of potatoes. Upon leaving the harbour in North Bay, the boat, loaded with potatoes, struck a rock in shallow water and sank. He managed to salvage the motor, drive shaft and propeller, which he transported to the River in a Volkswagen bus. He completely overhauled the equipment and sold it to Ralph Murray who installed it in his lobster boat. The ingenious builder suggests that an excellent product could be produced if work were completed indoors under controlled conditions. See **Plates 210** and **211**.

Sail Making

Captain Anselm Sampson, my great-grandfather, while fishing his schooner in the Bay of Fundy, noticed a vessel from D'Escousse trimmed with a new set af sails. He admired the way the sails worked in the wind and inquired as to who had made them. He was advised that it was a certain young Frenchman answering to the name of Emile Touesnard, who had recently come to D'Escousse. Anselm invited him to the River in the fall to make sails for his vessels. Emile later married Anselm's daughter, Minnie. This union produced all the Touesnards in River Bourgeois. Most fishermen made their own sails during the winter months.

Agriculture and Farming

In the past, most River Bourgeois residents operated a small farm with a vegetable garden, a cow, other beef animals, a sheep, a pig and either an ox or horse to do the heavy work. Fortunately soil conditions were such that with the application of readily available fertilizers such as manure, lobster shells, fish and kelp, the soil yielded generous crops. Soil conditions are described in an early Agriculture Report.

Plate 210–Courtesy of Vincent Kendall

Plate 211–Courtesy of Vincet Kendall

The soil surrounding Grand Gullet, the island and River Bourgeois is classified as belonging to the Woodbourne series. The topography of this classification ranges from rolling hills to hilly and some land has steep slopes. Surface drainage is usually rapid and the steeper slopes are easily eroded. Internal drainage is usually moderately rapid. The principal trees are red spruce, white spruce, wire birch, red maple, sugar maple, and some poplar.

Some excellent crops of hay, pasture grain or vegetables are grown on these soils. They respond well to fertilizer, and lime seems to be necessary for best results. On slopes that have been in hay or pasture for many years, much of the surface soil has been removed by sheer erosion, and it is necessary to build up the organic matter when these soils are cultivated.

The sale of agricultural products to surrounding communities is confirmed in the Petition[8] for *The Construction of Two Wharves and a Boat Carriage at the Little St. Peter's Harbour.* An excerpt from this documents, dated March 24, 1842, reads:

Your Petitioner also begs leave to state to your Honourable House that many of them are put to great inconvenience when they arrive with the produce of their farms at the Haul-Over on their way to and from Arichat, D'Escousse and River Bourgeois, partly owing to the want of a wharf, being obliged to back the produce from their boats in the water in inclement seasons of the year and then to carry at the Haul-Over on their backs a distance of nearly half a mile.

Residents continue to enjoy planting gardens, however few maintain farm animals since beef, dairy and poultry products are readily available in nearby supermarkets. Milk is now delivered to the door on a regular schedule and for a number of years a butcher has been selling select quality meats door-to-door .

Farming

Allain Touesnard, Church Point, was the largest local full-time farmer. He continued the farm begun by Joseph Deslaurier in the late-1800s. (Joseph died on May 24, 1927 aged 80 years, and his wife Philisité died in 1952 aged 85). Allain's operation included beef, pork, poultry and milk. During the early 1950s, Allain's son, Alfred and I delivered many bottles of milk to St. Peter's. The Cosy Corner Restaurant was his main client. The farming operation is continued on a smaller scale by his sons, Alfred and Edward. Edward works part-time on the farm specializing in beef cattle. Others involved in farming at that time on a commercial basis included: Tom Morrison (Sporting Mountain), Gerard Touesnard (Oban and Seaview), and Bennie Konning who operated a piggery in Sporting Mountain.

Oxen were the earliest animals used to help inhabitants remove stumps, plough fields and haul carts, wagons and sleighs. Farmers bred cows for milk and beef. Andrew Boudreau and Gerard Touesnard were trained to use these animals around the farm (see **Plate 212**). By the beginning of the 20th century, draft horses such as the Clydesdale and Shire were commonly used. Allan Touesnard was one of the first to own a farm tractor, a steel-wheeled *Massey Harris*.

Fr. Pierre Robitaille operated a small farm and owned the first threshing machine. He sold it to Marshall Digout who sold it to Simon Fougere. Simon travelled around the River threshing oats and grain. A four-horse power stationary gas motor powered the machine which was towed by a team of horses or Baptist Landry's tractor. When the floor was strong enough, the machine was hauled into the client's barn. A threshing machine was on exhibition at the River Bourgeois Museum for several years. René Louis, who lived close to St. Peter's, frequently came to River Bourgeois with his threshing machine. **Plate 213** shows Simon Sampson towing a threshing machine.

Lumbering

One of the earliest historical notes of River Bourgeois refers to St. Peter's inhabitants coming to the River to cut firewood and timber in the mid-1700s. During the last century, large quantities of wood have been sold for pit props to the Sydney and Glace Bay mines and for pulpwood to *Bowater-Mersey Pulp and Paper Company* and *Nova Scotia Forest Industries*. In recent years, there was a pulp yard in St. Peter's close to Cottons, and pulp was shipped from the Canal to Europe. A downturn in the economy and the pulp and paper industry along with the Spruce Budworm infestation of the 1980s, has reduced this business considerably. According to predictions, it will take 30 years for the trees to fully recover from the Spruce Budworm attack.

Water–powered sawmills

River Bourgeois boasted one water-powered sawmill in its history. This small shingle mill operated by Joe Robinson, was located in Cannes, along the brook which bears his name. Its source of water was a dam situated above the Number 4 Highway. Part of the dam was removed during the construction of the new highway in 1931–32. Many stones from its walls were used to build a foundation under Charlie Pottie's store, which had to be relocated to accommodate the new road. Robinson supplied the local communities and surrounding areas with shingles.

Before the water–powered mill, shingles were hand-made using draw knives and a holding device such as that being used by my son John Samson in **Plate 214**, taken at the Habitation in Annapolis, Nova Scotia. The preferred wood for making shingles was cedar or douglas fir, but black spruce was

Plate 212–Courtesy of Gerald Touesnard

Plate 213–Courtesy of Margaret Digout

Plate 214–Taken by Garvie Samson

used as a substitute. To obtain the best product, trees were felled in the fall and left to air-dry during the winter with the branches attached to the trunk. Black spruce shingles, when treated with linseed oil, provided great service as they did did not crack, warp or rot.

Steam–powered sawmills

Hugh MacLean operated a steam-powered sawmill and a shingle-mill in Thibeauville. Upon his retirement, his sons Jack, Hector and Stewart managed the operations. Sam Burke recalls that both sawmills operated from the same boiler. Amos Thibeau, who lived close by the mills, recalls working there as a teenager in 1918. He loaded logs on the jack and removed slabs from the saw. One day the boiler sprung a leak and had to be patched. It lasted two more years then was replaced by an Acadian stationary gas engine which was capable of operating both mills simultaneously or seperately.

The family sold the mill to a Mr. Samson from Louisdale who replaced the stationary motor with a car engine. Gerard Touesnard purchased the mill from them and set it up in Oban where he operated a mill for several years. When he returned to the River, he brought it with him and sold it in 1990 to a Mr. MacLeod (86 years of age) from Sterling Mines. Apparently, the mill is still in operation.

Andrew Fougere had a mill located in his field 50-yards west of his house which was purchased from the Dunphy family in Point Tupper. Leo Fougere, Andrew's great-grandson, met an elderly John Cook from Point Tupper several years ago who recalled driving a team of horses to Cannes with the boiler loaded on a freight wagon.

As a child, Sam Burke (born 1909) worked around the Fougere's mill. He remembers the boiler measured 5-feet in diameter and 8-feet in height. It was fitted with gauges and control mechanisms and contained a series of metal tubes which carried steam to a one–piston engine. The carriage was pulled back and forth by steel cables, powered by the steam engine, and had a 16-inch diameter blade with removable teeth. To saw thick logs, it was necessary to make two passes with the blade, one on either side of the log. Slabs and miscellaneous scraps stoked the boiler. Sam Fougere transported much of the milled lumber to Stevens in Sydney.

The mill was sold to a Scotsmen from Oban. A new mill was established in the field below George and Lizzie DeWolf's house which was equipped with a gasoline motor. It operated from this site until 1945.

I have discovered documents referring to a small steam sawmill operated by M.J.T. MacNeil in 1886. He occupied property presently owned by Robert Bouchie, at Church Point. There is little more known of this operation.

Motor–powered sawmills

The Digout family was very much involved in the lumber industry. One of the earliest mills was owned and operated by Marshall Digout in his field below the Number 4 Highway. George DeRoche recalls that the mill was operated by a 10-horse power *Fairbanks Morris* motor. This engine was unique in that it had a magneto and was primed with gasoline, however it could operate on either gasoline or kerosene. Fred Digout called it a "one lunger", it was huge. To start it, one stood on the fly-wheel, of which there were two, each weighing 500 pounds. The saw-blade measured 42-inches in diameter and had removable teeth.

Fred Digout purchased his Uncle Marshall's mill in 1948 and operated it from the original location for 15 years, then sold it to Terry Boudreau from River Tillard who set up the mill in River Tillard but never operated it. He sold it to a man from L'Ardoise where it is believed to be still operating. Fred replaced the old mill with a modern mill on the Marshall site, then relocated it above the highway, close to the shoe repair shop of his father, Victor. With his new mill, he could saw and dress lumber, make shingles and saw 3,000 lathes per hour.

Willard Pottie's mill was located at the head of the River close to Lorenzo Pottie's original home. The mill was actually operated by Raymond, Willard's son. After several years of operating in this location, Raymond set up a mill on the South Side behind the Point.

Archie Morrison's sawmill was located in River Tillard just south of the railway tracks, close to the River and below the existing roadway. It was operating in 1922 according to researched documents. Gerard Touesnard recalls seeing the remnants of the concrete walls used to support the motor. Herman Morrison, whose father owned the mill, recalls the mill being sold to Messrs. MacKinnon and MacLeod from Framboise in 1936. They came with a team of horses, slept overnight and returned the next morning to Framboise with the mill loaded on a sled. Fred Digout believed it was a small shingle mill.

Ross's mill was located in Seaview and listed by R. G. Dunn & Co. as operating in 1910, with a business volume under $500 per year.

Gerard Touesnard operated a small sawmill in Oban. His carriage was the original used by Hugh MacLean in his steam operated mill in Thibeauville. Gerard's son Adrian also operated this mill in Seaview for a short time.

Cross-cut Saws

Cross-cut saws cut wood unsuitable for logs into short lengths to burn in kitchen stoves (such as the Bridgewall, Enterprise and Mansfield), and in pot-bellied stoves and fireplaces. Every resident owned a bucksaw, and many cut their own firewood. However for convenience, and at a reasonable price, portable cross-cut saws were available. George DeRoche believes that the first motor operated cross-cut saw was owned by Martin Dugas, who sold it to Simon Fougere. It was powered by an *Acadia Stationary Motor*. John Sampson (the diver), from Church Point, also owned a cross-cut saw.

The typical apparatus included a stationary motor transported on one wagon and a saw-jack mounted on another. Vincent Sampson used his father's (John Sampson) apparatus in the early 1940s following his father's death. He recalls the difficulty loading and unloading the heavy stationary motor from the wagon and understands why so many men were injured doing this job.

A typical work contract required the operator to transport the stationary motor in his wagon, while the client was responsible for transporting the saw-horse. The operator attended to the operation of the equipment, while labour to load and manipulate the saw-horse and remove the wood was supplied by the client. Normally the labour team included five men. The operator charged $1 per hour for his equipment. The heavy stationary motor was eventually replaced by the farm tractor fitted with a power take-off. Tractors, such as the Ford owned by Allan Touesnard, could be fitted with a cross-cut mechanism. They were powerful, portable and fast.

Wool Carding

In addition to his sawmill, Hugh MacLean established a carding mill[9] in Thibeauville in 1878 while living with his father (Laclin) in Belmoral. Hugh had worked in a carding mill in Millinocket, Maine, and brought the technology to River Bourgeois. He constructed a new home close to the mill and moved from Belmoral to Thibeauville on January 29, 1880.

The Thibeauville site was ideal for a water–powered carding mill. The stream had an adequate flow of water, having several tributaries (one of which included Hill's Lake). The banks along the creek were high and the brook narrowed, forming a natural site for a dam and reservoir. Fortunately Clarence LeBlanc and his wife Elsie took a keen interest in the Mill and provided me with valuable information. In addition, Anthony Rousseau shot a video of the Mill and the MacLean family in 1952.

The building enclosing the carding equipment was three stories in height, with a peaked roof running at right angles to the stream. It measured 32-feet x 26-feet. The main entrance to the building was on the second floor opposite the paddle wheel, which faced the house. Carding equipment was located on the same level and spare parts, such as rollers, belts and pulleys, were stored on the third floor. Details concerning the construction and operation of the mill can be found in **Appendix 3. Plate 215**, taken at the Wile Carding Mill in Bridgewater, shows carding equipment similar to that used at the MacLean Mill.

A Little Bit Of Pleasure

To women, having their wool carded was a real treat and time saver, as most of their families were very large and there was always work to be done. A carding machine could process 12-pounds of wool per hour, the equivalent amount by hand would take 12 days. The cost of carding went from 4 cents per pound in 1884 to 7 cents per pound in 1918. Wool was used to produce basic clothing such as sweaters, blankets, socks and mittens.

Many of those I interviewed, especially the elderly ladies, spoke of the mill in Thibeauville with excitement. Everyone recalled the large gaps between the floorboards, the movement of the building to the rhythm of the wheel, and the sound of rushing water. As the mill grew older, with its creaky worn-down wooden pulleys and rollers, and slapping leather belts, the apparatus sounded like a threshing machine. It could be heard half way to River

Plate 215–Courtesy of Garvie Samson

Bourgeois. All recall making the three–mile trek to Thibeauville with a bag of wool on their backs. While awaiting their wool to be carded, they watched the water dive off the wheel, visited relatives in Thibeauville, or dropped in to see Maggie MacLean who was always prepared to serve a cup of tea and a milk biscuit. During the summer, Maggie proudly walked visitors through her extensive flower garden.

Hector MacLean, who treated the Carding Mill with "pride and joy", was a bit of a character. He always had a wad of chewing tobacco in his mouth, and according to many, most customers' wool was anointed with some of his *Pictou Twist*[10]. He was easily distinguished from his brothers by his trademark "ball of wool" tucked behind his ear. The mill closed in 1954 following Stewart MacLean's death.

Secondary Industries

Blacksmiths and Forges

There was a substantial population growth in River Bourgeois during the mid–1800s as a result of immigration and the Catholic church encouraging parents to have large families. Industries expanded in response to the new demand and blacksmiths were inundated with work. Every industry used some piece of hardware which had to be fabricated, renewed or repaired. The blacksmith, with his knowledge of metals, could usually repair the part or make a new one.

Peter Robertson[11] was the earliest known blacksmith. His forge (**Plate 216**) was first recorded[12] in 1882 along the shore road leading to La Pointe à

Nanonne. The field where the forge was built was later owned by Fr. Samson, James Richard and Amable Fougere. Most of his business involved fabricating hardware for the fishing industry and it is believed he fabricated some of the metal fencing which surrounds the cemetery and metal crosses. Elliott Robertson, Peter's grandson, recalls his father, George A. Robertson (diver), relating stories about the long hours Peter spent working the hot metals. *His hands were so tough, he could remove the red-hot covers off the stove with his bare hands. You could see the smoke coming off the callouses.*

Plate 216–Courtesy of Annie Mae Bourque

Willie Robertson (Peter's son), continued operating the forge and relocated it 200-yards east of the original site, where he also built his home. The forge was recorded[12] under the name of W. H. Robertson, Blacksmith, between 1920 and 1932 with the volume of work produced worth between $500–$1,000.

Some of the tools used in Robertson's forge were taken to the LeNoir Forge[13] in Arichat for safekeeping and exhibit. **Plate 217** shows the original bellows used in Peter Robertson's forge, manufactured in 1882. Some of the tools used in the forge were on display in the River Bourgeois Museum which was converted to a Senior Citizens Centre in 1994. Willie Robertson died on June 3, 1965 at the age of 84 years; his wife was Mary Boudreau (1879-1967).

M.J.T. MacNeil's forge was located on Church Point at the end of the lane where Alex Bouchie and now Robert Bouchie resides. This forge was shown on the A.F. Church map of 1888.

Another forge was situated next to the most easterly of the three Bissett warehouses. There is no record of who operated it, however it may have been a Samson as there were five brothers living in this area. The forge is shown on the A.F. Church map of 1888. A small building stood at the same location in 1903.

Charlie Burke advised that there was a small forge located at Bissett's Land, located below Arthur Doary's, in the early 1900s.

There were two Robinson forges in Cannes. Joe Robinson had a forge located

Plate 217–Taken by Garvie Samson

along the shore on the west side of what is presently known as Joe's Brook, 50-feet below the bridge shown in **Plate 218**. George DeRoche, who lived close by, showed me where the rock foundation remained until it was destroyed by equipment used to construct a new wooden bridge over the brook several years ago. William Boyd's original house can be seen in the background.

Joe's forge was established before 1886 and remained open until his death on January 15, 1912[14]. Amos Thibeau recalls visiting the shop on numerous occasions to see Joe make horseshoes, hinges and steel rims for buggy and

Plate 218–Taken by Garvie Samson

wagon wheels. Charlie Digout recalls bringing an old skate to Joe who made a spear out of it for him.

The second forge was owned and operated by Matt Robinson, Joe's son. It was located at the entrance of Gerry Fougere's driveway. Fred Digout recalls it was a very small forge and could have been Joe's old forge relocated, since there is no recollection of both forges operating at the same time. Matt lived across the road from this forge. The Robinson lineage is: Joe, Matt, Fred and Ray. Ray now resides in the old homestead.

Woodworking shops

William LeVesconte owned a shop measuring 25-feet x 50-feet on the northwest side of the Lobster Pond, next to the lighthouse. This shop was used for general maintenance, repairs and for boat storage. The small motorized tender boat, *Thora*, was stored there in the 1920s. On the shore below LeVesconte's barn, a short distance away, are the remains of an old vessel believed to have been owned by Willie Boudreau. (Willie was Andrew Boudreau's father.)

Steve Smith and Elias (Robert) Cooper Restin opened a small shop in what later became the Smith's residence, across from where Robert and Mary Pettigrew live. Their intentions were to establish a small window manufacturing plant, however there wasn't sufficient business to support the operation and they closed the shop. Robert returned to Halifax and Steve settled in River Bourgeois. Steve was very much involved in sports and spent all his spare time helping the youth of the community.

Carriage works

Joseph Fougere clearly recalls his uncle Andrew Fougere's workshop. Joseph Lavallee had given Joe a dog and harness and his uncle Andrew made him a beautiful sleigh. Andrew's shop was next to his sawmill and here he made carriages, including the wheels. Joe recalls seeing his uncle whittling away, making a hub for a wagon wheel. He used to paint a very thin line on each spoke, the trademark of a real craftsman. Wheels were fitted with steel rims to protect the wood. To install the steel rim Andrew had his own small forge. He built and repaired many wagons, especially for the Scotsmen from the Mountain who came to him because of his fine craftmanship.

Coopering

Fishermen used a large number of puncheons and barrels of all sizes to preserve and ship fish. It is believed that there was a small cooper shop located in one of Bissett's buildings close to the lighthouse. I saw one of the steel mechanisms used for holding the barrel staves together at the LeNoir Forge in Arichat.

Harness Shop

A Mr. Bulger made harnesses and items of leather in a small shop in River Tillard where Michael Boudreau, and later Charlie Fred Sampson lived. Not much is known of this individual.

Endnotes/Comments

1) Soil Survey of Cape Breton Island, Report No. 12, Nova Scotia Soil Survey. Truro, Nova Scotia, 1963. *The Kingsville Soil Series occupies two percent of Cape Breton Island. At depths greater than three feet the soil is dusky-red, very plastic with a pH of 8.0.*

2) In 1740, Michael's father was transferred to Port Toulouse where Michael and his mother joined him from Bordeaux, France. They remained in St. Peter's until Wolfe's forces captured Fort Toulouse in 1758 and shipped the French soldiers and their families back to France. The noted information was written by Michael in his Report entitled *Port Toulouse,* obtained at the Nicholas Denys Museum in St. Peter's. The name Port or Fort Toulouse is derived from Compte De Toulouse, an illegitimate son of Louis XIV. Saint Peter's was also called San Pedro, Sainte Pierre and Port Toulouse. Nicholas Denys was born in Tours, France, in 1598.

3) George Edward Bissett (1801-1861). George's grandparents were Jacques and Jean who came to Halifax in the spring of 1752 on board the *Betty*. Jacques's son, Frederick, was from Lunenburg and George spent some time in Cole Harbour located outside Dartmouth. Later generation included: George Henry (1827-1921), Halifax, who married Virginia Lee Boudreau of D'Escousse (1830-1918); Dr Charles P. Bissett, MD (1866-1916) River Bourgeois, who married Emma Cameron of St. Peter's; William Cameron P. Bissett (1899-1973), Saint Peter's who married Ann Agnes (1901-1970), of Glace Bay; Charles P. Bissett (Wynndot, Michigan); and Charles W. Bissett (Camarillo, California). Mary Jane Boyd, daughter of Donald and Anastasia O'Toole, married George Bissett. Their children included Clarence, Clara, Marjorie and Hazel.

4) William LeVesconte's 1879 diary. Public Archives of Nova Scotia, Halifax.

5) *Richmond Record*, Marshall Bourinot, February 27, 1985.

6) Jack LeVesconte, whose father William was a business partner with Tom Leslie from D'Escousse, related details regarding the factory during interviews on March 27, 1988, and December 13, 1990.

7) The Registry for vessels constructed in Cape Breton opened in Sydney in

1786. *Sally*, a 35-ton vessel constructed in Louisbourg, was the first vessel registered that year. The Arichat registry opened in 1842. Vessels entering the various Ports were required to pay Harbour Master's Fees, under the provision of the Dominion Acts of Parliament for the appointment of Harbour Master at specified ports from December 3, 1886 to January 12, 1920. Elias Camille Bouchie was the local Harbour Master and kept Harbour Masters Records from 1888–1916. Lenova (Bouchie) Sampson, his granddaughter, provided information from his Harbour Master Journals on vessel traffic to and from the Harbour. Docking fees were less than 50 cents, depending on the size of the vessel. Camille died February 10, 1921 aged 78 and his wife, Edesse Bourque, died November 15, 1928 aged 78.

8) PANS Series "p", RG 5, Vol #44, 102, March 24, 1842.

9) The first satisfactory carding mill was invented by Sir Richard Arkwright in 1775. Intended to be used in the cotton industry, with some modifications it became extensively used in the wool industry. Carding involves the straightening and untangling of wool fibres in preparation for spinning. The carding machine produced a higher quality product than the hand cards and at a much faster rate. Prior to the invention of this machine, in large industrial centres carding was performed by child labour. The average sheep produced five to eight pounds of fleece.

10) *Pictou Twist* was a favourite chewing tobacco. It resembles a piece of flat black rope.

11) Peter Robertson (1826 – Sept. 14, 1909), married Rebecca Dugas (c. 1840-1908). They raised a family of 16 children. Peter's father was Samuel Sands (b. 1787) originally from the West Indies, He changed his name to William Robertson and married Mary Beaver.

12) Mercantile Agency Reference Book, Dunn Wiseman & Co., Dalhousie University Archives.

13) Thomas LeNoir opened a forge in Arichat in 1793 to provide ironwork for the bustling fishing and vessel construction industry.

14) Joe Robinson had a heart attack while gathering fire-clay at the shore below Isaac Burke's, in Cannes. Isaac carried him home by horse and sleigh. Martha DeRoche recalled the day it occurred.

15) Canadian Historical Magazine, Vol. 1, no 4, page 2188.

Miscellaneous terms used in this chapter

Packet – A little pack or small parcel. Parcel as of letters hence mail. A fast ship or boat, originally one under government control, for conveying mails and passengers at stated times. A vessel making regular trips.

Sloop – A fore-and-aft rigged boat with one mast and a single headsail jib.

Smack – A small coasting or fishing vessel, commonly rigged like a sloop.

Chapter III
Religion and the Parish Community

The Church was unquestionably the most important institution in the community. From it the inhabitants drew spiritual strength and guidance and its physical presence was a constant reminder of their religious obligations. The parishes of Arichat and L'Ardoise, which worked closely during the development years, provided all the missionaries before 1869.

Missionaries

Because of its geographical location and excellent port, Arichat developed into the industrial centre of Cape Breton in the early 1800s and became the headquarters for missionaries to L'Ardoise, Christmas Island and River Bourgeois. One of the earliest missionaries in Cape Breton and eastern Nova Scotia was Father Bailly de Messein, who came from Halifax in 1771. He boarded in Arichat on four separate occasions during that year, and is considered to be Arichat's first priest. In 1786, the earliest chapel was built under Father Joseph-Mathurin Bourg, the first Acadian priest, originally sent to Halifax as Vicar General by Bishop Louis-Philippe D'Esglis, the eighth bishop of Quebec. In 1786 there were 140 Acadian and Irish families living in Arichat; by 1811, the population had grown to 1,095.

Rev. Doctor William Phelan became Arichat's first permanent priest, serving from June 13, 1786–April 16, 1792, when he was removed from his duties by Superior Father Jones of Halifax. On September 28, 1792, Father François Lejamtel arrived in Arichat and conducted missionary work throughout Cape Breton while serving as pastor of Arichat until June 23, 1819.

Bishop Denaut of Quebec, the first Bishop to visit Arichat, arrived in early July of 1803. In a letter to Bishop Plessis, his co-adjutor in Quebec, he recorded the missions[1] served by Father Lejamtel as having 203 communicants and 128 children in Arichat, and 38 communicants and 20 children in River Bourgeois. This confirms that there was a substantial congregation established in River Bourgeois by the year 1800.

In 1815, Bishop Plessis visited Arichat and the eastern Nova Scotia parishes. The Bishop and his suite were pleased to engage the services of Captain Ignatius Foret and his elegant 75-ton schooner, *Lively*, for the return passage from Arichat to Halifax. Captain Foret offered to provide the service free of charge, since he was transporting a cargo of coal to Halifax. The bishop insisted on paying him $2/day for the baggage, to which he agreed. This incident is one of many which confirms the respect paid to clergy by merchants and citizens.

During Bishop Plessis' visit to Arichat, he appointed Father Gaulin as missionary of Antigonish and on July 4, 1815, he provided him with a list of duties to be performed in the community. There is no record of Father Gaulin's register, if he kept one, however records at Tracadie recorded his first baptism in Antigonish as being on July 16, 1815.

Arichat's third parish priest was Rev. Remi Gaulin who was transferred from Cheticamp where he had served four years. He remained in Arichat from July 1819–September 1822 when he was replaced by Father Hyancinthe Hudson. Father Henry McKeagney was appointed Fr. Hudson's assistant on January 1, 1823. (Father Gaulin was the first pastor of St. Ninian's Parish in Antigonish.)

Father McKeagney moved to L'Ardoise in early 1823 and helped establish the Parish of L'Ardoise. L'Ardoise served as the base from which River Bourgeois, St. Peter's and all the Micmacs Indians in Cape Breton were served. In 1823, Fathers Vincent de Paul and Henry McKeagney went to Chapel Island to hear confessions of 300 Micmacs assembled there to make their annual mission in preparation of the feast of St. Ann. Father McKeagney remained in L'Ardoise until January 9, 1825, at which time he was charged with the new mission of Sydney. The wardens of L'Ardoise and River Bourgeois were disappointed with his transfer and sent a Petition to Bishop Plessis in protest, to no avail.

Upon Father McKeagney's departure, the missions of L'Ardoise, River Bourgeois and the territory in-between once again became Arichat's responsibility. Father Hudson administered to the missions from Arichat until July 17, 1825 when Father Vincent de Paul[2] came to L'Ardoise. Beginning in July 1825, Father Vincent de Paul was the missionary priest for River Bourgeois. He remained in L'Ardoise until July, 1826. Father Hudson returned to Quebec and Father Jean Baptiste Potvin replaced him as Pastor of Arichat until 1828.

Other priests serving from Arichat before River Bourgeois became a separate parish included: Pierre Roy (1828–1832), Charles Lairez (1832–1835), Jean Baptiste Maranda (1835–1840) and Louis Alexis Bouret (who served for two months in 1840). Arichat's 10th resident pastor was Father Jean Baptiste Marande who served between 1840 and 1850. He was appointed Vicar Apostolic of Nova Scotia by Bishop Fraser, with Father Zephrine Leveque as his assistant.

On September 23, 1844, Arichat became a Diocese with Father William Fraser as the first Bishop, elected by decree of Pope Gregory XVI. The Arichat church canonically became a Cathedral on the same date and Father Maranda was appointed Rector and Vicar General of the Diocese.

River Bourgeois as a Separate Parish

Rev. Julien Courteau was appointed pastor of L'Ardoise in June of 1841 and remained there until 1869 when he was succeeded by Rev. James Quinan. The high esteem in which Father Courteau was held by his peers was expressed by Bishop MacKinnon in his report to Rome in 1860, when he wrote of the *assiduity and care which Father Courteau had, for 20 years, watched over the spiritual and temporal well-being of the Cape Breton Micmacs.*

By 1869, there were approximately 900 inhabitants in River Bourgeois being served by Rev. James Quinan from L'Ardoise. He was also responsible for the missions of St. Peter's, Red Islands, and the Micmacs. As a result of his numerous obligations, his schedule was to minister at L'Ardoise for the first two Sundays of the month and to visit River Bourgeois on the third Sunday; a schedule unacceptable to either parish. Considerable pressure was placed on Bishop MacKinnon to establish River Bourgeois as a Parish before leaving for Rome to attend the Vatican Council. The Parish was established by canonical decree under the patronage of Saint John the Baptist by Father Guillaume-Marin LeBlanc on August 8, 1869, which is so inscribed in the church registry.

Parish Priests

The first parish priest was **Rev. Guillaume-Marin LeBlanc** (1834-1907). He was born in Arichat on April 5, 1836 and attended Arichat Academy, St.FX College and the Grand Seminary of Quebec where he was ordained on April 22, 1866. Father LeBlanc served the parish from August 8, 1869–November 5, 1877. In 1877, Fr. LeBlanc[3] received notice from Bishop Cameron that he had been transferred to Port Felix. He was not pleased with the Bishop's decision and argued that the parish of Port Felix was too extensive and he was not a worthy replacement for the incumbent. Bishop Cameron, who was very strong-willed and determined, would not be told how to administer the diocese. During Father LeBlanc's pastorate at the River, the parish debt had risen to $500 and Fr. LeBlanc felt obliged to remain as pastor until the debt was eradicated. He felt so strongly over the issue that he expressed his desire to retire, rather than transfer to Port Felix. Bishop Cameron refused and a confrontation ensued.

Fr. LeBlanc was suspended and forbidden to say Mass or to exercise any priestly functions until he fully repented and repaid furnishings sold from the glebe and pew rents collected for 1878. During this confrontation period, wardens were appointed to manage parish affairs. Upon considerable deliberation and soul-searching, Father LeBlanc decided to reconsider his position and accept the transfer. Bishop Cameron would not reinstate him, however, until all financial matters were resolved. Fr. LeBlanc's suspension was lifted and he became pastor of Port Felix on December 3, 1878.

Father Charles-Pierre Martel was born in Arichat on December 8, 1828, and was ordained to the priesthood in Antigonish on May 28, 1860. He was transferred from Tracadie to River Bourgeois in 1877 and remained as pastor until 1888 when he retired to the Joseph Deslaurier Residence, because of poor health. He died on March 21, 1891 in River Bourgeois and is buried in the local cemetery. Father Martel was Fr. LeBlanc's uncle.

Father Michael MacKenzie was born in Red Islands and ordained in Quebec. He became the third pastor and served from 1888 to 1891. He retired to the Deslaurier Residence where he died in 1891.

Father Donald J. Cameron was born on December 17, 1863. Ordained a priest on October 18, 1891, he was appointed the parish's fourth pastor. He served from 1891–1893 when he retired to the Deslaurier Residence where he died April 3, 1893. He was buried in the local cemetery and the encryption on his headstone indicates the respect in which he was held by parishioners. *In loving memory of Rev. D.J. Cameron, whose mortal remains here repose. This monument is affectionately erected by his loving parishioners and factful friends ...*

Father Hugh P. MacPherson (1867-1949) made frequent visits to River Bourgeois between 1892 and 1893, while he was posted in L'Ardoise.

Father Amable-Evariste Mombourquette (1863-1949) was born in L'Ardoise and ordained in Montreal. He served the parish from 1893–1895.

Father Alexander M. O'Handley served between 1895 –1902. He was relieved of his duties because of problems with alcohol.

Father Gustave Treunet was originally from France. He served between 1902–1904 at which time he was succeeded by Father Chouinard.

Father Joseph Louis de Gonzague Chouinard (1895-1959) was born and educated in Quebec. He served as pastor when major renovations were being made on the Church between 1904–1909. He is remembered for his strict adherence to religious principles in vogue at the time. Dancing, except at weddings, holding hands, boys and girls swimming together and like activities, were considered to be against religious principles and would not be tolerated. During one of his more emotional sermons, he pounded the pulpit exclaiming, *There will never be a priest come out of River Bourgeois.* Apparently, his inflexibility in dealing with prominent parishioners resulted in his being transferred to Petit de Grat in 1909. He also had a conflict with Mr. Terriot who had completed the renovations to the church. He died in Rimouski in 1959 at the age of 84 years.

Father Joseph Pierre Robitaille's (1874-1949) obituatory read:

> *April 29—Rev. Robitaille, beloved parish priest of River Bourgeois-Port Felix parish, died today after a brief illness. Born at L'Ancienne–Lorette, Que., in 1874, he would have been 75 years of age on June 28. Father Pierre was ordained at his native town by Cardinal Begin on Dec. 28, 1902. He was educated at Ancienne, St. Joseph's College in Memramcook, N.B., and Grand Seminary, Que. He served as curate at Arichat from Jan. 15, 1903, until November the following year when he was named curate of D'Escousse. On Jan. 10, 1907, he became parish priest at Port Felix, and in 1909 was placed in charge of River Bourgeois, where he served until his death. He was a son of the late Jacques Robitaille and Marie Hamel of Ancienne. He was one of the best known and respected priests in the diocese. Surviving members of his family include two brothers, Rev. Joseph Edward Robitaille, Edmonton diocese, and Dr. Theophile Robitaille, Quebec City. Requiem, High Mass was held in River Bourgeois, however he was buried in Quebec.*

Father Pierre operated the parish farm and shared his extensive knowledge of farming with parishioners. He was very influential in maintaining the French culture, and in this regard formed the *Cape Breton Historical Society.* The purpose of this society was to encourage and support research into the French origins of Cape Breton and to promote and manifest them. His brother, Edward, served as curate in Arichat and made frequent visits to the River. Parishioners were very fond of both priests.

Father Flavien Samson was born in L'Ardoise on December 22, 1899. He served as parish priest between 1950–1965. He was educated in Memramcook and Quebec where he was ordained at the Grand Seminary on May 6, 1928. He was sickly early in his career, spending 13 years in Cheticamp Hospital. Upon his arrival at the River, he identified the needs of the community, in particular those of the youth. He was amazed at the generosity of parishioners and embarked on a series of projects which had a lasting positive effect on the community. He supported the establishment of the Consolidated School, the Parish Centre and baseball field, the construction of a new glebe, the conversion of the old glebe to a convent for the *Filles de Jesus*, looked after refurbishment of the church and vestry and the erection of the large wooden cross and statues overlooking the cemetery.

On August 31, 1965, the Sisters became suspect when Father Samson did not arrive at the vestry for morning mass. Father Rodgers of L'Ardoise was summoned and together with James Richard and Whitney McPhee, the glebe door was forced open. Father was found dead in his chair, the television playing and a cigarette butt lay clenched between his fingers. He is remembered as a kind and devoted priest.

Father Joseph Marinelli was born in Glace Bay. He was fluent in three languages, loved to sing, and was highly respected by parishioners. He served from 1965–1973.

Father Thomas Morley served from June 1973– July 1979. He is remembered as a very warm priest who loved singing.

Father Hugh A. MacDonald served from July 1979–July 1981. He was instrumental in bringing religion back into the schools and revived many of the traditional religious celebrations.

Father John J. MacDonald served from July 1981–August 1988 and was certainly one of the most likable priests. He brought back the French mass and was very involved in the Credit Union and Co-op. He was transferred to D'Escousse where he remains as pastor.

Father Hugh D. MacDonald served from August 1988–August 1991. During his term, a considerable number of restoration projects were undertaken on the church.

Father Charles Gordon Brewer served from September 4, 1991–1993. He was born in Ingonish on December 20, 1930 and educated at St.FX University and Holy Heart Seminary in Halifax. He was ordained to the priesthood on May 23, 1959 in Antigonish. Father served as chief librarian at St.FX and provided pastoral services throughout his priesthood as an assistant in several parishes. He was a great supporter of the history of Antigonish and obtained a Master of Arts in History at U.N.B. in 1971. Father Brewer died on May 27, 1993 at the Community Health Centre in Sydney, at the age of 62. In response to his request, he was buried in River Bourgeois where 60 priests attended his funeral.

The following priests also served the Parish: **Rev. A. Doucet**, **Rev. Gerroir** and **Clarence MacDonald**.

Father Bernard A. MacDonald was appointed Pastor on May 30, 1993. He was originally pastor of St. Joseph's Church, Southwest Margaree and St. Patrick's Church in Northeast Margaree. He is highly respected by Parishoners.

First Chapel

It was very important, especially for Catholic Acadians, to have a place of worship and a suitable meeting place for the visiting missionary. The chapel was located in Gallitan Valley[4] in Les Etangs, where the first permanent settlers established themselves. This locale was one of the closest crossing points from Isle Madame and landings were protected by Cascaret Island.

First Church

A pastoral report from Arichat dated May 1825 mentions River Bourgeois as one of the four missions served, with a *church* built there prior to that date. The indenture in **Appendix 5** relates to land[5] being allocated specifically for a church.

The first trustees of the church as recorded on July 2, 1830 were: John Burke, Peter Burke, John Beranger, and Simon Landry. Father Joseph Narcisse Trudel of L'Ardoise was clerk and missionary priest of St. John the Baptist Church. According to historian A.A. Johnson, the first chapel on Church Point was located close to the seawall on lands donated by Abraham Sampson, father of Thomas Sampson. The chapel, constructed in 1825, was located south of the present church in line with the lighthouse.

Second Church, Site of the Present Church

Confirmation of a chapel existing in the early 1840s is found in the parish registry regarding the blessing of the bell[6]. The document reads: *1843– Blessing of the new bell, Jean the Baptiste.*

Father Courteau, who missioned to River Bourgeois from L'Ardoise beginning in 1841, recorded that the Church Bell was *baptised* (given a name according to the church ritual) on November, 20, 1843. For the ceremony, the bell's Godparents were Jean (John) Bourg and Marie Poirier. They gave the bell its name, *Jean-Baptiste.*

Additional evidence which confirms the existence of a chapel before 1850 was discovered in a Hydrographic Field Note Survey[7] which shows a *chapel* in the general area of the present church.

Bell of 1878

There is no record as to what happened to the first bell. A second bell[8], blessed in 1878, was installed in the present church. This bell, shown in **Plates 300** and **301**, was blessed on May 12, 1878 by Monseigneur John Cameron accompanied by Rev. D.I. McIntosh (pastor of L'Ardoise), Rev. James M. Quinan (pastor of D'Escousse), Rev. Archibald McKenzie (pastor of Hawkesbury) and parish priest Rev. Chas P. Martell. It bears the name *Saint John the Baptist*, along with all the ceremonies of the Roman Ritual.

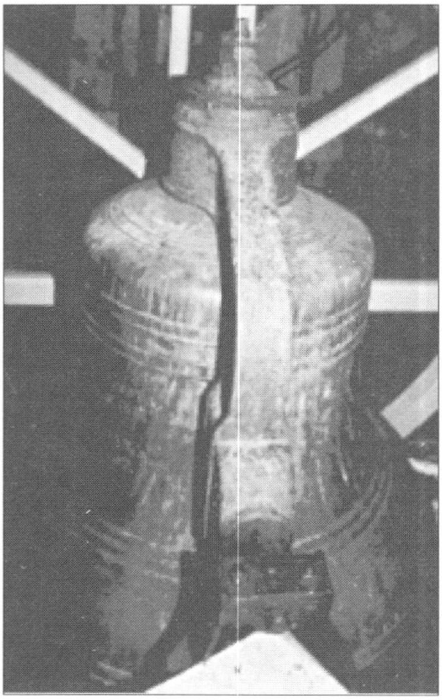

Plate 300–Courtesy of Anselm Sampson

Honoured Godparents: Acetic Beetroot and Eusebe Beetroot, Mrs. George H. Bissett, Mrs. Patient Bouché, Duncan Cameron, Mrs. Elias Cordeau, Mrs. Lucien Cordeau, Abraham Fougere, Mrs. William Fougere, Hen. H.H. and Marie Antoinette Fuller, Edwan Hearn, John Kite, Patrick Kite, Mrs. André Landrie, John Landry Jr., Mrs. Noel Landry, Pierre LeBlanc, James Morrison Jr., Mr. and Mrs. James Morrison Sr., Mrs. Simon Pettipas Sr., John Richard, Mrs. Charles Sampson Sr. and her son John, Daniel Sampson, David Sampson, Isidor Sampson, Mrs. Julie Sampson, Mr. and Mrs. Placide Sampson, Mrs. Thomas Sampson, Urban Sampson, Mr. and Mrs. John Sutton, Mr. and Mrs. Robert Sutton, Mrs. William Toole.

The following is engraved on the bell:

Ste. Joannis Baptista, Rev. C. P. Martell 1878
U. Samson, D. Samson, D. Cameron, U. Boudrot

On July 13, 1994, the bell was removed from the tower following recommendations of A.H. Roy and Associates Limited from Antigonish,

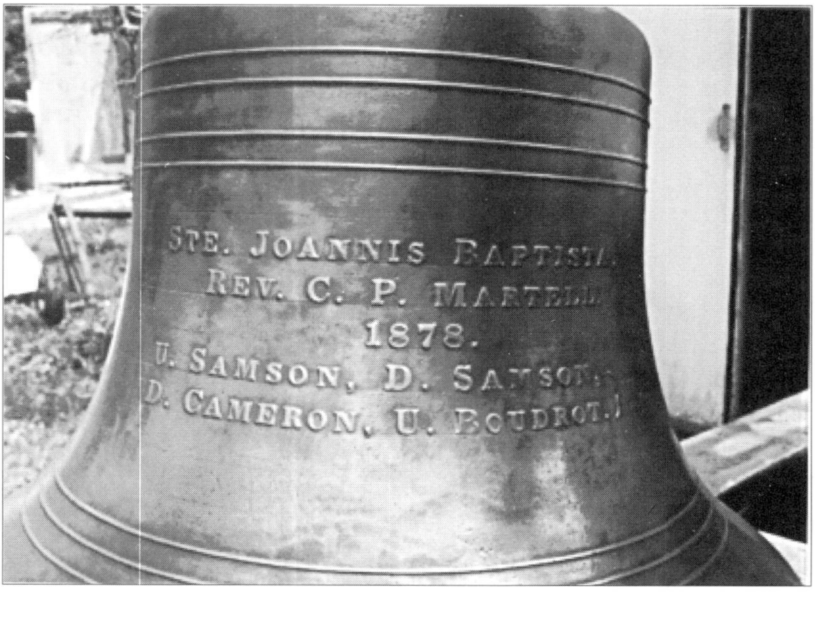

Plate 301–Taken by Garvie Samson

who questioned the structural integrity of the tower, as it had experienced considerable water damage over the years. Workmen participating in lowering the bell, directed by Anselm Sampson, included his brother Bernard, Arthur Bouchard, Albert Burke, Rock Filion, Danny Landry and George Landry. The bell will be mounted for public display.

Existing Church

A number of major alterations were made to the church between 1903–1909. The current church, which can be identified by the five windows along the side, is shown in **Plate 302**. **Plate 303** taken in 1947, and **Plate 304** taken in 1953, show the remodelled interior and exterior. The renovations included lengthening the church and increasing its height to facilitated the installation of a balcony, pulpit, and window over the altar. Numerous refurbishing projects undertaken over the years have been summarized in **Appendix 6**.

Rectories

The original rectory, shown to the right in **Plate 302**, was constructed in 1869. It served as a residence, office and meeting place for the priests and parishioners until 1954, when a new rectory was constructed. In that same year, the parish was honoured with the arrival of Sisters from the Congregation of *Les Filles de Jesus*, who came from Arichat to teach in the new school. The Sisters occupied the old rectory until 1968, when they moved to Louisdale. The old rectory was closed and Lawrence (Bucky)

Plate 302–Courtesy of Russell Fougere

L to R. Ann Samson, Victoria Samson, Maude Lethizer, "Nanonne" Samson, Amable Samson, Willie Robertson and Bennie Samson.

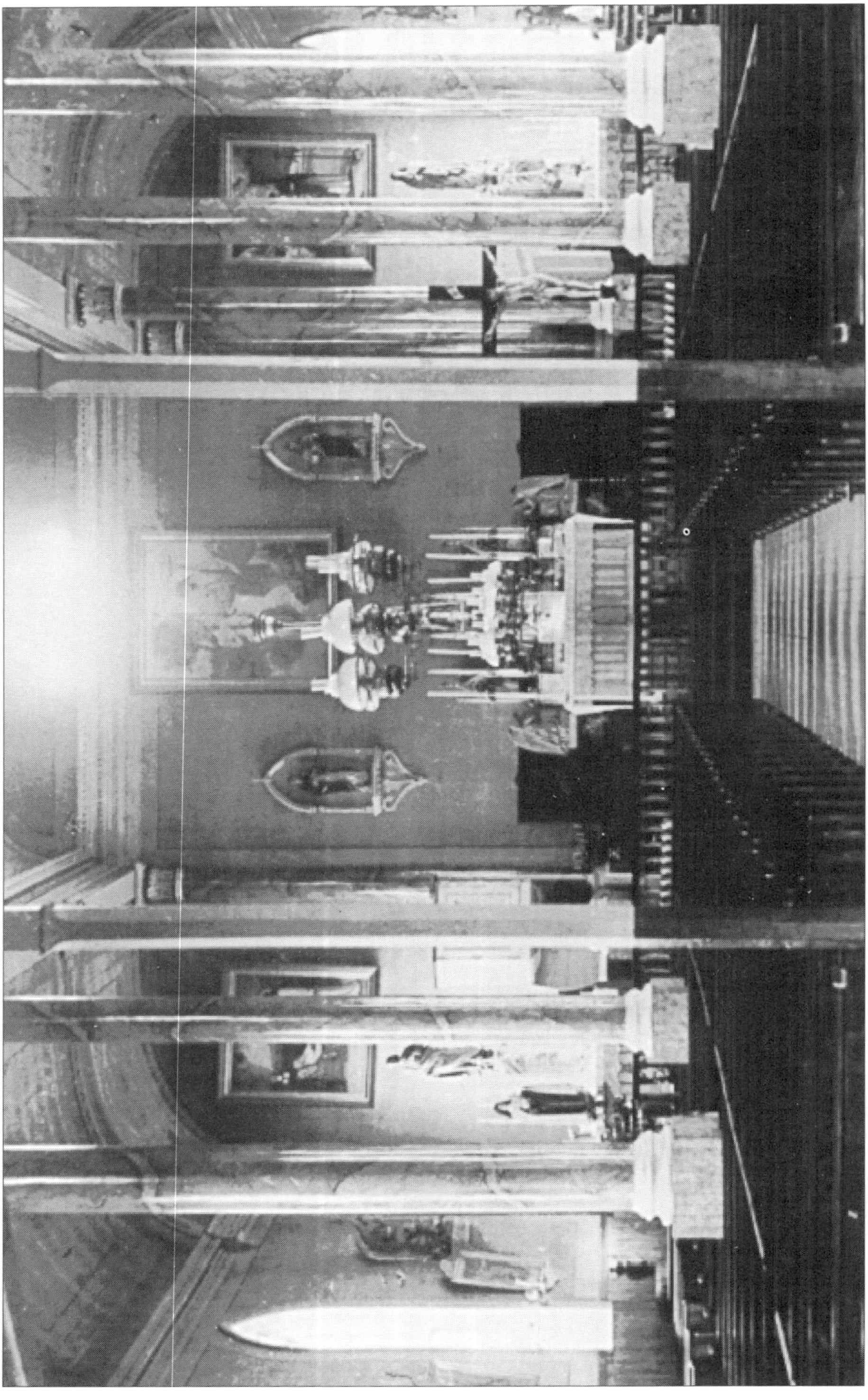

Plate 303–Courtesy of Marguerite Fougere

B. Martin photo

Plate 304–Courtesy of E.G.L. Wetmore (PANS)

Sampson purchased the building and hauled it across the road where it was converted into a triplex. It sits on land originally owned by Thomas Sampson.

Lighting and Chimes

Lighting was originally provided by kerosene lamps suspended on brackets at various locations around the perimeter of the church. The ornate lamp assemblies, with oval shades and silver reflectors, were attached to the walls with metal brackets. The central areas of the church and balcony were lit by three beautiful chandeliers containing clusters of six lamps each. The fixtures were fitted with a recoil mechanism which enabled them to be lowered for refuelling and lighting. Wall-mounted units were provided at the stairs, entrance lobby, and vestry. The caretakers were responsible for lighting and fuelling the lamps. Sarah Digout was fortunate enough to obtain one of these lamps as a souvenir and counts it as a prized possession.

When electricity came to the River in 1939, electrical wiring became a priority in the church for lighting and the furnace. The church was wired in 1939 and electronic chimes were installed in 1953 through the generous support of the C.W.L. During their many years of operation, the chimes could be heard throughout the parish. They were used to sound the Angelus, play music at feasts such as Easter and Christmas, and during the church services. The loudspeakers[9] are mounted in the bell tower while the electronic consoles are located on the west wall of the Vestry.

Parish Farm

Priests were given a bare subsistence allowance for their services. In an attempt to make ends meet, many resorted to the operation of a small farm. Father Robitaille kept five Jersey cows and two horses in a two-story gambrel-roofed barn which measured 28 feet x 32 feet. The animals occupied the first floor and the second story was used for hay, straw and grain. The main floor and walls were constructed of concrete. Hay was unloaded from the wagon with a horse-drawn hayfork. Father Robitaille or a servant boy would transport the cream to the River Tillard railway flag station by horse and wagon and it would be processed in Sydney or Antigonish. In later years, as the roads improved and vehicles became available, cream was taken to MacIntyre's Lake to expedite delivery. Farm equipment included a mower, raker, wagon, carriage and a threshing machine. The priest owned several parcels of land which were used to provide hay for his cattle and additional requirements were purchased from parishioners. Remnants of the barn's foundation remain to this date.

The farm also included an icehouse measuring 16 feet x 20 feet, located north of the barn, close to the existing school. Ice cakes came from a pond in Marshall and Victor Digout's field, off Joe's Brook in Cannes and Lindloff Lake in St. Peter's. Anselm Sampson worked on the farm as a teenager in the early 1940s. One of his duties was to keep the glebe's ice box filled with fresh ice. There were two chicken coops located southeast of the barn which housed 2,000 birds. Chicks were purchased in New Glasgow and sold at maturity in Sydney. There was a small vegetable garden and a carriagehouse east of the glebe.

Cemetery

The Parish cemetery is adjacent to the church on a very steep slope visible from most of the parish community. In 1956, a large cross and several statues were placed in close proximity to burial plots of four priests. The cross is lighted and can be seen from great distances on a clear night. Problems regarding the size and location of the cemetery were first voiced by E.C. Bouchie, Harbour Master, who lived on the adjoining property to the west. He expressed his concerns in a letter[10] to the Province on February 25, 1895.

Problems concerning the limited cemetery space were expressed in the Sunday Bulletin of May 20/21, 1989, by Father Hugh D. MacDonald.

> *As you well know, we are getting very short of cemetery space. It is urgent that we make a move to obtain some land very soon. A great deal of work has been done on this project already, and various possibilities have been investigated. The Department of Health has strict rules and regulations (rightly so) as to the location of a cemetery. So it isn't an easy project to get suitable land properly located, etc. The Parish Council is seriously considering an 18-acre piece of land across from the Tower Road (on the St. Peter's side of the Community Centre). The asking price for this piece of land is $12,000. At the present time, we are awaiting approval from the Dept. of Health as well as checking out other aspects of the land.*

Concerns regarding the cost and location of land to expand the cemetery were eliminated in 1989 when Edward Touesnard donated a parcel of land to the parish. This land, located on the east side of Church Point Road across from the school, is ideal with its close proximity to the church and the old cemetery. The land has not been used to date as there is still space in the original cemetery. River Bourgeois parishioners are truly grateful for this most generous gift.

Deslaurier Residence

Joseph and Philisité's (Samson) residence, now owned by Edward Touesnard, was once the home of several retired priests. Some suggest that it was once used as a glebe, however I am unable to confirm this as the old glebe has been in place since 1870. Cletus Touesnard recalls being told that Joseph Deslaurier used to drive priests and others in the community in his horse-drawn wagon.

Cletus's aunt Philisité said that the kitchen was added to the house by David Samson (Old Captain David). The roof trusses in this addition, as well as those in the main house which was built by 1880, are labelled in Roman numerals and secured with wooden pegs. The trusses were likely prefabricated in Boston and transported to the River by vessel.

James Richard boarded at Joseph Deslaurier's house with Amable Bona in 1939. He recalls that on the south side of the second story, there was a large open room which the retired priests used as a chapel. Florence Touesnard showed me this room with old pictures of priests and saints, as well as the wooden mantle that served as an altar.

Funeral Home

In recent years, funeral homes have all but replaced the family home and church vestry as the traditional resting place to mourn and respect the deceased. The church vestry had often been used for this purpose, however the threat of fire became an increasing concern and alternatives were considered. A committee, headed by Father Hughie D. MacDonald, was selected and met on April, 30, 1989. (Leo Digout died on this day.) In attendance were: Kenneth Cosman (chairman), Glen Sampson, Neil Burke, Arthur Doary, Danny Landry, Albert Burke, Rita Fougere, Anselm Sampson, Tony Sampson, Stanley McPhee, Mary Touesnard and George A. Landry.

Following months of research and visits to other facilities, plans were drawn by Arthur Doary which incorporated the most desirable features. Land was obtained from Mrs. (Fraser) Catherine Boyd and Blaise Boyd on the Number 4 Highway in Cannes (see **Plate 305**). Construction began on May 14, 1990 and was completed by September. The official opening of the non-denominational,

Plate 305–Taken by Garvie Samson

40 x 40 foot funeral home was held on September 30, 1990. Dignitaries included: Fr. Hugh D. MacDonald, P.P., Richie Mann, MLA, Madeline Libbus, Warden/ Councillor, and Kenneth Cosman, chairman.

Construction of the facility was headed by Donald Webb, carpenter foreman from L'Ardoise. Local workmen included: Maurice Landry, Blaise Boyd, Lee Burke, Tony Sampson and Basil Bourque. Arthur Doary provided consultation as required. Financing was provided by a government grant which covered one-half of the cost, while parishioners contributed through the Funeral Home Fund and personal donations. Other parishioners donated sodding for the landscaping, a kitchen set, furniture, plaques, and photos. The greatly-needed facilities is also benefiting surrounding communities who rent it for a minimal charge.

Religious Whose Parents were from the Parish

Name	Parents
Rev. David Bona	Edith Monica (Savage) & Andrew Bona
Rev. Leo Curdo (Cordeau)	Mr. & Mrs. John Curdo
Fr. Meade	Elizabeth Jane (Digout) & Arthur Meade
Rev. Kenneth Leo Robertson	Florence Mary (Power) & Alexander Alfred Robertson
Rev. Lloyd Joseph Robertson	Florence Mary (Power) & Alexander Alfred Robertson
Rev. Gregory Sampson	Lottie (Boucher) & Danny Sampson
Brother Pius Sampson	Harriet (Fougere) & Henry Sampson
Fr. Earl Smith	Margaret (Burke) & Gerald Smith
Rev. Richard Thibeau	Sophie (Burke) & Gilbert Thibeau
Rev. John Yake	Theresa (Burke) & Earl Yake
Sr. Elizabeth Beranger	Mary (Burke) & Damien Beranger
Sr. Maurice Boudreau (Anne)	Adèle (Boucher) & Pierre Boudreau
Sr. Regis Boudreau	Suzanne (Bourque) & Maurice Boudreau
Sr. Jeanne Boucher	Harriet Jane (Sampson) & Lewis Boucher
Sr. Helen Burke	Clara (Fougere) & Harry Burke
Sr. Lola Burke	Alvina (Beranger) & John P. Burke
Srs. Geraldine, Agnus and Anastasia	Mr. & Mrs. John Curdo
Sr. Lena Landry	Angèle (Boudreau) & Anselm Landry
Sr. Veronica MacNeil	Mary Mathilda (Boudreau) & Ernest MacNeil

Sr. Adèle Robertson	Rebecca (Dugas) & Peter Robertson
Sr. Helen Elizabeth Robertson *(Sr. Mary of Irene)*	Florence May (Power) & Alexander Alfred Robertson
Sr. Loretta Sampson	Josephine (Beranger) & John J. Sampson
Sr. Madeleine Thibeau	Margaret Anne (Boudreau) & John H. Thibeau

- **Sr. Ann Samson** was born February 5, 1891, the daughter of Philomen (Bourque) & Thomas Samson. Now aged 103, she resides at *Filles de Jesus Motherhouse* in Moncton N.B. See **Plate 1811** taken on December 11, 1991 (Aged 99 years and 10 months).

Servant Girls and Caretakers

- Annie Ranson originally from Poirierville served for several years under Fr. Pierre Robitaille.
- Little Nanonne Sampson was well-known and remembered because of her small stature.
- Katie Ann (Sampson) Burke worked for Fr. Samson. She was recommended by Sr. Lola who was in Cheticamp teaching at the time he was convalescing in the Cheticamp Hospital.
- Emily (Landry) Boucher currently assists the priest with cooking and household chores.

Caretakers at the turn of the century (including Thomas Sampson, Beni Samson and Charlie (Tom) Sampson) attended the furnace when the church was heated by a steam boiler fuelled with coke. Water for the furnace came from the cistern. There was a small pot-bellied stove in the vestry where weekday masses were offered. When Father Samson arrived, he installed an oil-fired furnace in the vestry. E'phrem Boudreau worked at the glebe in 1921 when he was a student at the River Bourgeois school. In an article in *Le Courier Section du Cape-Breton* on December 17, 1986, he recalled earning his keep while going to school. Some of his duties included: lighting the fire at the vestry, caring for the farm animals, and ringing the Angelus. Father Pierre Robitaille was pastor at the time.

Choir Members and Altar Servers

One of the earliest organists was Bruno Beranger, the first school teacher. He had been studying to be a Trappist Monk and was very familiar with the Gregorian Chant sung at the time. Other choir directors included: Mrs. D.D. Boyd (formerly Catherine MacIsaac), John Bona, Annie Boyd, Cecilia (Boyd) Fougere, Katie Ann (Sampson) Burke, Sisters from the *Filles de Jesus*, and

Henrietta Doary. Singers included John J. Sampson, Charlie Sampson, Peter Digout and Amable (à Noré) Burke. Jack Adams, a friend of Charlie Sampson[11], used to come from St. Peter's to sing on special occasions. Anthony Landry recalls singing with his brother John at Ephrem and Julia Boudreau's wedding. I recall singing next to Tony and Bennie Konning during the early 1950s when Gregorian Chant was still in common use. Victoria Bouchie was paid $15/year for singing at daily mass. Pauline Bond also sang for years.

Current **Altar Servers** include: Chris Boudreau, T.J. Burke, Stephen Burke, Jackie Digout, Joseph Doary, Krista and Ryan Dorey, Melinda Doutaz, Christopher Fillion, John Grimes, Chad Landry, Gordie Landry, Janice and Laurie Landry, Daphne LeBlanc, Amanda MacDonald, Ann McNamara, Andrew Touesnard and Krista Touesnard. Charlie Digout was a servant boy between 1923–1944 and received $2/month for his service.

Parish Council

The Parish priests have been assisted throughout the years by the Parish Council. This year's members are: Fr. Bernie A. MacDonald, Mimi Fougere, Theresa Burke, Ann MacNeil-Landry, George A. Landry, Carmen Fougere, Anselm Sampson, Art Bouchard, Michael Boudreau and Danny Landry.

Plate 306 -Taken by Garvie Samson

Present Choir (left to right)
Front Row–Madeleine Cook, Vera Landry, Lynn Grenier, Blanche Comeau, Mary Cosman, Ann Sampson.

Second Row–Henrietta Doary (director and organist), Ethel Stone, Josephine Morrison, Marlaine Burke, Margaret Morrison, Betty Park, Robert Park (vocals and guitar).

Third Row–Michael Owens (vocal and guitar), Delore Burke, Mathilda Boudreau, Lillian (Lilly) Smith, Joan Owens, Mary Touesnard.

Religion Teachers

The religious congregation, *Les Filles de Jesus*, which had opened a convent in Arichat in 1902, were invited to teach in the new River Bourgeois school in 1954. They taught regular courses, religion classes, chanted for morning mass, directed the choir, prepared serving boys, assisted the priest, cared for vestments, and did household chores. They lived in the River Bourgeois rectory until 1967, in Louisdale Convent until 1970, then moved to L'Ardoise where the lived until 1983. They finished teaching in River Bourgeois in 1977.

Religion classes continue to be taught. Teachers include: Therèse Digout (who teaches and organizes classes), Lucille Boudreau, Joan Owens, Ethel Stone, Margie Gullickson and Florence Sampson.

Religious Celebrations

One of the most memorable historic celebrations was the *Feast of The Assumption* celebrated in a different parish each year, on which occasion the Bishop was in attendance. Parishioners were honoured by the Bishop's visit with his entourage of dignitaries and guests from surrounding parishes. They were proud of their community and expressed it by making a special effort to tidy their properties, adding a fresh coat of paint to their houses and whitewashing their fences. Each household flew a small flag and the church was decorated with flowers, wreaths and banners. The choir, singing in Gregorian Chant, was specially prepared for the occasion. Following the liturgical celebrations, parishioners were treated to a supper at either the school or one of George Bissett's buildings located by the Government Wharf.

Children usually feasted in the afternoon while the adults dined in the evening when the festivities concluded with music and dancing. This was one of the rare occasions that priests tolerated dancing. Sister Lola Burke recalls these celebrations very well as Laura Boyd used to teach the children different songs and dances to perform during these occasions.

Confirmation

Confirmation was a very special day in the lives of children and their parents. It was for some the end of Sunday School, but for many a step into adulthood. The Bishop only went to individual parishes once every four years for this celebration. On July 14, 1861, Bishop MacKinnon confirmed 55 at River Bourgeois and 87 in Arichat.

Mi-careme

The Mi-careme, frequently mentioned by parishioners during interviews, was celebrated on Monday and Shrove Tuesday before Lent. During the celebration, people masqueraded and performed at night, going door to door as children now do on Halloween. The crowds announced their presence with sustained high-pitched shrill chants then residents would welcome their guests. Every effort was made to identify individuals while fiddles, accordions and mouth organs played for dancing and entertainment. In some instances, it is rumoured that liquor was served with tea, coffee and fresh pastries. Such festivities would be incomplete without pranksters overturning outhouses, freeing cattle from their pastures, or setting rowboats adrift.

Silver Jubilee

On December 28, 1927, parishioners showed their deepest respect for Father Robitaille on the 25th anniversary of his ordination to the priesthood. The organizing committee included Mrs. Annie Boyd, President and Mrs. Daniel Samson, Vice-President. Father Robitaille was assisted at mass by Father Leo Keats (St. Peter's), Father Abraham Boudreau (L'Ardoise), Father Wilfred Boucher (D'Escousse), and Father Theophile Paul Millet (West Arichat). The choir was directed by Mrs. D.D. Boyd (formerly Catherine MacIsaac). A superb banquet was held with Fabian Landry as head cook. Head table guests included the priests, John P. Burke (Municipal Councillor), Alex Sampson (Postmaster), Eugene Digout, Captains Anselm Sampson and Frédéric Bourque, Léonard Fougère and Thomas Poirier (D'Escousse).

125 Years of Faith and Commitment

On August 7, 1994, under the direction of Father Bernie A. MacDonald, Saint John the Baptist Church celebrated its 125th Anniversary as a separate parish. *(It is noteworthy that missionaries provided spiritual guidance and administered the sacraments to inhabitants before 1794.)* Parish Council President, Ann MacNeil-Landry, welcomed Bishop Colin Campbell, Father Hugh MacDonald, Father Francis Cameron and the congregation, inviting them to participated in this important celebration. In his homily, Bishop Campbell commended the parish for its spiritual development throughout the years and wished it every success during the next century. **Plate 307** shows the celebrants.

To mark this occasion, the community called upon its talented people to undertake a variety of church-related projects. They included:

- Sunday afternoon mass and reception at the Tara Lynn Community Centre.
- Unveiling of the first set of stained glass windows designed by Sheila (Sampson) Caissie, daughter of Basil and Virginia Sampson, and constructed by Arthur Doary.
- Unveiling of a banner designed and made by Francis Digout with a stand constructed by her brother Ernie Bourque (**Plate 308**).

Plate 307–Taken by Garvie Samson

- Unveiling of a stole for Fr. J.J. MacDonald designed by Arthur Doary and sewn by Pennie Pottie.
- Publication of an information booklet by Committee members (Francis Digout, Thérese Digout, Gerry Fougere, Gerard Touesnard, Fr. Bernie MacDonald and Sylvia Pottie). **N.B.** – I was pleased to provide my research information to the Committee and I thank them for their acknowledgement.
- Commemorative plaques designed by Arthur Doary.
- Construction of a platform and erection of a sign on the Number 4 Highway at the entrance of Church Point Road, to post the mass schedule, completed by Anselm Sampson and Arthur Doary.
- A lunch served at the Parish Centre by the Parish C.W.L.

Stained Glass Window, Donors and Dedications

The first stained glass windows were installed at the north side of the church adjacent to the side entrance door (See **Plate 309**). Donors and dedications were as follows:

- The west half of the window section was donated by the Sampson family and Leo Doré–dedicated to James and Mary Sampson and daughter Lena Doré.

Plate 308–Taken by Garvie Samson

Plate 309–Taken by Garvie Samson

- The second section was donated by Francis Mary Digout–dedicated to Leo Digout and daughter Yvonne, Hilaire, Ida and Claude Bourque.
- The uppermost triangular section was donated by Marlaine, Albert, Stephen, Neil and Allen Burke–dedicated to Delphis Alzear Landry.

Church Identification Crest

Above the main entrance to the church was placed a crest bearing the name of the church, Saint John the Baptist, the year it was established as a parish, and the year the last bells were installed. The crest was designed and constructed by Anselm Sampson and installed in 1990. The cost of the crest was funded by the estate of Marie Boyd, a former school teacher and one of the community's most active members, always ready to share her time and talents.

Contributions of Workmanship

The fine craftsmanship of our ancestors has been preserved by men such as Ernie Bourque who are continuously donating objects of their work to the church. His contributions include five statue pedestals, one of which supports the statue of the Blessed Virgin, two altar server chairs, as well as an altar and tabernacle at the vestry. Ernie's brother, Claude, constructed an oversized priest chair, complete with armrests and carvings. The multi-talented Arthur Doary contributed numerous items including the main altar in the church and steps at the altar railing. He is currently fabricating the stained glass windows and an altar for the sacristy.

Other

Throughout the years, the contributions made by parishioners to maintain the church, and assist with mass as singers, altar servers and caretakers, has been enormous. Without such assistance, the parish would not function.

I would be remiss if I did not officially thank Anselm Sampson who was an invaluable asset to my investigations of the church properties during the last several years. Together we scaled walls and ceilings, crawled into crevices and measured everything we felt noteworthy, in an attempt to record the history of the church.

Endnotes

1) A.A. Johnson, page 203, Volume II.

2) Father Vincent de Paul was born in Chalamont, near Lyons, France, on October 29, 1768, a son of Claude Merle (a physician and surgeon) and Louise Garner. At baptism he took on the name of James. He was ordained into the Trappist Order at Val Sainte, Switzerland, on October 13, 1805. He journeyed to Boston, New York, and finally to Halifax on May 10, 1815, where he was provided hospitality by Father Burke. Father Vincent's ship sailed to England without him while he was procuring provisions.

3) Reference book; Bishop John Cameron, R.A. MacLean, 1991.

4) The area received its name from Gallitan Richard, an early resident.

5) Arichat, July 2, 1830, Book C, page 315.

6) Parish registry, 1845-1885, page 28, Rev. Coudreau.

7) Hydrographical survey map of 1850, Bedford Institute of Technology.

8) This bell was manufactured by Meneely & Kimberley Founders, Troy, N.Y. and measures 32 inches in diameter and 24 inches in height.

9) Church Speakers–The belfry is constructed of 16 sides and contains eight louvres. The eight speakers are mounted such that most face the more populated area of the parish, namely towards the North, East and West, as viewed from the tower. Data on chime equipment installed in the vestry: Carillonic Bells, Model 180 Series, Schulmeric Carillon Inc., Sellerville, P.A.

10) Letter written by E.C. Bouchie in 1895 concerning the encroachment of the cemetery on his property. Information provided by Lenova (Bouchie) Sampson, Camille's granddaughter.

11) Charlie drowned at River Tillard on December 23, 1937, as a result of a motor vehicle accident. His wife was left to raise a young family of seven boys and seven girls.

Chapter IV
Education

Provincial School Act of 1826

Educational conditions in Cape Breton in the early 1800s were best described by Lawrence Kavanaugh Jr., Member of the Legislative Assembly of Nova Scotia, in his 1824 official survey[1] for the Provincial Government. He wrote:

> *There is no Regular School in the County of Cape Breton that I know of, except one in Sydney and one at Arichat, but I am not competent to say the number of Children that attend the former, nor the allowance paid the Master for Tuition.*

River Bourgeois is recorded under L'Ardoise for which he reports: *At River Bourgeois, there are 30 families and about 40 children fit for Schooling. The people are poor and not in circumstances to support a Teacher.*

Kavanaugh's provincial survey was the basis upon which the Assembly passed the School Act of 1826. It decreed that each Section maintain a school (at the expense of the parents), and that the minimum salary of the teacher be 50 pounds/year. Cape Breton was to receive 220 pounds, and the town of Halifax 300 pounds (100 pounds each for the National, Acadian, and Catholic schools).

Beginning of School System

The first professional educator to be paid from public funds was Bruno Beranger, a young postulate monk from France attending the Trappist Monastery in Tracadie. Deciding not to take his final vows, he settled in L'Ardoise. After returning from Rome to obtain his dispensation he moved to River Bourgeois where he spend the rest of his life teaching and assisting the clergy. Bruno quickly learned that teaching was the easy part of his profession; convincing parents that education was more important than assisting with household chores or helping dad on the fishing schooner, was his real challenge. His contributions and dedication to service in both communities was acknowledged in Petition[2] dated January 20, 1869.

> *To the Honourable The House of Representative of Nova Scotia now in General Assembly convened. The Petition of John Beranger of River Bourgoise in the County of Richmond School Teacher,*
>
> *HUMBLY SHEWETH, that your petitioner opened a school in L'Ardoise under the patronage of the Revd. Priest McKeagney on the 25th day of July in the year 1825 and continued as a teacher for three years. After that period petitioner removed and settled in River Bourgoise, and a few years after opened a school at*

the said place under the patronage of the Revd. Julian Courteau, a trustee of said school. Your petitioner has to observe that when he commenced teaching, there was scarcely a youth of 15 years of age that could speak English in either of the above named places.

YOUR PETITIONER had many difficulties to contend against, as the Inhabitants were imperious and ignorant, they would give but little encouragement to a teacher, your petitioner after some time succeeded to impress on their minds the necessity of having their children educated. At last a large and respectable school was established in River Bourgoise your petitioner has been teaching at the said last named place for these last 30 years.–And petitioner is proud to say that many of the young men that he had the pleasure of teaching, are now respectable members of society in different districts that they reside in, as they can read and write both the English and French language with ease.

YOUR PETITIONER is getting feeble from old age, and in consequence cannot give his service any longer for the public good. Your petitioner has to observe that he was the first teacher 44 years ago that took the youthful French of the said two Settlements in hand to cultivate their minds, and teach them to write the French and English language also to speak the latter with fluency, and poorly remunerated for his teaching services by the inhabitants, owing to their want of means.

YOUR PETITIONER under those existing facts, most respectfully approach Your Honourable body by petition, praying that You will be pleased to consider petitioner's long and useful service in teaching school at L'Ardoise and River Bourgoise, and in Your Kind administration of justice be pleased to grant petitioner whatever You may think proper to allow, to assist and support petitioner's declining years, for his long and faithful teaching.

AND YOUR PETITIONER'S in duty bound will ever pray. Vc Vc Vc
J. Courteau, P.P. River Bourgoise, January 20, 1869.

We the undersigned have known Mr. John Beranger for a number of years, and during that period we are well aware that he was a sober, honest and steady person, and very exemplar in conducting his school teaching.

M.J. Kavanaugh, J.P., R.G. Morrison, J.P., Donald Boyd, J.P., Duncan Cameron, J.P.

There is early evidence that Bruno[3] was poor and in dire need of any financial assistance he could obtain. On December 5, 1842, when he purchased a one–third acre lot from John Quinn[4], he already owed him 490 pounds. His poor financial circumstances were most likely a result of his 50–pound annual salary.

Schools

The earliest schools and education in the community were in the Lower End close to the Catholic Church, where the Priest had a strong influence on education and where Bruno lived. In 1839, there was no school building nor money to build one, so Bruno instructed students outdoors and in his home. Frances Digout recalls her mother chatting about the days they spent in Bruno's field learning to read and write in French and English. Frequently, when Bruno grew old and weak, his students assisted with his chores such as planting and harvesting.

The precise location of the first school is open to discussion, though all agree that it was situated close to Dennis's Brook. Elderly residents Hilaire Bourque and Beni Samson along with French author Ephrem Boudreau[5], refer to Henry Sampson's field as the site of a school in 1888. **Plate 400**, taken in 1991, shows the old building still standing in Edward and Florence Touesnard's field. This one-room school was purchased by Joseph (Josi) Deslaurier[6] in the 1890s. It either served as a school before 1887, or as a temporary school from 1887-88 while a new school was constructed. Since then, it has been used as a storage shed, a weaving workshop for Jose's wife Philisité (Samson), a pig house and as an abattoir. It measures 18 feet, 6 inches x 20 feet, 6 inches with a clear ceiling height of 8 feet. The attic has 1-foot, 6 inches knee walls and a 6-foot ceiling. This space was used for storage and as emergency sleeping quarters. Wood pegs secure the rafters and floor joists. Hemlock boards, some measuring 16-inches in width, clad the exterior walls and roof.

Plate 400—Taken by Garvie Samson

School Burns

In August 1887, just after summer vacation, the Lower End school burned. Inspector M.J.T. McNeil, B.A., made reference to the incident in his Report[7] for the year ending October 31, 1888:

> *The County of Richmond has been victimized by the fire-fiend to an unusual extent during the last year. No less than three schools have been burnt. viz: One in River Bourgeois in the second week of the scholastic year; a second in Black River in April last and the third at Port Richmond about the middle of June.*
>
> *The last mentioned was caused by a brush fire and plainly accidental. In the second case rumours of foul play were heard, but they were probably unfounded. In the first case, however, there is unfortunately too much reason to believe that the torch of some miserable incendiary did the cowardly work. Circumstances point so strongly in that direction that probably the services of a detective would not have been in vain, but it seems the perpetrator must escape present punishment, at last.*
>
> *It is a sad commentary, however, on the educational public spirit of a community when a miserable personal squabble over the engagement of a teacher can engender such a demonical spirit of pure malice. The injury caused by such fiendish work is simply incalculable; it is not to be computed in dollars and cents. Here is a large and important section that has been in consequence without school last Winter Term. School was kept during the Summer Term in a building temporarily provided and provision has been made at the recent Annual Meeting for the erection of the exterior shell of a school house.*

New School Constructed

The superintendent of Education's Report[8] in 1889 confirms the replacement of the school destroyed by fire in 1887: *A new school house has been erected in River Bourgeois, Richmond Co., to replace the one destroyed by fire. It is considerably larger, and when finished inside, will be much more commodious than the old one, though not strictly up to the requirements of the Section.*

Fortunately, in every community there are those who realize the importance of historical documents and preserve them. Such is the case regarding the blueprints for the new school and the 1893-94 School Registry. These items were found by James and Jean Richard behind a heat shield, while renting Alex Sampson's house. These articles were presented to the Public Archives of Nova Scotia, in Halifax, for reference and safekeeping. The new school is shown in **Plate 401.**

Some information found in the Registry is noteworthy. For example:

- The school term ran from September 4–July 4.

Plate 401 courtesy of Anselm Sampson

- John W. MacIsaac, Principal, earned a salary of $190 for the term and his assistant was Elizabeth Beranger, a grade-8 student whose grandfather was Bruno Beranger.
- There were 64 students from grades one to nine and the curriculum included reading, grammar, French and arithmetic.
- M.J.T. MacNeil was Inspector of Schools and the trustees were Joseph Burke, Charles Landry and John Bona with Rev. A.E. Mombourquette as pastor.

From the blueprints, I have determined that the mansard roof school measured 44 feet x 35 feet on the first floor, and 44 feet x 36.5 feet on the second floor. The ceiling heights measured 11.3 feet at both levels. The first floor included two classrooms and a porch while the second floor included one classroom and an auditorium, which featured a stage running across its entire width.

The number of students attending school from 1889 to 1954 varied, in accordance with the population. In 1891, the population was 1,120 which remained constant until 1941 when it dropped to 896. The population number has remained approximately the same to the present day.

Following the school's closure in 1954, Allen Touesnard purchased the building to expand his poultry operation. The building's generous ceiling heights allowed the construction of a mezzanine floor which increased the usable floor area. Some observers suggested that chickens occupying the mezzanine level, received a *higher education*. The old school was dismantled by Allen Touesnard in the early 1960s.

Plate 402–Taken by Garvie Samson

River Bourgeois Consolidated School

Closing the Cannes and Lower End Schools and replacing them with a new central school was not supported by every member of the community. For the residents of Cannes and the South Side in particular, it meant students would have to be bussed over three miles and parents wouldn't see their children at lunch, as they had in the past. It also meant that they would lose the presence of the school and teachers in their locale. There was also apprehension as to how children from the two closed schools would adjust to being among a much larger number of students. For those with grown up children in Cannes and the Lower End, the new school did nothing for their morale.

Notwithstanding the controversy, the River Bourgeois Consolidated School, also known as the *Stell Maris School*, was constructed at Church Point, to the east of the Catholic Church and adjacent to the cemetery. Opening in the fall of 1954, it boasted five classrooms, a large auditorium complete with stage, and an enrolment of 180 students. The first principal of the school was James T. Richard. Over the years the school was expanded, so that by the time of its closing in the summer of 1994, it contained at the lower level: three classrooms, a music room, canteen, gymnasium, washrooms and a mechanical room, and at the main level it contained: five classrooms, a library, a reading lab, teacher's room, washrooms and service rooms. The maximum school enrolment at River Bourgeois Consolidated was 230 with a minimum of 28 students in 1994.

Furnishings and appurtances from the building were transferred to schools at St. Peter's, Arichat and L'Ardoise in August of 1994. The future of the school remains uncertain. **Plate 402** shows the school in 1994.

School Teachers

During my research, I found several lists of teachers who taught in River Bourgeois schools. These teachers (with years where possible) include: John Bruno Beranger (1839-1869), Stephen McPherson (1870s), Amable Burke, Alvina Beranger, Hattie Fougere (1914-15), Helina MacNeil (1920s), Nellie Burke (1921-1923), Sophia Burke (1921-23), Evelyn Campbell (1933), Ida

MacEachern, Ida Delahunt, Minnie Doucette, Stella MacDonald, Francis (Bourque) Digout, Sarah Burke, Camille Bouchie, Gertie Boyd, John (Willie) Sampson, Hollie Fougere, Louis Langlois, Evelyn Campbell, James T. Richard (1939-1957), Colin Pottie, Sister Lola Burke, Francis Digout (she taught for 38 years, her first school was Port Felix in 1933, her last year was River Bourgeois Consolidated in 1977), Jean (MacNamara) Landry, Stanley McPhee, Elaine Richard, Fred Sampson (Daniel Sampson's son, brother to Ida–Hilaire Bourque's wife), Leona (MacDonald) Campbell, Tobie Baccardax (Principal), Thérese (Baccardax) Digout, Paul Baccardax and Myra Felion. **Plate 403** shows a class from 1910.

Cannes Schools

Information regarding the earliest education in Cannes is limited, so one might speculate that initially children came from Cannes and surrounding areas to receive instructions from Bruno, or that on certain days he met with children in Cannes. The earliest known teacher was Felix Bourque. He lived

Plate 403–Courtesy of Annie Mae Bourque

River Bourgeois School, September 1910
1st Row–? Bourque, Raymond Samson, Charlie Landry, Willie Landry, Eddie Boudreau, Eddie Bouchard, Willie Digout, Alexander Digout, Florence Boucher, ??, Lena Landry, Eva Landry.

2nd Row–Raymond Boucher, ??, Bastian Landry, ??, Murdock Samson, Mabie Burke, Amable Landry, Charlotte Landry, Florence Boudreau, Margaret Samson, ? McNeil, Miss MacGillivray (teacher).

3rd Row–Mabel Burke, Ruby Beranger, ??, Charlie Boucher, Simon Burke, ??, ??, ??, Florence Boudreau, Louise Samson, Mary Jane Burke, Alvina Landry.

4th Row–Leo Landry, Clifford Fitzgerald, Mariah MacNeil, Gertie Boyd, Lillian or Hilda McNeil, Minnie Samson, Girtie Morrison, Florence Boyd, Phyllis Burke (anté), Stella Boyd (teacher).

very close to the first school and his father was one of the first settlers in Les Etangs. Felix, my great-grandfather, is known to have constructed the first school benches. The A.F. Church map of 1888 (see map at front of book) positions a school on the South Side Road between the residences of Mrs. S. Bourque and Felix Bourque, below Sam Fougere's residence. Andrew Fougere purchased the old school, using the materials to enclose his sawmill.

Plate 404 courtesy of Marie Fougere

Cannes School Class–November 1909
1st Row–Cornelius Pottie, Vander McPhee, Joseph Amos Burke, Peter McPhee, Alexander Boudreau, Hyacynth Pottie, Jim Boyd, Sam McPhee, Bref Thibeau.

2nd Row–Bernie Burke, Sam Fougere, Elizabeth Burke, Melinda Thibeau, Amy Burke, Lizzie Ann Richard, Loretta Boudreau, Robbie Thibeau.

3rd Row–Bill LeBlanc, Henry Landry, Sam Dugas, ??, Alex Ranson, ??, ??, Henry (Vital) LeBlanc, Sam Richard, Matt Thibeau.

4th Row–Cameron Boyd, Terry Thibeau, Joe McPhee, Henry Pottie, Victor Pottie, Peter Fougere, Joe Digout, John Boyd, Russell Boyd, Alexander Landry, Wilfred Thibeau.

5th Row–Laura Boyd (teacher), Catherine Ronson, Ida Mae Landry, Atlanta Fougere, Jadie Fougere, Christina Dugas, Marie Boyd, Margaret Mae Pottie, Viola Pottie, Katie Fougere, Vina Landry.

6th Row–Christine Boyd (teacher), Jessie Bell MacLean, ??, Lizzie Jane Digout, Mary Agnes Pottie, Hattie Fougere, ??, Hattie Burke, Marie Ronson, Olive Ronson, Lena Richard, Rachel Landry, Celeste Ann Burke, Rachel Sampson, Mary Louise Landry, Minnie Thibeau, Minnie Burke, Annie Mae MacLean, Lizzie LeBlanc, ??, Charlotte Ann Pottie.

The second school, with two classrooms, was built on the site of the original school and closed in 1954. Adrian (Hogan) Bourque purchased the school in 1955 with the intention of constructing a house from the materials. In the interim, he found a suitable house in West Arichat and sold the school to Alzear Samson from Petit de Grat who constructed a house there, from the materials. Ironically, Adrian's wife, Priscella Boudreau, taught in this very school. **Plate 404** shows pupils from the 1909 class in Cannes.

Cannes school teachers included: Felix Bourque, Angus Joseph Boyd, Christina Boyd, Sarah E. Boyd, Pat Thibeau, Sarah Burke (1927-1931), Sadie MacNeil, Laura Boyd, Annie (Hureau) Boyd, Cecelia (Boyd) Fougere (1927), Francis (Bourque) Digout (1936-37), Raymond Samson from L'Ardoise, Hattie Bourque, Professor Wilfred Thibeau. In 1927, Elizabeth Landry taught grades 1–4, with 62 pupils; Sarah Digout taught grades 5–10 with 45 students between 1927–31, and Marie Boyd taught the same grades with 60 pupils. Other early teachers included: Thérese (Baccardax) Digout, Alfred Baccardax, Stella MacDonald and Jessie MacLean (one year).

Seaview Schools

There were two schools in this small community. The first was located at the Cross-Roads, and the second where it is today, below what was once Lionel LeBlanc's and Gerard Touesnard's farm.

Thanks to Lorenzo (Peter) Pottie, I visited the old school on July 15, 1994 and took several photographs. **Plate 405** shows the front of the school and **Plate 406** shows Lorenzo Pottie inside. These photographs confirm that the building is in a deplorable state, and one heavy gale will bring it to the ground. Vandals have removed the hardwood and spruce sub-flooring and the interior cladding. The walls are bulging and the tongue-and-groove hardwood ceiling is about to collapse. Two chalkboards remain at the front of the room, one on either side of the stovepipe thimble located three feet below the ceiling. The room is extremely well-lit, with numerous windows

Plate 405–Taken by Garvie Samson

Plate 406–Taken by Garvie Samson

positioned at the sides and the rear of the room. At the back, the windows have been boarded-in, though no pane of glass remains intact, and the suspended brick chimney hangs dangerously on metal straps. The classroom's interior measures 23 feet, 6 inches x 18 feet, 4 inches with an 11–foot ceiling height. The exterior building height measures 21–feet.

Lucille (Martell) Boudreau, originally from Sampson's Cove, taught here between 1954-56. Her class included 26 students from grades primary to 10 inclusive. The room was arranged with two rows of seats, one on either side of a large Waterloo stove, both facing a blackboard. There was one bookcase and one chemical toilet. According to Lucille, all the students did very well and the fact that there were many grades in the same room did not stop the students from learning, rather it helped them learn to concentrate on their own work.

School teachers at these schools included: Dan Alexander MacDonald, Henrietta Cameron (St. Peter's), Vida Proctor (Whiteside), Mrs. Emma England (Mulgrave), Peter Thibeau (Thibeauville), Annie MacDougall (The Points, West Bay), Lorena Bona (River Bourgeois), Jessie Urquhart (Pictou), Jessie Mitchell (Pictou), Vincent Kennedy (Queensville), Rita MacDonald (Whiteside), Annie Mae MacDonald (Inverness), Marie Boyd (River Bourgeois), Annie Mae MacLean (River Bourgeois), Mary (Latimer) Ferguson, Elizabeth Steel (Judique), Angeline MacLennan (Big Pond), Eunice MacPherson (Big Pond), Roy Morrison (Seaview), Nellie MacPhee (River Bourgeois), Elizabeth Landry (River Bourgeois), Thérese Digout (River

Bourgeois), Yvonne LeBlanc (Seaview) and Lucille Boudreau. The last teacher was Yvonne (LeBlanc) Sampson who taught in 1957, at which time the school closed.

Other River Bourgeois teachers

There were other teachers from River Bourgeois who may not have taught at one of the local schools. They included: Harriett (Hattie) Burke, Pat Thibeau, Charles Bissett, Caroline LeVesconte, Peter LeVesconte, Charlie LeVesconte, Annie MacLean (Peter MacLean's daughter), Gladys Burke, Elizabeth Burke, Walter Bouchie, Sr. Ann Samson, Sr. Lauretta Beranger, Abraham Beranger, Arthur Doary and Stanislaus Laurence Digout.

Religious contribute to education and community life

When Father Samson came to River Bourgeois in 1950, he recognized problems in the education system. The schools were in a state of disrepair and students had to commute to St. Peter's for grades 11 and 12. Father Samson convinced the Municipality to construct a new school and obtained the teaching assistance of Les Filles de Jesus. (Les Filles de Jesus, an Order of teaching sisters originating in France, were prevented from teaching in 1902 by an anti-clerical government. Following the ban, the sisters came to Canada in search of work and established their first Foundation in Eastern Canada in Arichat.)

Sisters who provided invaluable service to the community in various capacities included: Marie Ann-Joseph, Josephine Marie, Prisca-Marie, St-Etienne-Marie, Gustave-Marie, Marie de L'Emmanuel, Marie St-Lidvine, Marie de St-Lucie, Marie Charles, Marie Luce-Emmanuel, Rosaire-Marie, Marie Florentine, Ursula-Marie, Marie Leonard, Marie Therese-Emma, Richard Marie, Marie de St-Benoit, Mathilde Marie, Marie Evelina, Marie Andronique, Marie Jean-Gabriel, Marcelle Marie, Marie Adelina, Bertha Marie, Marie Antoine de Jesus, Marie-St-Fiacre, Valerie-Marie, Marie St-Venérande and Sister Anthony-Mary. Between 1957–1970, there were a total of eight religious serving the community, all of whom lived in the presbytery. From 1970–1977, they lived in L'Ardoise and commuted to the River.

In addition to teaching, the Sisters assisted the priest by singing at daily mass, teaching catechism, training altar boys, directing the choir, establishing a music program in school, caring for all the church vestments and attending to the domestic needs in the glebe, such as cleaning and cooking. By their actions and good deeds, they served as role models to students and lay people. The success of their students is a fitting testimony to their work.

Private school

One of the most prominent and respected families in the community was that of William Isaac and Ethel May (Shaw) LeVesconte. They were strong supporters of education and encouraged their children to pursue careers in this field. Known to have open minds regarding religion, they transcended religious barriers and enrolled their daughter, Caroline, in the Arichat Convent. Here, under the Filles de Jesus who would come to teach in the River some 50 years later, Caroline earned her grade 11 certificate and returned to River Bourgeois. She established a classroom in the attic of her parent's spacious Victorian home, because the local school was crowded and it was a considerable distance for small children to walk. In the attic, adhering to the regular school curriculum, Caroline taught her brothers, Peter, Jack and Charlie, over a two-year period.

Night school

In the mid–1920s, many of the older men who did not have the opportunity to attend school as youngsters because of family obligations, expressed an interest in learning to read and write.

One of the educated residents, D.D. Boyd, volunteered his services. He rented the MacLean Store, located across the road from George Boudreau in Cannes, where he taught adults to read and write in the evening. Francis Digout recalls passing the store one evening, while returning with a pair of shoes from Victor Digout's, and hearing D.D. Boyd urging his students to spell and repeat words aloud. He would say, *If you can say it, you can spell it.*

Pencil Cape

Pens, pencils and paper were scarce, expensive and not to be wasted, so chalkboards and slates were used extensively for writing and arithmetic. Dennis's Brook, a favourite spawning stream for smelts which ran beside the Lower End School, was close to *Pencil Cape*, a slate outcropping

Plate 407–taken by Garvie Samson

200 yards upstream. Students congregated there to collect finger–shaped pieces of stone which they shaped into markers for their slates. A favourite rendezvous point during recess, lunch and after school was a large boulder located in the brook, 50 yards below the school. The boulder, shown in **Plate 405**, must have been something special, as it was recognized by all the older residents and engendered fond memories of their school days.

There was also a slate outcropping in Cannes. It was situated close to Henry Landry's on the South Side. Louise (Burke) Smith recalled when children would go there to collect pieces of rock for their slates. The slate board she owned had a wooden frame for protection and ease of carrying.

Student Conveyance

Prior to construction of the Consolidated School in 1954, several residents drove students with their own cars. Cameron Boyd drove Cannes students in the 1940–50s while Joseph Boucher and James Richard drove from the Lower End. James drove Marianne and Jeannette Fougere, Elaine Digout and Shirley Burke. He was required to obtain a bus driver's licence to carry students in his car and he still retains this licence.

David Touesnard provided the first bus service in the community in the fall of 1954 when he conveyed children from River Tillard to the Lower End school, pending the official opening of the new school. David drove for the School District with his own 54-passenger bus until 1961, when the County assumed the bus service. He drove for the County until 1964 when he retired and they purchased the bus. Terry Boudreau drove until he became Councillor then his brother George drove for some time. Lawrence Stone drove students from the South Side and Hawker until he became ill.

Calvin Burke, who now lives on Church Point, began driving the school bus in 1986. He drives students to St. Peter's Elementary and High School from Louisdale, Kempt Road, Cleveland, Roberta, West Bay, Dundee and Sampsonville. Calvin took over from Bill Calder of St. George's Channel who retired in 1986 after driving for 30 years.

In 1992 with the French School amalgamation, several school busses were used to transport students from River Bourgeois. In 1994, students in grades 7 and 8 were conveyed by bus to L'Ardoise while grades 9–12 were taken to St. Peter's. The last term for grade 9 students in the River Bourgeois School was in 1981. Following the school's closure in Seaview, students were transferred to St. Peter's School. Drivers included: James Grant, Fred Digout, Gerard Touesnard, Lester Burke and Lester Robertson.

Observation

The social effect of closing the River Bourgeois Consolidated School will be felt as the years pass unless some similar use is found for the premises. The School was a very important institution; one that unified the community particularly when religion was an integral part of the curriculum. Unfortunately, efforts to streamline the system, caused by economics and declining enrolment, forced the closure of this important River Bourgeois institution.

Education Trivia

- Suggested annual salaries–N.S. Superintendent of Education Report, 1857. First-class male–$120; First-class female/second-class male–$90; Second-class female/third-class male–$60; third-class female–$45.
- The average cost of registering pupils in 1872 was $5.59, a slight increase over 1871.
- School construction costs in 1871: 39 schools for $45,895.
- School Sizes Report–October 31, 1872. Inspector Remi Benoit to Rev. A.S. Hunt, M.A., Superintendent of Education— *The ratepayers think they have done all that duty requires of them, all that need be done, by erecting a building 25 feet x 20 feet, for the instruction of 100 to 150 children.*

Endnotes

1) A.A. Johnson's, *A History of the Catholic Church in Eastern Nova Scotia.*
2) Petitions - Public Archives of Nova Scotia (PANS), RG5 Series P, Vol. 77, 1869.
3) Bruno married Olive Landry, originally from D'Escousse, on July 12, 1841 in L'Ardoise.
4) John Quinn was originally from Halifax. Registry of Deeds in Arichat.
5) Euphrem Boudreau published two books on River Bourgeois namely: *Rivière-Bourgeois*, 1984 and *Glossaire du Vieux Parler Acadien*, 1988.
6) Joseph (José) Deslaurier was originally from Tracadie where he worked with Fr Martell. He purchased the farm presently owned by Edward Touesnard in 1880.
7) PANS, LB, N85, 1888.
8) PANS, LB, N85, 1889.

Chapter V
Communication and Electrification

Postal

The earliest form of written communication was carried on by merchants in their daily business. The first organized delivery system in Nova Scotia was in 1754, as described in the following excerpt[1].

> *Irregular postal service in N.S. was apparently begun on April 23, 1754 by Benjamin Leigh, a Halifax stationer. In the following year the Britain Post Office, in an attempt to improve military communications between Britain and North America, began a monthly packet run to New York. From there, any available vessel carried mail to Halifax. This service, disrupted during the American Revolution, ended, and after March 1788, regular packets called to Halifax. The Postal Service in British North America remained a British charge until 1851 when it was relinquished to the Provinces.*

Mail for River Bourgeois was carried by coastal vessels, while urgent dispatches over short distances were sent by land courier; usually Micmac Indians. Communications between Halifax and Sydney, where the Post Office was opened in 1785, were carried out by vessels on a fairly regular basis.

Prior to Cape Breton's annexation by the Province in 1820, postal service was poor because of inadequate roads. The need for regular mail service increased as Arichat, a major shipbuilding and trading port, developed. By 1824, postal facilities had been established in Arichat and the Gut (Strait) of Canso.

Lieutenant Governor Sir James Kempt realized the importance of constructing suitable roads between the mainland and Arichat for trade and communications. Passable roads were essential for an efficient and reliable Postal System. In 1831, with Kempt's support and tenancy, a roadway was completed from Port Hastings to Arichat.

The first organized Post Office in Nova Scotia, and in Canada, was established at Halifax in 1854. It was operated by the Colonial Office and the General Post Office in London. Postal affairs[2] did not come under Nova Scotia control until 1851, however by 1855 there were 52 Post Offices and 169 Way Offices. One year after Confederation, the Dominion assumed control of its own postal system. By 1913, there were 2,014 offices in operation, one for every 300 persons, but by 1983, with the introduction of Rural Routes, that number had been reduced to 350 where it remains.

Way Stations and Packets

Way Stations were the ancestors of present day Post Offices. During early development of the colonies, way stations were established for the convenience of businessmen and later for public use. Mail was carried from one Way Station to the other via sailing vessels called *Packets* or *Paquets*. The demand for a communication delivery service is confirmed by a number of petitions including the following:

> January 14, 1843; Petition from Isle Madame and adjacent parts *praying for funds to a packet between Arichat and Halifax.* Petition of Felix LeVache of Arichat, Richmond County, 1844 for *aid to a pacquet between Boston and Halifax*, and a second petition from Mr. LeVache for *aid to run a pacquet between Arichat and Halifax.*

Packet service by vessel was still in demand in later years as confirmed by a petition from Petit de Grat in 1911.

> The Petitioners requested; *a small amount of public purse or a subsidy for the establishment, between Halifax and Petit de Grat, of a packet service by sailing vessel.* The petitioners mention *the satisfactory service that they had occasionally received at the hands of Capt. Placide Bouchard of River Bourgeois, in the staunch and well-appointed schooner,* J. E. Collins *and considered him suitable and desirable for such a packet service.*

There were two Way Stations[3] established in River Bourgeois. The earliest was operated by George E. Bisfet (Bissett) in 1845; located on the peninsula where the lighthouse was constructed in 1903. The second Way Station was at Fred Caree's in Cannes. Fred was the original owner of the store later owned by John Fortune, Mary Fortune, Peter MacLean and Tom Morrison.

One of the benefits Way Station operators enjoyed was the *Franking Privilege,* which entitled them to send their personal mail, postage free.

River Bourgeois (Church Point)

The earliest Canada Post[4] record of an active River Bourgeois postal service was in 1838. This date confirms several other references made to the Way Station operated by George Edward Bissett. At that time, his business was established at the harbour entrance, where the lighthouse was located.

By 1845, George relocated to new buildings below where Thomas Sampson later lived, and he probably continued operating the Way Station from this new location. Postal service changed hands frequently during the next decades. Operators were: George H. Bissett (1869–1877), J.J. McNeil (1877–1884), and G.H. Bissett (1884–1890).

Plates 500 &501–Courtesy of Delore Burke

The oldest remnant of an actual post office building, is shown on **Plate 802**. This post office/store was located on Church Point, 50 yards south of the existing church. It was first operated by Thomas Sampson, then by his son Alex who operated it from 1890–1943. The oldest discovered stamped envelope[5] was addressed to Josi Deslaurier in Tracadie, Nova Scotia, from his wife Marie Anne in River Bourgeois. It is dated December 7, 1879.

In 1943, Delore Burke established a store which he constructed from a small storage building purchased from his parents, Amable and Mathilda Bourque, across the road from John and Caroline Doucette (**Plates 500 & 501**). He operated the store/Post Office business with his wife Hilda until 1951, at which time they sold it to Walter Bouchie whose sister Helen operated it until 1958 when she married Bennie Konning. The Burkes repurchased the businesses and hauled the store next to Lewis and Lilly Smith's home.

In 1964, for convenience and efficiency, the store and Post Office were relocated to the basement of the Burkes' new house. In 1967, a new Crown-owned Post Office was constructed on a small lot owned by Allain Touesnard, which he had purchased from Amable F. Bourque. Delore became postmaster and remained there until he retired in August of 1980, with over 30 years of dedicated service. Carmen Fougere became the new postmaster in September 1980, and remains in this post.

Cannes

Postal records show the earliest Cannes Post Office operationed in 1884. According to Peter and Arthur Digout, Tranquil Digout operated the Post Office for at least 40 years until he died at the age of 90, on October 15, 1926.

The small building used for postal service was located at the bottom of Tranquil's field, where Charlie Digout's house is situated.

Susan Landry (wife of George) took over the Post Office following Tranquil's death. She operated it from their home until a small building was hauled across the ice from the South Side around 1928, and placed in the bottom of their field, close to Boyd's Lane. Susan was Postmistress from 1926–1955, when her daughter Eileen took it over. Eileen operated it until 1970 when the Rural Route System was put in place.

South River Bourgeois

Vital LeBlanc operated the first Post Office in the early 1900s and it was continued by Philomen Burke until 1943. Rita Landry operated it from 1943–1945 at which time it was taken over by Philomen's son, Victor Burke and his wife Evelyn, who operated it with their small store until 1970 when the Rural Route System was established.

Mail was transported between the Cannes Post Office and the South Side. Some of the carriers included: Remi Fougere, Henry Fougere and Henry Landry. They used boats when the water was open, crossed the ice when it was passable, and at other times used the roadway.

False Bay/Hawker

Prior to 1928, the community was known as False Bay because of the shallow waters of its inlet. The name of the Post Office was changed to *Hawker* shortly after it opened in 1928. This name originated from a military aircraft which had crashed, resulting in the loss of many lives.

Simon McPhee was the first Postmaster. He operated the Postal Service from his home between 1918–1928. Martin and Seraphine Pottie ran the service from their home between 1928–1951. Leo (Simon McPhee's son), and his wife Mae agreed to take over the operation in 1951, mostly as a convenience for residents. They maintained the service and a small store until 1970, when Canada Post established the Rural Route Service.

Mail for False Bay was delivered to Cannes Post Office where the operator was required to collect it on Tuesdays, Thursdays and Saturdays. This was normally done by horse and wagon or sled. In the 1940s, when Martin Pottie went to fish pogie each spring in Boston, Seraphine, despite her old age, walked to Cannes to deliver and collect the mail.

River Tillard

Mary (Bourque) Young was the first Postmistress at River Tillard. She was diminutive, but energetic and fearless. In order to collect mail at the Flag

Station[6] located on the St. Peter's side of River Tillard, she had to traverse the open railway trussel suspended 25 feet above the river. Crossing the bridge in the light of day was frightening; walking over at midnight during a snowstorm with a lantern in one hand and a mail bag in the other would have been an unthinkable task for most men. Walking another half mile to her home, through a narrow roadway lined with trees, was possibly the least frightening part of her journey. To do this morning and night, six days per week, and to mind the Post Office, she was paid a salary of $8 per month.

Mary was married to Alex Young from Martinique on Isle Madame. She was a sister to Hilaire and Maurice Bourque. She operated the Postal Service from the 1920s until her death in 1944.

Following Mary's death, Mathilda Boudreau operated the Post Office from 1945–1970. She received a 25-year Award Plaque for her dedication to service. Mathilda did not have to collect the mail from the Flag Station; it was delivered to her by courier.

Thibeauville

The first Post Office was located at Lauchland MacLean's Carding Mill, within a quarter mile of the Sporting Mountain Station. Lauchland began the service following the installation of the station in 1903, then his daughter, Maggie, ran the Post Office until the early 1940s. John (Chink) MacLean, Peter MacLean's son, recalls the operation; the MacLeans had a small counter and a cabinet with pigeon-holes, each labelled with the name of a Thibeauville family.

Henry and Margaret Thibeau assumed the Post Office following World War II. Tom Thibeau, Jack's brother, used to pick up the mail at the railway station. Peter and Mary Thibeau operated the post office for a few years.

Seaview

The following people operated a small postal service in this community, located within one mile of Sporting Mountain Station: William Sutherland, Christie Sutherland, Donald Morrison, John N. Morrison, Mrs. Lionel LeBlanc and Cecile Touesnard. In later years, the mail came from Hawker. Couriers included: Serita MacLellan, Donald MacDonald and Roddie Morrison.

Couriers

In the late 1800s, upon completion of the Cape Breton Railroad through MacIntyre's Lake, the mail was collected there and couriered to the community Post Offices. Some of the earliest couriers included: Thomas

Samson, Leander Boudreau, Tranquil Digout and Henry Fougere. Following completion of the section of railway from Port Hawkesbury to St. Peter's in 1903, mail and freight were sorted at Sporting Mountain Station.

Couriers collected the out-going mail at Church Point and stopping at the Cannes Post Office to collect mail already couriered there from the South Side and False Bay. Then they drove to Sporting Mountain Station, a distance of 2-1/2 miles. On the return trip, they stopped at Cannes. The Cannes mail included mail for the South Side and False Bay, which was place in appropriate mail bays for pick-up.

Jack LeVesconte *drove the mail* in the winter from 1936–1945. During the summer when he was working for the Department of Highways, Lawrence Burke drove for him. Jack remembers that the train was scheduled to arrive at Sporting Mountain at 5pm so he left home at 3:30pm. When the train was on schedule, he would be back home by 8pm.

At Sporting Mountain, there was an enclosed stable where the horse could be rested, fed, and kept out of the cold should the train be late arriving. Sometimes the train couldn't push itself through the heavy snow, which meant an overnight stay at the station. The station contained a pot-bellied stove and firewood for the convenience of passengers and couriers, and there was always a fire burning. One was never alone, as there were also couriers there from Thibeauville and Oban.

The station was sub-divided in two sections; one for passengers and one for freight. The passenger section was always left open. Mail came in separate bags for each Post Office and the baggage-master would not leave the mail bag unless the designated courier was there. The on-going mail bags and freight were collected first. Each railway station was provided with a telephone, and one could call *up-the-line* to stations such as Louisdale, Whiteside and The Junction (McIntyre's Lake), to verify the train's progress.

Couriers from the South Side included: Remi Fougere, Harry Adele Burke and D.D. Burke. Willard Pottie *drove the mail* from Sporting Mountain for several years with an old green *Willis Overland* vehicle. He removed the back seat so he could carry the mail bags and any small freight items. In the winter when snow was too deep for the vehicle, his small, fast mare and sleigh provided the service.

When the St. Peter's train changed its schedule to bi-weekly runs, the mail came from MacIntyre's Lake. Austin Letcher couriered the mail with a team of horses, and later a truck. Stanley Burns used to drive for Letcher but was killed when he hit the rear of an army vehicle in convoy which was moving from Halifax to Sydney during the war. Roddy Steele from Cleveland also drove for many years in a truck with a wooden box.

Rural Route

Many small Post Offices closed in 1970. In many rural areas, mail is now delivered to individual households. Robert Pettigrew began service which is currently provided by Claire (Bourque) Bouchard.

Telephones

On February 14, 1876, both Alexander Graham Bell and Elisha Gray filed patent applications for the telephone. Bell's patent was issued on March 7, 1876, however it was not until 1893, after considerable litigation, that the Supreme Court ruled in his favour. On March 10, 1876, the first sentence ever transmitted by electricity was sent by Dr. Bell, and now communication innovations appear endless.

Nova Scotia's first telephones[7] were installed in the Caledonia Colliery at Glace Bay in 1877. The telephones were supplied by G.G. Hubbard from Boston, Dr. Bell's future father-in-law. In 1879, the Dominion Telephone Company opened a central office in Halifax at 189 Hollis Street. In 1880, the Bell Telephone Company purchased the plant and rights of the Dominion Telephone Company. In May 1880, Bell Telephone issued the first list of telephone subscribers which contained 77 names. The first dial telephone in Canada was installed in Sydney Mines on November 26, 1907.

Maritime Tel and Tel was incorporated on April 22, 1910. On July 1, 1911, it purchased N.S. Telephone Company Ltd. which operated 12,051 telephones in Nova Scotia, and consolidated the major telephone systems throughout the province. By 1916, Maritime Tel & Tel operated 20,000 telephones in the province.

St. Peter's exchange opened on November 1, 1915. It had 10 subscribers and one pay station located at the Telephone Office operated by Mrs. D. Currie. By 1918, there were 15 subscribers and one pay station at the Telephone Office operated by Mr. G. Cheney. This exchange eventually served all of Richmond County east of Cleveland, excluding Isle Madame.

River Bourgeois Mutual Telephone Company

On Sunday, February 13, 1916, speaking from the pulpit, Rev. Pierre Robitaille, proposed there should be a telephone system installed in River Bourgeois and offered his support to the project[8]. His words are summarized as follows: *Could we not build a telephone line all around River Bourgeois, to St. Peter's?–If we can do so, why should we postpone it any longer?*

On February 21, 1916, a general meeting was held in the Lower End schoolhouse and 100 men claimed they were willing to install four poles each—enough for 10 miles of telephone line. An application was signed and forwarded to S.A. McMillan of Antigonish, the government-appointed inspector for rural telephones. The application was signed by: Rev. P. Robitaille, PP; Wm. LeVesconte, merchant; M.J. McNeil, Inspector of Schools; Capt. Anselm Samson and William F. Boyd, merchant.

On March 28, 1916, several days after receiving the Certificate of Incorporation, a meeting of all subscribers took place in the Glebe. The purpose of this meeting was to appoint Directors for the *River Bourgeois Mutual Telephone Company*. William F. Boyd was absent, having joined the *St.FX College Unit for Overseas Service* so Rev. Robitaille acted as secretary. Appointed Directors were: Rev. P. Robitaille, Capt. Anselm Samson, Vital LeBlanc, Martial Digout, John J. Sampson (the diver), M.J.T. McNeil and Wm. LeVesconte. It was moved and seconded that another meeting should be held to appoint officers of the Board of Directors. During this meeting on March 31, appointed Officers were: John J. Sampson–President, Rev. P. Robitaille–Secretary and Wm. LeVesconte–Vice-President.

During the third meeting, held in the glebe on April 10, 1916, Rev. Robitaille was asked to buy, without delay, materials for 8–9 miles of telephone line, including all boxes as per prepared list of materials. Materials were purchased from Northern Electric Co. Ltd. in Halifax. Initial financing for the project was provided by Father Robitaille. He was repaid by the Company as funds became available.

It was moved and seconded that John J. Sampson be empowered to install stakes along the line of poles. These should be permanently set and he should accept all necessary help to complete the work. On September 23, 1916, a meeting was held at the glebe to adopt rates for tolls and to establish the By-laws as follows:

> *There will be no charge for local calls for members in good standing, that is to say those having paid share on same box but remain under the obligation of paying 5 cents for reaching the St. Peter's locality. Subscribers paying no share in a box should pay 5 cents within the locality of R.B. and 10 cents for the locality of St. Peter's. That non-subscribers or strangers should pay 10 cents for calls within R.B. and 20 cents for the locality of St. Peter's.*

It was proposed by Capt. Anselm Samson and seconded by Martial Digout that subscribers should be credited, in the books of the R.B.M.T. Co., 85 cents for each pole on spot and 40 cents for each pole set up ($5 for 4 poles set up).

On January 24, 1917, a motion was passed requiring that all members pay a minimum of $5 in cash or provide the equivalent in labour or materials to the Company.

The First General Meeting was held on February 6, 1917 in the East End School with 40 members in attendance. Some of those participating at this meeting included: Henry Samson, Peter McLean, Eugene Digout, and Elie Samson. Peter McLean and Alex Samson were appointed the first auditors and J.D. Bourque was appointed overseer of the line at the rate of $2 /day while repairing the line. Main lines through River Bourgeois were put in operation and additional lines were added as described in the following.

Grand Gulley

Approval of the Grand Gulley line from the East End School to Archie Morrison's was granted on March 14, 1917. Apparently the line was only installed to Andrew Robertson's house so Archie undertook the installation of the remaining poles to his residence, for which work he submitted a bill to the Company in February of 1918. Upon a motion by Joseph E. Bourque seconded by Vital LeBlanc, the board unanimously rejected the bill.

Sporting Mountain

On February 12, 1918, a motion was proposed by Martial Digout, seconded by Alex Samson, that application be made to the Board to extend telephone boundaries to include Sporting Mountain. After considerable discussion among members, the motion was carried by a vote of 14 to 10.

During the 4th Annual Meeting held on February 10, 1920, an application was received from Thomas and Dan Morrison for membership in the Telephone Company. In their application, they offered to build the necessary extension of telephone line between the existing line and their homes. A long and argumentative debate ensued in reference to the extra heavy charges that this extension would bring to the Company. It was moved by M.J. McNeil and seconded by Archie Morrison that a vote take place on the question. The motion passed on a vote of 20 to 17.

The 23rd Annual Meeting on November 30, 1939, was held in the Credit Union Building. Members included: W.F. Boyd, Charles A. Burke, Peter Landry, Eugene Digout, Vital LeBlanc and Sam Fougere. Sam Fougere was appointed to replace Capt. Anselm Samson who had died on March 5, 1938. John J. Sampson retired from the Company on November 4, 1940 for health reasons, having served as it's President for 24 years. He died in 1942. He was succeeded by William F. Boyd, while Victor Digout was appointed Vice-President. Other Board members included: Simon A. Fougere, Abraham

Beranger, Eugene Digout, John L. Boyd, Peter Landry, Whitney McPhee, Charlie Fred Sampson and Alex McPhee.

South Side

Telephones were installed on the South Side years before Sam Fougere was appointed to the Board. Evelyn Fougere recalls how people from the surrounding area used the telephone at all hours of the night.

Central Exchange

St. Peter's was the central exchange for the adjacent communities and included R.B. listings for the first time in October 1947. Subscribers included: Abraham Beranger, Mrs. Charlotte Bourque (Cannes), Mrs. Virginia Bourque, Mrs. Annie Boyd and W.F. Boyd (Cannes), John P. Burke (River Tillard), Simon F. Burke (Cannes), Lawrence Burke, Eugene Digout, Andrew Fougere, Mrs. Alvina Landry and Peter Landry all of Cannes, Wm. LeVesconte, Mrs. Patrick Morrison (River Tillard), William Robertson, Rev. P. Robitaille, Alex Sampson, D.A. Sampson, John J. Sampson and Mrs. Mary Young (River Tillard).

Secretaries

Marie Boyd became the first female board member on May 16, 1948 when she was appointed secretary. Marie served in this capacity until Gladys Touesnard was appointed and served as secretary and treasurer from February 1963–June 1974. During this time, most meetings were held at Whitney McPhee's residence.

Dial Service

On May 3, 1974, Gladys Touesnard was advised by E.P. Rice (Engineering Supervisor, O.P. Design, District 2 East), that on May 18, 1974, the St. Peter's exchange and all Mutual Telephone Companies would be converted to dial service. The official ceremony commemorating the occasion was held at St. Peter's District High School on May 21, 1974.

Telephone Sets

Plate 502 shows the development of the telephone beginning in 1871. In **Plate 503**, Martha DeRoche demonstrates the typical battery-operated set most commonly used in the 1940s and 1950s. To dial the operator, the user depressed a small button located on the side of the unit while cranking the handle.

Maintenance

Lawrence Sampson and Leonard Bouchie worked on the installation of new wires and poles between Alex Young's house and Cannes in the late 1930s. Abraham Beranger was in charge of the work and owned a pair of *creepers* which were used to climb poles to install insulators and wires. The term

Plate 502–Taken by Garvie Samson

transformer was used when the lower and upper wires were connected using a short piece of wire. Transformers were installed every 12 poles. The service provided by residents such as Whitney McPhee, Charlie Robertson and Fred Doary, who worked hard to keep the lines in operation, cannot be overlooked.

Plate 503–Taken by Garvie Samson

Telegraph

The Government Telegraph (Morse Code) operated in L'Ardoise[9] in 1906. It was operated by Margaret Finlayson at her father, Abe Finlayson's residence.

In River Bourgeois, one of the first Telegraph operators was Catherine Fougere, who later married Simon Landry. The Telegraph Office was located in Cannes next to Carmen Fougere's, and was in operation by 1917. Evelyn (Fougere) Burke relates that she was given the same name as the Telegraph Operator in L'Ardoise whose name was Evelyn (King) Lafford. Sarah Digout recalls that Simon Anselm Fougere's wife operated the telegraph from Henry Fougere's. She was a one of Walter Fougere's sisters. The house, which is still standing, is located just west of Carmen Fougere's property.

Maria Boyd (1888-1968), who had been employed as a Telegrapher by Canadian Pacific Railroad, was operating a telegraph at the River in December 1917. Martha DeRoche recalls seeing her Aunt Laura Burke walking towards the Telegraph office crying, on December 6, 1917, the day of the Halifax Explosion. Her husband, Simon F. Burke, was working on a ship in the Halifax Harbour. Thankfully, he was not injured.

Electrification

The first flicker of lights in Nova Scotia was produced by generators[10] located at Black's Wharf, Halifax, in 1885. The earliest local power was produced at St. Peter's in 1936, when the Power Commission installed a diesel plant and distribution system to serve the town. The plant consisted of a 24 hp, 3-cylinder diesel, driving a 18.7 KVA 2300-volt generator. The power line between Port Hawkesbury and St. Peters, passing through River Bourgeois, was constructed in 1937. Frank MacNeil from Port Hawkesbury supervised the installation of the lines and was the electrical inspector.

Rural Electrification Act

The availability of electricity in rural areas was assisted by the formation of the Rural Electrification Act[11] of 1937. The Act *allowed government help to extend distribution lines to be built throughout rural communities with energy available at five cents/kwh for the first 15 kwh/month and three cents/kwh for the remainder, plus $1.25 service charge.*

On Isle Madame[12] at Pondville, there was a 50 hp Bates, one-cylinder diesel, generating 25 kws serving the area in 1938. Initially, power was used for light between dusk and 1am. The demand grew as people purchased refrigerators and stoves. The main transmission line from Grand Anse to Isle Madame was completed in 1940.

River Bourgeois

Power was available to residents of River Bourgeois in 1939. During the first year, 22 families had electricity installed. Some of the first customers were: Peter Landry, Andrew Fougere, William LeVesconte and Angus Boyd.

During the initial installation, applicants and their families could obtain work on the Line such as cutting the right-of-ways, installing poles, and pulling cables. Workers were allowed to earn an amount equal to the cost of wiring their house, usually $50. My mother, Theresa, recalls Willie Robertson making a survey of households interested in having electricity. (My father, James, wired our house and Charlie inspected it). Charlie (Willie's son), had worked as an electrician in Bermuda, and returned to the River to wire most of the first houses. Following all electrical installations, final inspections were conducted by the Power Corporation. Gerald (Charlie's son), related that his father read anything that contained electrical data and his favourite reference book was *The Popular Mechanic*. One of the earliest wired houses in the River by Charlie Robertson was that owned by Sam Fougere. Evelyn Fougere recalls Mary Ann, Charlie's wife, photographing their house as a memento of one of his first electrical installations.

Street Lighting

In 1968, customers began requesting pole lights in front of their property. Eventually everyone wanted lights and began to apply political pressure. By 1970, most of the roadways had street lighting. Walter Fougere, County Warden, was influential in obtaining this service.

Endnotes

1) Information copied from plaque on Old Post Office building on Barrington Street in Halifax.
2) PANS, MG, 100, Vol 57, No 56.
3) Way Stations- See NAC, GPO/MG/40/L/12/36 and 40/L/59/207 Aug. 1842.
4) Canada Post Offices, 1755-1895 by F.W.
5) Information from Florence Touesnard in 1993.
6) To collect the mail at the Flag Station, the designated courier simply raised a Flag and the conductor slowed the train to collect or discharge the mail.
7) *The History of Maritime Tel & Tel 1877-1964* by Dr. A.M. McKay of Maritime Tel & Tel.
8) River Bourgeois Mutual Telephone Co. business meeting notes.
9) "Telegraph in L'Ardoise". Article written by Alice Burke, Oct. 15, 1978.
10) *Current News*, N.S. Power Corp., Spring 1994.
11) N.S. Power Corporation, F.W. Buckley Report, 1986.
12) Info from Mr. Francis Martell, retired Power Commission Supervisor, now residing in Poulamond, Isle Madame, Cape Breton, April 1993.

Chapter VI
Transportation

On Water

Schooners

The first settlers in Nova Scotia were fishermen who built their homes and fishing shacks along the province's extensive shoreline. Most families owned a small fishing vessel or a rowboat to transport passengers or light cargo. Large fishing schooners frequently sailed directly from fishing grounds to ports such as Halifax and Boston with their catch, returning with cargo for local merchants. Schooners known as *Coasters* travelled on regular schedules to ports along the coast of Cape Breton and the Mainland, delivering and collecting merchandise and produce.

In the mid-1800s, it was common to see several dozen schooners anchored in the River Bourgeois harbour. Some returning from the Gulf of St. Lawrence or the Grand Banks, were loaded to the gunnels such that from a distance, they appeared ready to submerge. Others, preparing for a fishing trip without ballast, rode so high that the slightest wind seemed sufficient to capsize them. At Arichat, one of the busiest ports in Nova Scotia, it was common to count 100 schooners moving in and out of the harbour. Such pictorial seascapes became only a vision of the past with technological developments having a dramatic influence on the shape and types of vessels.

Motorized Vessels

During the latter part of the 18th century, the use of steam, diesel and gasoline motors to propel vessels had a marked effect on the commercial mode of transporting merchandise and people. The new generation of vessels offered so many advantages that fishermen had no choice but to wean themselves from the historically reliable schooner. Petitions such as the following confirm the beginning of this transition and the importance of government subsidies to assist the local communities.

> *The Petition of the undersigned Inhabitants of Arichat, dated 1877, in the County of Richmond humbly therewith:*
> *That much dependence for steam communications between this harbour and the different harbours and places on the coast from Halifax to P.E.I. is placed upon adequate subsidizing of a Steam Packet to perform such service. That during the prosperous years, your Honourable House encouraged the establishment of a line of steamers touching at the above ports by the grant of a subsidy of $200 and*

during the last year $175 as per trip. That the granting of said sums induced the owner of the steamer M.A. Starr *of Halifax to service the said route. The people of this place as well as the people of other ports at which it called found her of incalculable benefit to them on account of the expedition and safety she assumed in the carriage of merchandise and passengers. That your inhabitants observe with alarm the reduction in subsidy to the sum of $50 per trip as set forth in the estimation of expenses for the year placed before your Honourable House, etc.*

The importance of transportation from River Bourgeois and D'Escousse is verified by numerous Petitions requesting subsidies such as those in 1909, requesting Steam Charter Boat Service be continued from St. Peter's, D'Escousse and River Bourgeois. Schooner service, however, was still required as is verified by a Petition in 1911 requesting the continuation of service offered by Placide Bouchard of River Bourgeois. The Petition makes reference to Mr. Bouchard's vessel as *a staunch and well-appointed schooner* J. E. Collins, and continues, *your Petitioners take the liberty, which it hoped may be pardonable, of mentioning that vessel and her captain as suitable and desirable for such a pocket service.*

William Robertson had a government contract to ferry passengers to and from D'Escousse. Initially the rate was $1 per crossing. Many of his passengers were salesmen who often carried samples of their merchandise. When boat motors became available in the early 1920s, he provided the service with a small motor boat. Joe DeRoche offered the service from Simon Burke's store in Cannes to D'Escousse for a rate of $2 per crossing. On occasion, William LeVesconte used his power boat the *Thora,* (shown in **Plate 600**), to transport businessmen to D'Escousse.

By the 1920s, the number of schooners attempting to compete with the

Plate 600–Courtesy of Jack and Ada LeVesconte

motorized vessels was reduced to a handful. The last of these included Anselm Sampson's *Rosie M.B.*, and Placide Bouchard's *J.E. Collins*. Larger commercial steamers such as *The Richmond* and *The S.S. Margaret* travelled regularly from Sydney to Halifax, stopping at ports in-between to collect cargo and passengers. Locally they docked at Boyd's or LeVesconte's, depending on the wind and tide conditions.

Main Roads

Development of a Regional Network

The movement of merchandise and people was most conveniently done by water, however as new settlers such as lumbermen and farmers arrived, the need for roads to the interior became a priority.

On a regional scale, Lieutenant Governor Sir James Kempt and Chief Justice John Marshall realised the importance of roadways, particularly between Sydney, Arichat, and the Mainland. They held "high office" and used their influence to expedite road construction.

The first section of roadway to be upgraded ran between River Inhabitants and Grandigue Ferry. John Luce, a well-known land surveyor residing in Arichat, was commissioned to survey this section in 1827. Upon completion of the survey, Alexander Grant, with a crew of workmen from Pictou, undertook and completed the roadway in May 1828. Residents were unhappy with the influx of workmen from Pictou working in their "backyards", however Grant completed the work without incident and on schedule. This section was named the *James Kempt Roadway.*

The section of roadway between River Inhabitants and Port Hawkesbury was named the *Ship Harbour Road*. It was aligned by John Munroe of Pictou and built by Alexander Grant in 1832. This segment represented the remaining connecting link between the Mainland and Arichat. Sir James Kempt's dream of providing a roadway from the mainland to Arichat had finally been realized.

The roadway linking *James Kempt Road* at Grand Anse to River Tillard was named the *St. Peter's Road.* Construction was again undertaken by Alexander Grant and the road was completed while Dr. Andrew Madden from Arichat was Commissioner. Because of funding restraints, some of the work was completed using Statute Labour[1]. This section of roadway was not completed without incident, as it traversed precious farmland. Residents, such as Hugh and Charles McLean, wanted compensation before construction began through their land. Grant, however, with the support of farmers such as Laughlin McLean, managed to overcome all obstacles and the roadway was complete in 1829. The first River Tillard Bridge[2] was constructed in 1827.

Boat Carriage at St. Peter's Canal

Trading was practiced between communities and inter-provincially as confirmed by the Petition dated March 24, 1844 entitled, *Petition for the construction of Two Wharves and a Boat Carriage at Little St. Peter's Harbour*. The Petition also stipulated that *the wharves and boat carriage are for the use of the Public, that it is one of the greatest thoroughfares in Cape Breton as people are continually migrating from all parts of Nova Scotia and the Island of Prince Edward to the Bras D'Or Lake.*

Another section of the petition expresses *the need to transport produce on the way from Arichat, D'Escousse and River Bourgeois. That owing to the want of a wharf, farmers are obliged to back-pack their produce from their boats over a distance of one-half mile, then haul their boat overland. That the provisions of a wharf at the Lake side and one at Little St. Peter's as well as a Haul-Over, will allow the farmers to increase their trade and obtain a better price for their produce.*

Community Roads

Robertson's Road

One of the earliest established roads[3] was located along the east side of the entrance channel, between Grand Mary's Point and the Church. It was used daily by residents from the South Side, Cannes and Hawker, on their way to LeVesconte's store and Sampson's Post Office and Store, or to the Church. In addition to pedestrian traffic, horse-drawn carriages plied the roadway to and from the forge, warehouse buildings and wharves. Heavy traffic and constant erosion from the sea necessitated regular maintenance.

On March 30, 1916 a Petition was presented to the Government in Council, House of Assembly, entitled *Repairs to Road from Robertson's Shore to Grand Mary's Point*. It read as follows:

> *The Petition of Rev. P. Robitaille and 100 others asking for aid for road in River Bourgeois. We the undersigned PETITIONERS, resident taxpayers of River Bourgeois, in the County of Richmond, and Province of Nova Scotia, HUMBLY SHEWITH:*
>
> *First:* *That there is a road from William Robertson's shore leading to Grand Mary's Point which is impassable.*
>
> *Second:* *That the above road is used by two-thirds of the Parish.*
>
> *Third:* *That the above is the road which people take to go to church every Sunday and other days during the year.*

Fourth: *That it is also the road used by two-thirds of the Parish to go to the general Post Office of River Bourgeois.*

Fifth: *That the crib work placed there 15 years ago is entirely destroyed, and the high tides go over the road and prevent people from passing.*

Sixth: *That the road is cut up by the tides and is in such a soft condition that people cannot pass without getting wet.*

Seventh: *That this is one of the roads used the most of any in the District, as it is the only means whereby two-thirds of the people can conveniently go to Church, General Post Office and store.*

Eighth: *That the rowboats used by these people cannot be conveniently landed at any other point on account of the tides falling so low.*

We sincerely hope and appeal to you, as our Representative, that you may use your strong efforts to have some money granted for the purpose of repairing this road which we, the PETITIONERS, consider an urgent need, and your PETITIONERS as is duty bound will ever PRAY.

Signatories included: Alphonse Beranger, Willie Beranger, John Bona, Elias Bouchard, Peter Bouchard, Placide Bouchard, Amable R. Bouchie, Willie Bouchie, Charles Boudreau, Elias Boudreau, Henry Boudreau, Sam Boudreau, Wm. S. Boyd, Abram J. Burke, Capt. Alex Burke, Amable Burke, Amable A. Burke, Amable F. Burke, Amable H. Burke, Amable I. Burke, Amie Burke, Amos Burke, Charles D. Burke, Charles F. Burke, Clifford Burke, Damian Burke, Daniel Burke, Deserie Burke, Dominick Burke, Elair Burke, Felix Burke, Fred D. Burke, Freeman Burke, Isaac F. Burke, Isaiah Burke, John Burke, John B. Burke, John C. Burke, Joseph Burke, Josime Burke, Louis Burke, Michael Burke, Pacien C. Burke, Peter Burke, Placide Burke, Simon F. Burke, William Burke, William J. Burke, Dan Digout, Eugene Digout, Marshall Digout, Tranquil Digout, Victor D. Digout, Dennis Dugas, Isaiah Dugas, Matheau Dugas, Placid Dugas, Stephen Dugas, Vital Dugas, Andrew Fougere, Charles Fougere, Charles E. Fougere, Edward Fougere, Henry Fougere, Maurice Fougere, Murdock A. Fougere, Patrick Fougere, Remie Fougere, Simon Goyetche, Charles Grimes, Amie Landry, Andrew Landry, Docity Landry, Edmond Landry, Edmund Landry, Geo. Landry, Geo. H. Landry, Henry Landry, Jeffery Landry, Joseph H. Landry, Peter Landry, Peter A. Landry, Simon Landry, Simon P. Landry, Theodore Landry, Vital Landry, William Landry, Chas. LeBlanc, Henry LeBlanc, Vital LeBlanc, Ben LeBlance, Fiddel LeBlance, Wm. I. LeVesconte, Gilbert MacDonald, Peter McLean, Simon McPhee, Francis J. Pate, Martin Pate, Charles Pottie, Jerry

Ranson, Jule Ranson, Maria Ranson, Charles Richard, Elair Richard, Isaiah Richard, Peter Richard, Elias Richards, Wm. Richards, A.C. Robertson, Fred Robertson, Matthew Robertson, Wm. H. Robertson, Rev. P. Robitaille P.P., A. Sampson, Alex Sampson, Chas. J. Sampson, Elias A. Sampson, Paul Sampson, Thomas Sampson, Beni Samson, Angus Thibeau, Edward Thibeau, Henry Thibeau, Jacob Thibeau, James Thibeau, P. J. Thibeau, Patrick Thibeau.

The roadway was joined at the Government Wharf by a road serving warehouses owned by George H. Bissett, and homes owned by several Sampson families. It terminated at the main road leading to LeVesconte's residence and Patoune's property. Eva (LeVesconte) Clare recalls travelling this road in the early 1900s on her way to her father's store. (See A. F. Church map of 1886 at beginning of book.)

North Side (Lower Road)

Upgrading on the Lower Road, between Joe's Brook in Cannes to the Lower End School, was completed by Kennedy Construction of New Glasgow in the late 1920s. Beach gravel was purchased from residents on a per-cubic-yard basis. Gravel was gathered from local beaches and transported to designated areas along the shore. The stockpiled materials were hauled to the roadway by horse-drawn wagons and carts.

The contractor set up a stable at the bottom of what is presently Frances Digout's property and a cookhouse in Frederick Bouchard's field next door. John P. Burke, who was bookkeeper for the contractor, had his office in what is now Frances Digout's house.

North Side, Upper Road, Route 4

Prior to 1932, travellers between St. Peter's and Grand Anse passed through River Bourgeois along the Lower Road, from Damien Beranger's to Joe's Brook, or they crossed inland via the *Saint Peter's Road,* more commonly known as the *Post Road.* The first section of roadway to be improved, undoubtedly the most difficult, was River Tillard. In 1930-31, the section of roadway referred to as *Burke's Hill* was improved at an expenditure of $4,677.73. Amos Thibeau recalls working on this section of the road with a horse and cart. John P. Burke and Simon McPhee were road foremen.

On August 25, 1931, tenders were called for a five-mile section of highway running from River Tillard to Grand Anse, which included improvements to the alignment, width and surface of the road. Tenders were received from Wm. T. Clow, John Latimer, E.R. Orlando, Canadian Paving Company, M.H. McManus and Andrew Wheaton & Sons. Wm. T. Clow was the lowest tender at $80,199.25, with John Latimer second at $92,381.30. Clow had accepted a contract covering another section of work and was asked to withdraw. Latimer was awarded the contract on September 1, 1931.

Construction began immediately, with a completion date of June 30, 1932. The work came under *Joint Expenditure for Relief of Unemployment*, and being a section of the Trans-Canada Highway, the Dominion of Canada paid 50 per cent of the cost. Under this same program, considerable work was completed on roadways to Sydney during the early 1930s. George DeRoche recalls that the bridge at Doctor's Brook had the year 1932 marked in the concrete, and that Latimer's construction camp was located in Bastien Landry's field, close to Riverview Villa. In the early 1930s, improvements were also made to the road on the South Side.

Roadway materials were obtained from Archie Morrison's beach, where a small steam shovel loaded a crusher. (My father, James, worked as night watchman). Materials were not obtained from Sporting Mountain as gravel had not been discovered there at that time. Road construction equipment consisted of picks, shovels and bars. Horses and oxen pulled carts with dump boxes and truck-wagons with removable floor panels. Stumps were extracted by horse teams; men used *stump pullers* such as that owned by John Sampson (see Plate 601.)

The motorized device used on road construction was a Caterpillar 20 Dozer. This small-tracked machine was equipped with a push blade and a sturdy tow bar. Ropes were used to tow stumps and large rocks, such as those removed from the dam at Joe's Brook. Some of these rocks were used to

Plate 601–Courtesy of Vincent Sampson

Plate 602–Taken by Garvie Samson

construct the foundation wall under Charlie Pottie's store. Small dozers towed graders, such as that shown in **Plate 602**, which were used to maintain road surfaces and drains after the roads were built. The gravel roadway along Route 4 from Hawker to River Tillard was paved in 1939. Gerard Touesnard recalled his brother, Davey, had purchased a new 2–1/2 ton Ford truck which he used to haul asphalt on this project.

Church Point Road

The existing road from Route 4, to and around the cemetery, has remained virtually unchanged except for re-alignment when the new wooden bridge was constructed at Dennis' Brook. The entire roadway was upgraded in 1961, with improvements such as widening, excavation of gutters, installation of culverts, and the application of an asphalt surface. The main highway was also paved at this time. The contract was awarded to Martell's Construction of North Sydney and my father, James A. Sampson, was superintendent.

River Bourgeois Bypass

Beginning in 1977, major re-alignment and improvements were made to Route 4 from Louisdale to River Tillard, bypassing River Bourgeois. Access ramps were constructed at River Tillard and Sporting Mountain Road. Access to the Thibeauville Road from the new roadway is cumbersome and dangerous.

Intended to improve safety and traffic flow, the bypass had a negative impact on small business in River Bourgeois. Construction of an access ramp in Hawker would have allowed motorists an opportunity to view the wonderful natural scenery of the community, so often photographed by amateur and professional photographers such as the late Robert Norwood. Construction of the Trans-Canada Highway from Port Hasting to Sydney in

1965, via Baddeck, also dramatically reduced traffic volumes and business through communities such as Port Hawkesbury, Louisdale, and River Bourgeois.

Modes of Transportation

Stage Coaches

Early improvements in roadways resulted in an increased volume of traffic, and demand for more and improved carriages, maintenance shops, and accommodations. Businesses providing such services in St. Peter's included:

1882: T. S. Lindsay & Co. Stages (also in Antigonish) volume $40,000–$75,000. John Morrison, wheelwright, volume $1,000– $2,000. John Morrison, Hotel & c, no volume shown.

1897: John Morrison Hotel, Stages & c, volume $3,000–$5,000. Malcolm McLeod Hotel (wine and liquor dealers, hotel and saloons) volume $2,000–$3,000. A.D. McDonald Carriages, volume less than $500.

1902: John Morrison Hotel, Stages & c, volume $3,000–$5,000. John W. Morrison, wheelwright, volume $1,000–$2,000. A.D. McDonald Carriages, volume less than $1,000.

1906: John Morrison Hotel, Stages & c, volume $3,000–$5,000. E.G. Lescombe, Harness, volume less than $500. Other motels operating at a later date included the Radio and the MacDonald Hotel.

Railway

The most significant on-land innovation in the movement of merchandise, people, and development of the municipality, was the railway linking Port Hawkesbury to St. Peter's. One of the earliest supporters of a Nova Scotia railway system was *Sam Slick* (Judge T.C. Haliburton). He told his readers in 1835, *a railway in an area could work a miracle; for it is river, bridge, road and canal—all in one. It saves what we haven't got to spare; men, horses, carts, vessels, barges, and what's all in all—time.*

Construction of the St. Peter's Railway began in July, 1901 and the 30.65-mile section of track was completed on September 8, 1903. The arrival of the first train in St. Peter's was a day of celebration. Businessmen such as George W. Kyte (an up-and-coming lawyer and politician), Charles W. Bissett, M.D., and A.A. Morrison, were some of the more prominent citizens in attendance for the inauguration of the railway service.

The new freight and postal service was considered a *God-Sent*. To maximize access, stations were provided at Sporting Mountain, Grand Anse, Whiteside,

Plate 603–Courtesy of Alfred and Maude Burke

Basin Road, Evanston, and Chapel Road. Flag stations were located in areas such as River Tillard, to facilitate incoming and outgoing mail. **Plate 603** shows passengers waiting for the train's arrival at the Sporting Mountain Station. Local residents called the train the *Blueberry Express* because it went so slow that passengers could jump off to pick blueberries along the track and still catch the moving train.

On January 30, 1959, it was announced[4] that effective March 1, 1959, CNR would discontinue passenger service on two sub-divisions in Nova Scotia: Port Hawkesbury–St. Peter's and Port Hawkesbury–Inverness. The article confirmed the community was already served with bus service, and provided twice-daily direct Rail-liner and other main-line train connections. There would be no change in freight service with carload lots moving by rail and less-than-carload lots by CNR highway vehicles; express shipments and mail would continue to be handled by CNR road transport. Traffic continued to decrease and without pomp or ceremony, the last train rolled out of St. Peter's in July of 1977. We congratulate the citizens of St. Peter's for recycling the Railway Station. It is now the meeting place of the *Bonnie Brae Senior Citizen's Club* and other social groups.

Passenger Cars

Although automobiles[5] were manufactured in Nova Scotia as early as 1898, it wasn't until the early 1920s that cars were purchased and registered[6] by local residents. The first cars were purchased between 1924 and 1926. Owners included: Charlie Pottie with his Model "A" Ford sedan with wooden spokes, Father Robitaille who used his car to transport milk to St. Peter's and Port Hastings, Sam Fougere with a Touring Chevrolet, William LeVesconte's Chrysler, and Angus Boyd's Buick. Batiste Burke and John P. Burke also owned cars. The closest thing to manufacturing cars in River Bourgeois was a *touring car* Jim Bouchie and Charlie Robertson made from one of Tom Morrison's old cars. Ernie Bourque made numerous modifications to a 1926 Chevrolet truck with wooden-spoked wheels. He eventually sold it to a man from French Cove.

Trucks

Trucks were not as prevalent as cars because they were more expensive. The earliest truck owner was David Touesnard who purchased a 1932 six-cylinder Chevrolet in Sydney. In 1937, trucks were purchased by Jack LeVesconte and James A. Sampson. Anselm Fougere also owned a truck. The most popular trucks were GMCs and the Chevrolet Maple Leaf. The dual–wheeled trucks were rated at 2-1/2 tons capacity, however they often carried seven to eight tons. Trucks were loaded by hand until the late 1930s when steam shovels came into common use, especially around the Cabot Trail.

Busses

In 1915, Albert (Bert) Sampson, originally from Louisdale, began driving a horse and wagon taxi for Peter MacDonald in Sydney. In 1925, he operated the first bus service from St. Peter's to Sydney, with a seven-passenger Studebaker bus. The six-day/week service left Sydney at 9am and stopped at the Radio Hotel in St. Peter's for 2-1/2 hours, before returning to Sydney where the driver stayed overnight. The bus[7] went to Grand River twice weekly.

Plate 604–Courtesy of Herman Burke

Eddie Gordon, who drove the bus for Albert Sampson, eventually bought-out the business and Studebaker for $600. Albert wanted to become more involved in the taxi business in Sydney. As demand increased, Gordon purchased a couple of buses and had the chassis modified (by Angus Gillis in John Cashe's garage in

Sydney) to suit his needs. Two of the early bus drivers for Eddie Gordon were Herman Burke (**Plate 604**) and Walter Fougere. Walter was the principal driver from 1938–1951 while Herman drove from 1942–1944. Acadian Lines now serves the rural areas. Gussie LeBlanc provided a bus service from Arichat to Sydney for some time.

Taxis

There wasn't sufficient business in the community for full-time taxi drivers. Those who provided this service did only to supplement their normal work. One of the earliest taxi drivers was John P. Burke who taxied in 1926, mostly for family and friends. Anthony Landry drove taxi with his 1939 Mercury for two years; another one of his cars was a 1946 Chevrolet which he drove for 10 years. He recalls that during the war years, taxis were issued *gasoline coupons*, some of which he kept as mementos. Others drivers included Jack LeVesconte and Lawrence Burke. In 1945, return fare from River Bourgeois to St. Peter's was 35 cents.

Trivia

Drive to the Right

It may be of interest to know why Nova Scotians, who originally drove on the left-hand side, now drive on the right-hand side of the road. The tradition was broken as of 2am, April 15, 1923, when motorists and horse-drawn vehicles were required to switch driving from the left-hand to the right-hand side.

The new rule broke with British tradition, but brought the province in line with Germany, France and the United States. New Brunswick and British Columbia had changed one year earlier, while Prince Edward Island remained unchanged. The change had merit since most cars were being built for right-side drivers. One of the major incentives, however, was the fast-emerging tourist business with the U.S.A.

Dust, Asphalt Paving

With the advent of automobiles, dust became a major nuisance on unpaved roadways. Beside the obvious dirt aspect, dust caused numerous carbonator problems and it was difficult to maintain a smooth driving surface. In 1931, more than 415 miles of roadway in Nova Scotia were treated with a *dust layer*–calcium chloride and Malagash salt. The use of Malagash salt had to be discontinued as no satisfactory application method could be found. In 1931, a committee headed by Dr. F.H. Sexton was appointed to study the question of dust layers.

One of the obvious solutions to the dust problem was to apply a waterproof covering over the gravel sub-surface. The surface most widely used today, namely asphalt[8], was being applied only on an experimental basis in the early 1930s. It took years of experimentation before suitable mixes and satisfactory application equipment were developed. Asphalt was first used to treat railway beds in 1943.

Roadway Never Materialized

George DeRoche advised me that there was a roadway laid out from Sporting Mountain to Number 4 Highway before the new bypass was constructed. It was surveyed and the centre line went through Hattie (Burke) Johnson's driveway in Cannes. The roadway construction actually began, with some of the road made for one of the paper companies. The project was discontinued and George, whose land the roadway traversed, requested and received some assistance for repair work. The land obtained from Hattie Johnson was also repaired.

Inverted Wharf

In 1961, Martell's Construction was awarded the contract to improve and extend the Government Wharf on Church Point. I was fortunate to have worked on this project with my father, James. Following the removal of loose materials under the intended crib location using a boom crane and clam bucket, soundings were taken and cross-sectional drawings were made. The crib was built on the shore upside down, and many observers wondered what in heavens we were doing. The formidable-looking craft was launched, righted, positioned and filled with ballast. It rested perfectly flat and remains intact to this date.

Endnotes

1) Statute of Labour. PANS, RG 1/337/48 Status of Nova Scotia, 1826, c3, s2.

2) In 1827, the first bridge was built with government funding. The River Tillard Bridge was constructed at a cost of 100 pounds by John Brown McNeil of River Tillard, a recent immigrant from Scotland. He later became one of the ringleaders in the St. Peter's Riot of 1847.

3) "Roads and Bridges", RG 5 Series P, Vol 115.

4) Halifax Chronicle Herald, January 30, 1959, *CNR will discontinue Passenger Service.*

5) The first automobile built in Canada was named *Victorian*, and manufactured in Hopewell, Nova Scotia, in 1898. The MacKay Motor Co. (1910-1914) operating in Amherst, Nova Scotia, was one of North America's most successful automobile manufacturers.

6) Motor Vehicle Registration: 1914–1,710 vehicles, 1920–12,450; 1930–43,507; 1940–59,454; 1941–64,410 and in 1945–59,442 vehicles. The first year for motorcycle registration was in 1924 when there were 137 registered. In 1923, 1,453 chauffeur licences were issued and in 1928, 1,039 beginners licences were issued. There were 1,504 gasoline licences issued in 1929.

7) Information on public transportation system from Alfie Sampson in Dartmouth and Herman Burke in Halifax.

8) Asphaltic Paving 1933–28.2 miles, 1934–47, 1935–193, 1936–378, 1937–678, 1938–804, 1939–960 and in 1940–930 miles.

Chapter VII
Medical Services

Medical services were virtually unavailable to the first inhabitants, the mortality rate was extremely high, and large families were necessary to offset the inevitable deaths. There were no doctors to service the communities of Arichat, River Bourgeois, St. Peter's and L'Ardoise, until the late 1830s. If someone became seriously ill, residents with practical experience did their best to relieve the afflicted by administering local remedies. Many people died during the harsh winter months, because of inadequate treatment. In the late 1800s, the Arichat Hospital began providing treatment, with serious cases sent to Antigonish, Sydney or Halifax.

One of the first physicians to establish in Arichat was Dr. Andrew Madden. In addition to his medical practice, he found time to work for the community by serving as Road Commissioner, Justice of the Peace and Councillor. In 1839, he came under great pressure when a severe outbreak of Smallpox overtook residents of Arichat and Isle Madame. The following Petition, dated February 4, 1840, confirms the extent of the disease and the efforts made by Dr. Madden to assure the needy received medical attention.

> *In Petition of Andrew Madden of Arichat in the County of Richmond, Surgeon. Humbly Showeth: That during the latter part of last year, Arichat was visited with the Smallpox, which increased to an alarming degree, and in many cases proved fatal. That in order to prevent the disease from spreading, Vaccinate was recommended by the Board of Health and your petitioner vaccinated upwards of 800 persons. That by the attached list your Honourable House will perceive that there are 543 persons who have received the benefit of vaccination, chiefly fisherman and their families, and who your petitioner considers unable to pay. And it is under these conditions that he feels confident that your Honourable House will take into consideration his services in connection with the efforts made and grant him such a sum as will be fair.*

This is one of many examples of exemplary work performed by doctors in small rural communities. In the late 1800s and early 1900s, improvement in roadways, the completion of the railroad from Port Hastings to St. Peter's, and the installation of telephones were of tremendous assistance to the sick. Physicians could be contacted sooner and acute cases could be transported to Arichat, Antigonish or Sydney Hospital where they could receive specialized care.

River Bourgeois was not large enough to support a physician and relied entirely on doctors residing in St. Peter's and Arichat. The first doctors recorded[1] as working in St. Peter's were Dr. Charles Bissett (1866-1916), and Dr. John A. MacDonald, Sr. (1854-1925). Both began practicing there in 1897.

Home Visits

Obtaining the services of a physician from St. Peter's could be a major undertaking during the winter as the roads were mere trails, suitable only for saddle horses. There were no telephones before 1917, which meant that someone had to go to St. Peter's on foot or by horse, to fetch the doctor. Despite the adverse travelling conditions, doctors travelled far and wide, by horse and saddle, wagon or sleigh, to attend to their patients. The following are examples of visits and charges from Dr. John A. MacDonald's business records (1900-1924):

- November 10, 1890: John Sampson, diver, night visit and attendance, $4.50.
- November 11, 1890: James Sampson, diver, one visit to daughter & attendance, $4.
- December 3, 1891: William Beranger, to visit son and apply dressing, $4. On same date to examine and supply medication to Gilbert Beranger's daughter, $2 and to supply medication to mother-in-law $0.40.
- December 11 & 12, 1891: Alphonse Beranger, visit and attend to wife, $5.
- December 27, 1911: David Sampson Jr., examine and attend to wife, $1.50. (This must have been for an office visit.)
- March 12, 1921: Mr. Sampson, lighthouse-keeper in St. Peter's, pills $0.75.
- March 19, 1921: Willie Beranger, Cannes, visit, $6.
- January 22, 1921: night visit to Gilbert Beranger, $6, pills $0.75.
- May 5, 1922: Alex Sampson, lighthouse-keeper in Saint Peter's, confinement case, $15.

Midwifery

Because of the difficulty obtaining doctors, certain women in the community volunteered their services in time of illness and childbirth. These services, usually free, were especially important in River Bourgeois because of the distance from physicians in St. Peter's. The following chart of births was compiled from information recorded in the Registrar of Births and Deaths between January 1,1909–September 1919.

Year	Doctors	Midwives/other	Total Births
1909	10	23	33
1910	12	20	32
1911	7	23	30
1912	14	18	32
1913	12	12	24
1914	14	21	35
1915	14	11	25
1916	16	7	23
1917	18	11	29
1918	28	14	42
1919	9	2	11 (to Sept. 22)
	154	162	316

Some of the most prominent midwives and the number of births they are credited with include: Marin Burke–49, Simone Burke–25, Olive Dugas–26, Mary Richard–2, Eveline Samson–4 , Mary Sampson–5, Margaret McPhee–17, and Margaret Pottie–5.

One of the most memorable midwives, likely responsible for some of the 29 unaccounted births above, was Susan Sampson. She practically had a full-time job with her daughter Anti Minnie Sampson, who gave birth to seven boys and seven girls, some of whom were born during the sample time period. Eva Clare told me Susan attended to all the LeVesconte children born between 1906–1912, namely: Caroline, Peter, John, Eva and Charles. Susan died on June 8, 1938, at the age of 103 years, 10 months.

Hermit Medicine Company

John P. Burke businessman, councillor, orator, Justice of the Peace, raconteur and musician, made retreats at the Trappist Monastery located close to Antigonish, and established a friendly relationship with the German Trappist Monks[2]. Before they returned to Germany, as they were being replaced by the Augustinians, they provided John P. with recipes and authorized him to produce their *Hermit Liniments and Salves.*

John P. and his wife Alvina (Beranger) purchased their first property on the Church Point from George and Sophia Robertson on January 9, 1912. This property, located west of the cemetery, was known as Anselm's Field. John P. produced the first *Hermit Medications* in a small shop close to William Robertson's forge in 1917, the same year the trademark was registered. When John P. and his wife Alvina sold their property to Maggie and Edmond Landry, they moved to

Plate 700–Taken by Garvie Samson

River Tillard and took their original shop. A new shop was constructed later in River Tillard close to their home. It measuring 12 feet, 6 inches x 14 feet, 6 inches, and is shown in **Plate 700** taken in 1993. The shop was equipped[3] with a butter churn, apothecary (druggist) implements, jars, labels, a pot-bellied stove, desk, shelves, a typewriter and stationary.

Medicines were mixed by John P., however as business increased, he employed his nephew, Mary Jones's son, to help with the work. The shop was out-of-bounds to four of John P.'s children though the eldest, Philip and Xavier, helped on occasion. Herman and Sister Lola Burke recall their father working many long hours preparing orders for shipment. **Plate 701** shows several medicine bottles.

Plate 701–Courtesy of Richard Burke

Bottle were typically labelled with the inscription: *Hermit Medicine Company, River Tillard, Richmond Co., N.S., Suggested applications are for Cuts, Bruises, Chapped Skin, Cold Sores, Piles, Proud Flesh, & c..* Another section of the label read, *Hermit Eczema*

Remedy, A Remedy For Eczema and Skin Disorders. Each shipment included letters of Testimonial from satisfied customers, such as the following from Charles J. Sampson on April 3, 1918:

> *I have no hesitation whatever in recommending your salve for burns. My little boy, who had a bad burn on the arm which had been irritated by his clothing, found a complete cure after using several applications of your salve. For the benefit of others who may meet with such accidents, I give you full permission to publish this.*

Hermit Medicine Products were sold by commissioned agents in Sydney, South Bar, Ingonish, Cheticamp and on the mainland. In addition to local markets, products, including salves and tonics, were shipped in small quantities to destinations as remote as Jamaica. Salves were recommended for eczema, cuts, burns, cold sores, chapped skin, proud flesh, piles and all skin disorders. Tonics were recommended for coughs and colds. The ointment was usually placed on a spoon, heated to a liquid consistency, then applied to the sore. It was very effective.

Early Diseases

The 1870s were a decade of steady growth in the diocese with the formation of new parishes, the building of churches, and the ordination of priests. Bishop Cameron initiated many of these developments and helped out in events such as the smallpox epidemic which struck Arichat in 1872, claiming 17 lives. In 1883, 29 children died in Richmond County as a result of diseases: 26 from diphtheria, 2 from typhoid, and 1 from scarletina.

On May 6, 1931, the Minister of Health held a meeting to determine ways of controlling the *White Plague* (tuberculosis), in Cape Breton. Communities were given two options; they could construct a TB Annex in each district or provide additional facilities in their respective hospitals.

Common causes of death in the 19th century were recorded as: old age, heart weakness, Canadian cholera, ulcerated tongue cankerous, consumption, brain fever, kidney marble, apoplexy, whooping cough, inward trouble, croup, blood poison, tuberculosis, indigestion, pneumonia, paralysis, pleurisy, lung disease, liver disease, appendicitis and heart disease.

Local Remedies

Fried Onions

Eva (LeVesconte) Clare[4] recalls that when her brother Jack was a child, he became very ill with pneumonia during a terrible winter storm. It was impossible to access the doctor in St. Peter's, as there were no telephones. In the middle of the night, Jack's condition began to worsen. His father,

William, put on his long moccasins. His wife Ethel asked, *Where are you going?* to which he replied, *To fetch Doll.* With toboggan in tow, through waist-high snow, he headed into the darkness returning one-half hour later with Doll Sampson.

On her arrival, Doll requested certain medications which they didn't have, so she decided to prepare a poultice. She asked William for all the onions they had and he returned from the basement with two large bundles. Doll pealed and thinly sliced two large bowls and fried the first in lard. She placed the hot fried onions in a cotton pouch and lay it on Jack's chest. Later she prepared the second batch. Throughout the remainder of the night and into the morning she attended to him. As morning approached, the fever broke and his condition greatly improved. Within one week, he had completely recovered. The incident was ironic because Jack despised onions.

Eva never forgot the long moccasins, which her friend, Julie Anne Landry (Mrs. Pacien Landry), admired. Apparently Julie had great difficulty obtaining proper footwear because her feet were so large and she frequently asked William to pass the boots on to her, which he eventually did.

Balsam Gum

On January 20, 1990, Jean Pottie, whose parents were Marie and Remi Fougere, related to me a medication they frequently used to reduce swelling and to remove poison. The recipe consisted of the following:

- Boil a quantity of balsam gum to form a syrup
- To 3/4 teaspoon of syrup add one egg yolk and stir
- Refrigerate.

Recently, Jean accidently drove three knitting needles deep into her foot, so she tried the medication as a poultice. Within a few minutes she could feel the drawing effect, and in a couple of weeks her foot was completely healed.

Asthma Relief–Lock of Hair in Pine Door Jamb

Cut a lock of hair from the patient, drill a hole in a door jamb, insert the hair and fill the hole with a pine plug.

The above procedure was performed on me as a three-year-old child. The lock of hair and pine plug remain to this date in the door frame at my grandfather, David Sampson's old home. The remedy works–the asthma disappeared.

Mail Order Medications

Medication for various maladies were often obtained by mail order. Typical examples are those made by John Bourque[5] on January 9, 1911 and October 7, 1914 to Northrope and Lyman Co. of Toronto for *Asthma Remedy Pills*, and on April 3 and April 19, 1919, to T. Eaton and Co. for a box of *Dr. Kellog's Asthma Remedy*.

Denturist

To obtain a set of false teeth, residents had to go to Isle Madame. Dorothy Sampson recalls her mother, Mary Agnes (Aggie), saying she had gone to D'Escousse to have her dentures made. Later, people had their false teeth made by a Mr. Turner in Port Hawkesbury. Martha DeRoche recalls having her first set of dentures made by Mr. Turner.

In 1968, Walter Kendall had two open-heart operations and was advised to pursue a line of work which did not require heavy lifting. He enrolled in a three-year denturist program at the Associated Dental Laboratory in Halifax, followed by an apprentice training program at George Matheson's Dental Clinic on Charlotte Street in Sydney. He wrote for his denturist licence from Francis Marchand's Dental Shop in Port Hawkesbury, passed and retains the licence to this date.

In 1971, he operated a dental clinic in his home in River Bourgeois, across the road from Cletus and Mary Touesnard. In addition to local customers, clients came from as far away as Sydney and Antigonish, all through word-of-mouth advertisement. Many residents attest to his superior workmanship and service. He closed the clinic in 1981 because of competition from a number of clinics opening in Antigonish and Sydney.

Local Physicians

Dr. Charles P. Bissett (1866-1916) son of George H. Bissett (1827-1921) and Virginia Lee Boudreau (1830-1918) from D'Escousse. Charles married Emma Cameron of St. Peter's.

Dr. Andrew Bona, dentist, was the son of Felix and Elizabeth (Jackson) Bona. He was a World War II Veteran and obtained his education through the Veteran's Program. He attended River Bourgeois and St. Peter's schools and graduated from Dalhousie University. He married Edith Monica Savage from Moncton, N.B., and spent most of his career in Saint John, N.B.

Dr. Douglas J. Bourque (b. 1900) dentist, son of Hilaire Bourque (c.1878-1967) and Ida (Sampson), was a war veteran and went to Dalhousie under the Veteran's Program. He was in the navy during the war.

Dr. John Huntley Boyd (1898-1971) son of Angus Joseph (1854-1938) and Mary Fraser (d. 1915) of Cannes. He married Pauline Kyte (1903-1980) from St. Peter's in 1930. He practiced medicine in the U.S.

Plate 702–Courtesy of Sarah Digout

Dr. Joseph Digout (d. 1978) son of Eugene (1870-1959) and Mary (Fougere) (1873-1965) of Cannes. He attended St. FX and the University of Laval, graduating in the class of 1924-25. He lived in his father's residence for six months, then moved to St. Peter's. He married Sarah Burke in 1931 and practiced in St. Peter's until 1976 when he retired. During many winters when Dr. Jack MacDonald, the only other physician in town went to Parliament, Dr. Joe worked alone. **Plate 702** shows Dr. Joe and his wife Sarah and **Plate 703** shows the Digout residence and office at the left, and Richard and Muriel (Sampson) MacDonald's house to the right.

Dr. John Murdock Sampson (1900–1964) dentist, son of Anselm Samson (1862–1938) and Catherine Bouchard (1864–1937) of P.E.I., attended St. FX University and Dalhousie University School of Dentistry. He married Mary Hanrahan of Antigonish, practiced in the U.S.A. and retired in Monastery

Dr. Michael Morrison, son of Archie (C.L.) and Mary Ann (1851-1883), was born in Seaview and went to Dalhousie University. He worked in Canso and

Plate 703–Courtesy of Sarah Digout

Antigonish following graduation.

Dr. George Aden Boyd (b. 1937), son of William Fraser (1885-1955) and Mary Ellen (Bourque), attended Cannes, River Bourgeois, and St. Peter's Schools and Dalhousie University where he graduated with his M.D. He specialized in Eye, Ear and Throat at the Royal Victoria in Montreal. He now practices in Sydney, N.S.

Other physicians

In the early 1900s, there was a certain **Dr. Murphy** who lived at property presently owned by Bobbie Bouchie on the Church Point. Little is known of this doctor except that he did not practice in River Bourgeois and there is no record of him having an office in St. Peter's. He moved to Halifax around 1910 when Tina Burke, from Cannes, became his housekeeper.

Dr. de la Villegué lived at property originally owned by Jean Richard, above Charlie Pottie's house. He was killed below Ben LeBlanc's while driving with Maurice Fougere in his carriage. His family included five children: Arcade, Felix (Phil), Alma, Tillie, and Marie. My grandmother Tillie Bourque used to play with Tillie de la Villegué as a teenager, between 1902–1905. Following the doctor's fatal accident, the family moved to Sydney.

Doctors serving River Bourgeois from St. Peter's included: Dr. Charles Bissett, Dr. J.A. McDonald, Jr., Dr. J.A. (Jack) MacDonald, Sr., Dr. Patton, Dr. Fred McCaskill, Dr. Kemp Morrison and Dr. A. Curry.

Dr. Patton from Port Morien, a graduate of Dalhousie University, came to St. Peter's to relieve Dr. Charles Bissett, who had to leave for Europe to obtain treatment for a bone condition. Dr. Patton's most difficult assignment was to keep the residents under quarantine during the smallpox epidemic.

Dr. Deveau from Arichat came to River Bourgeois for the occasional house call. He drove a model **T** Ford which they called *un four carré* (a square oven).

In 1935, there were two doctors listed in the St. Peter's Telephone directory: Dr. J.H. Digout and Dr. J.A. MacDonald.

Residents of River Bourgeois now have to go to L'Ardoise for medical services.

Trivia

- Doctor's Brook was named after Dr. de la Villegué.
- On September 13, 1918, medical personnel gathered in False Bay to pick moss for dressings and pads to be used overseas. Some 300 bags of Sphagnum Moss were collected, and many more bags could have been filled[6].

Endnotes

1) Micro Biography, Business Records. *The Mercantile Agency Reference Book.* Dunn, Wiman & Co., Dalhousie Archives, Halifax, N.S. Their business volume was recorded as $1,000–$2,000 per year in 1897. The two doctors were still practicing at St. Peter's in 1906.

2) Father Vincent de Paul established the Trappistine Sister in 1822 and the Monastery in Tracadie in 1825.

3) Sr. Lola, Herman and Richard Burke provided information and documents regarding the *Hermit Medicine Company*.

4) Eva (LeVesconte) Clare was interviewed on October 20, 1990 and died suddenly on October 23. The only remaining member of William and Ethel LeVesconte's family is Jack (John), who lives with his wife Ada, in St. Peter's.

5) Information from John Bourque's diary was provided by Sam Burke, Fred, Pauline and Ann Marie Pitts of Halifax, November 1990.

6) Information from booklet, *Echoes of the Past, The Senior Citizen's Portrayal of Early Life in Richmond County*, compiled by Donalda MacDonald, Maxine Frost and Terri Manley.

Chapter VIII
Merchandising

Many will be amazed at the number of businesses that operated in the community over the years. To reduce confusion, I have organized them by location. Though I have attempted to mention every business, it is not my intention to describe each in detail, as many were similar in nature. Several are worthy of greater detail as they were recalled with considerable interest and enthusiasm by many elders. **Appendix 7** provides business statistics.

I Church Point and Lower End

The first businesses were located along the shores of the harbour, later to be graced by the River Inlet Lighthouse. The most prominent ones were owned by the Bissett, McLean, Caree, LeVesconte and Robertson families. Inland there were the Urquhart, Walker, Caree, Fortune, Boyd and Sampson family businesses.

Bissett family

One of the most influential business families in the community was that of George Edward Bissett. The Bissett family was to River Bourgeois what the Kanvanagh family was to St. Peter's. In addition to their local interests, the Bissetts owned land in Lunenburg, Cole Harbour and Halifax. When George purchased his first commercial land at the harbour entrance to River Bourgeois (discussed in **Industries**), it included three stores. These stores, which sold salt and fishing supplies, are considered to be the first of any significance to operate in the community. George's first locally-built vessel was the *Martha*, built in 1831.

George Henry (d. February 15, 1921), George Edward's son, continued the fish operation and was involved in buildings located on the northeast shore of the harbour, close to the Government Wharf. His earliest business reference is the acknowledgement of a ship's bond payment in 1862 from Peter DeCarteret in Arichat. His first locally-constructed vessel was the *Express*, registered in 1862. He is recorded by *Dunn Wiman and Co.* in 1882 as a Supplier. Mrs. George H. Bissett died on July 30, 1918.

George Henry's son, Frederick, operated his general store business from one of the stores shown in **Plate 202**. It was recorded in 1866 and in 1892 under F. W. Bissett, G.S. & Fish. In 1911, the Halifax Telephone Directory had listings under F. W. Bissett Co. Ltd., Fish Merchants, 135 Lower Water Street and recorded his residence at 43 Victoria Road in Halifax. Mrs. F.W. Bissett was listed on Portland Street in Dartmouth. The last of the Bissett buildings in River Bourgeois, located at the Government Wharf, was dismantled in the early 1940s.

James R. McLean

George Edward Bissett sold his property and businesses to John Burke who then granted the land to John McLean in 1845. The first of several vessels registered under James McLean was the *Martha* in 1862. The A.F. Church Map[1] shows James McLean as the owner of a fish establishment, located on the George Edward property in 1888.

LeVesconte family

The LeVesconte family is remembered with great respect by everyone in the community. Their local businesses were extensions of the parent company in D'Escousse. In the **Industries** chapter, reference is made to William LeVesconte's diary of 1879, in which he wrote that on June 30th, he spoke to a Mr. Burke and his son Peter (1861-1932) who were crossing to the River with small lots of herring and mackerel. Peter LeVesconte's first store was located next to Peter Robertson's forge, close to La Pointe à Nanonne.

The LeVesconte's large warehouse/store was located 100 yards west of the Government Wharf. The facility, shown in **Plate 800** included 13,600 square feet of warehouse and display area and included one of the few water lots in the community. Vessels moored alongside the wharf at high tide where a derrick was used to load and unload heavy cargo to the warehouse. Most products were packed in barrels, as even the heaviest ones could be rolled

Plate 800–Courtesy of Clara Dennis

anywhere within the warehouses. Bulk salt was stored close to the wharf on the main floor. The front section of the building was used for general business. A statement to Charlie J. Sampson dated 1920 (**Plate 801**), gives an indication of the numerous items sold in the store. Eva Clare, William's daughter, recalled them stocking items such as: coffin-cloth, gingham (checkered cloth with green/white or red/white checks), dried cotton in plain white weave, curtains, wall-covering, needles and thread. They sold gasoline at his store soon after William purchased his first car in 1926. Docité Landry from the South Side was a clerk at the store for 40 years. The LeVesconte girls never worked in the store as few woman did during that time period.

William and Ethel sold the store to their eldest son Peter in 1935. He assisted with the larger store and operated a small store across the road in the winter, as the main store was too large to heat. His stock included: kitchenware, cutlery, pots, pans and china. Clothing items included: ten-gallon hats, shoes, shirts and neckties while suits could be custom-ordered. This store can be seen in the background of **Plate 202**. It was removed from the site in the late 1930s while the main store was dismantled in 1942.

Thomas Sampson

Thomas Sampson's small store of 200 square feet, shown in **Plate 802**, was situated across the road from the church, in-line with the harbour entrance. It was first listed in 1892 under the name of Thomas Sampson at which time it had a business volume[2] under $1,000. It was recorded under the name of Alex Sampson in 1901 with a business volume less than $500. In 1906 sales were between $500–$1,000 and in 1920, 1925, 1930, between $1,000–$2,000. In 1922, the store was listed under *Alex Sampson Groceries and Confectionary.*

Plate 802–Courtesy of Valerie Goyetche

Many recall the interior of the building. Along the walls were bins containing flour and grains, while a shelf above displayed glass jars of candies like jaw breakers and licorice. The store stocked a variety of canned goods, molasses and kerosene, but of greatest importance to the men was a large variety of pipe and chewing tobacco. A small pot-bellied stove close to the back door provided heat and hot water for a cup of tea. The back wall contained shelving and a bank of pigeon holes for incoming mail. Family members

River Bourgeois, C. B. 1919-1920 191

M Charles Sampson S

BOUGHT OF **WM. I. LEVESCONTE**

— DEALER IN —

FISHING SUPPLIES & MERCHANDISE

LOBSTER PACKER

TERMS:

Interest charged on overdue accounts

	1919			
Nov	20	To 5 Lard @ 40 2.00 (27) 1 Pr O/Pants $3.25	5	25
Decr	23	2 P Lard @ 45 (24) 1 Pr Corset $1.50	2	40
Jany	1920 2	2 Bags Flour @ $7.00 (24) [illegible]	14	70
	26	5 Beans @ 15 1- 3 Tin Lard @ 40 1.20	1	95
		1 P Lard 45 1 Shovel 90 (28) Creoline 25	1	60
		Mts $1.35 (29) L Globe 15 Matches 15	1	65
	30	Tobb 45 (Feby 2) 1 Raisins 25 Emulsion 50	1	20
Feby	5	1 pckge Pepper 15 (5) 5 Gr Sugar 1.-		95
	9	10 Rice @ 18 1.80 1 Pr Chds Rubber 75	2	55
		1 Tin Milk 16 (10) 84 Bags @ 15 12.60	12	76
	13	5 Sugar @ 16 2 Raisins @ 25 (14) Tobb 20	1	50
		Cr. Tartar 10 2 F. Biscuit @ 18		46
			46	97
	21	5 Beans @ 16 80. 5 Sugar @ 18 1/4 Matches 45	2	15
	23	Tobb $1.20 (March 4) 5 Yds Galatea @ 40	3	20
		2 Spools @ 10 Towling 18 1 Middie Blouse $2.00	2	38
		Ginger 15 Lemon 30 BR Powder 45		90
March		D Cleanser 15 (12) 2 Elm Mts @ $1.40 = 2.80	2	95
	19	Tobb 85 (22) Emulsion $1.00 (23) 2 Lard @ 45	2	75
	24	Hay $15.00 (31) [illegible] 30 (April 3) G Dust 16	15	46
April	3	1 L Globe 15 (6) 1 Pr O/alls $2.75 Leather 55	3	45
		Tobb 50 (9) Emulsion $1.00 (22) Chds Rubber 75	2	25
		1 Wash bord 75 (27) 8 1/2 Bags @ 25 2.13	2	88
June	18	BR Powder 45		45
			85	79
July	13	Pork 2.62 (21) 4 B Sugar 20 3 Soaps @ 12 36	1	78
			87	57

Sept 10 Paid $10.00 to Levi on Account

Contra "Cr"

Feby	1920 10	By Butchering	3	00

Plate 802–courtesy of Patsy McKay

included: Alex (a school trustee and member of the telephone company), Norman, Bill, and Katie. Alex died November 26, 1948 at the age of 79 years.

Malcolm J.T. McNeil
McNeil's store was situated at the end of *Bouchie's Lane* on Church Point. In addition to his business, M.J.T. MacNeil was Inspector of Schools and Justice of the Peace. Information concerning this business is documented in a statement[3] of account to a Mrs. Pringle, which covered the time period January 29, 1877 to July 5, 1880. The heading on the stationary gives a good description of merchandise sold at this store.

> *M.J.T. McNeil, Dealer in Staples & Fancy, Dry Goods, Ready Made Clothing; Tinware, Hardware and Glassware, Flour and Meal, Groceries, Stationary, & & &*

The McNeil store stocked a variety of sewing materials. These were sold by the yard or by the bale and included: cottons, flannels, prints, lace, satins, buttons and dyes. Eggs cost 10 cents/dozen and butter 15 cents/pound, in 1880. People came here from far and wide because of the selection. In 1892, the recorded sales volume was between $1,000–$2,000. This building also housed a Post Office.

When his business closed in the early 1900s, Malcolm McNeil used the facilities to store his numerous books and wagons. Other owners included Dr. Murphy (who moved to Halifax where Hattie Burke was his housekeeper), Alex (à Noré) Bouchie, and the present owners Robert and Anita Bouchie.

Camille Bouchie
Camille Bouchie operated a very small store across the road from the main cemetery. He sold dry goods, fish, canned goods and candy. There was a small office upstairs where he registered Deaths and Births and kept the Harbour Master Records. The store was in operation until the 1920s.

Burke, Bouchie Store
Hilda and Anthony Delore Burke (my uncle, a musician, veteran, postmaster, and at one-time small sheep farmer in Cannes), operated a store/Post Office across from John and Caroline Doucet beginning in 1943. The origin of the building is discussed under Post Offices. Helen Bouchie worked part-time in the store until her brother Walter purchased it from Delore in 1951. It was listed under *Walter G. Bouchie, General Sales*, in 1956. Helen worked full-time from 1951 until 1958 when she married Bennie Konning. Delore and Hilda re-purchased the store from Walter and had it hauled east of their current residence. In 1964, for convenience and efficiency, the store and Post Office were relocated to the basement of their new home. In 1967, the existing Post

Office was constructed and Delore served there a Postmaster until 1980 while Hilda attended the store. In the summer of 1980, Delore retired as Postmaster and they closed the store.

Amable Pottie

Amable, whose third wife was Lizzie Sampson from Church Point, opened a small store from his house on LeVesconte's Road. It served his own purpose more than the public as few shoppers ever frequented this area. He stocked canned goods and cigarette among other basic supplies.

Richmond Gardens and Crafts

Bobbie (Robert) Bouchie and his wife Anita make a variety of wooden articles at their new workshop at the foot of Bouchie' Lane. In addition to this business, Bobbie works as a carpenter.

Maurice and Lucille Landry

Maurice and Lucille returned from Boston in 1980 and opened a store with stock from Delore's store. The store was located across the road from Hilaire and Ida Bourque's house on the southwest corner of Charlie and Beatrice Landry's field. They stocked a variety of canned goods, dry goods and meats. The store closed in 1989. Maurice works as a carpenter.

Amable A. Fougere

This store was located in the Lower End, 100 yards northwest of the school, along the lower road. The original store sold mostly dry goods such as grain, oats, barley and flour. Amable's son, Joe, clearly recalls the beautiful sign, about 20 feet long, entitled, *A.A. Fougere, General Merchant,* which laid in their barn when he was a child.

Besides operating the store, Amable was a sales representative for W.T. Raleigh Medicine Company. He travelled from one end of the province to the other, by horse and buggie. When he was away on business, Dan Samson (Damien à Leon) from L'Ardoise attended the store. While Amable was still alive, Catherine opened an Ice Cream Parlour to supplement their income. Amable died in 1927.

Catherine (Katie's) Ice Cream Parlour

This business was very well accepted in the community and became a popular meeting place, especially for the children attending school next door. It operated between 1920–1937. In the mid-1920s, there was a similar business operating in St. Peter's by Mrs. A.J. Hill whose husband, John Hill, operated a butcher shop. Joseph (Joe), Catherine's son, described the operation to me in our interview on December 27, 1991.

Ice cream was purchased from *Brookfield Dairy Products* in Truro, transported by rail to Sporting Mountain, and couriered by Leander Boudreau to the store. The manufacturer placed the product in 5-gallon steel containers which were placed in wooden tubs. The tubs were tapered from 2–1/2 feet in diameter at the top to 2 feet at the base and fitted with a removable canvas jacket with rope handles. Prior to shipment, the ice cream containers were packed in chopped ice and additional ice was added on the train if required. Upon arrival at the store, the steel containers were placed in a four–compartment display chest and packed with ice. Salt was added to the ice to lower the freezing temperature.

Ice was stored in the basement of the house which was insulated with eel-grass. A hatch and shoot from the main floor provided access to load and retrieve ice. The neatly stacked ice cakes were covered with sawdust to reduce heat loss and to prevent them from freezing together. The basement floor and display chest were fitted with drains. Joe recalls his mother purchasing ice harvested from a fresh water lake in Martial Digout's field above Victor Digout's shoe repair shop. Two-man saws were used to cut the ice which was removed from the lake with large thongs and hauled to the Lower End of the River by horse and sled.

Joe's chores included chopping ice for the ice chest. On one occasion, he hit his knuckle with the axe instead of the block of ice. A scar on his left hand is a reminder of this occasion. The cost of an ice cream cone, served using a spring and lever metal scoop, was 5-cents. The most popular flavours were vanilla, chocolate and strawberry. Joe always had many friends, and this number increased when the containers where almost empty, *Children would congregate on the old swing by the house and eat every last drop.* Peter Sampson was especially fond of ice cream.

Damien Beranger

Beranger's store, shown on the wharf in **Plate 803**, was located 125 yards

Plate 803–Courtesy of Peter Digout

north of the Fougere store. It originated from a fish storage shed. A lean-to was added to the back of the store for bulk kerosene, which was in great demand for lamps and heating. A small building was constructed at the front, close by the road, to store molasses and vinegar. As business grew, the carriagehouse located above the roadway was turned to face the road. A storefront replaced the carriage entrance and this became the store most people recall. The exact date the store opened is not certain, however Damien purchased the land[4] in 1874 at which time he was classified as a fisherman.

Records show that the *P.D. Beranger General Sales* store had a volume between $1,000–$2,000 in 1921, and between $500–$1,000 in 1932. In 1956, the store was recorded under the name of *Abraham Beranger General Sales*, with no volume recorded. The store was still recorded under Abraham's name in May of 1960. Throughout its operation, the store sold bulk molasses, flour, dry and canned goods, candies, and some school supplies. This was one of the few stores to sell gasoline. During its operation, there was stiff competition with the A.A. Fougere store close by. Abraham was always ready to engage in a political conversation. Damien's wife, Marie (Bourque), died March 19, 1942 at the age of 84 years.

Edward Sampson
Abraham's store was purchased by my uncle Edward Sampson in 1959 and operated by Leo Sampson from its original location in 1960. It was then sold to Theresa (Mrs. Whitney) Sampson and hauled by my father, James, with a bulldozer to a location below the property previously owned by Father Robitaille, George Landry, Alfred Sampson and the present owner, Dorothy Sampson. The store was operated from this new location for a couple of years then sold to Valerie Goyetche who had it hauled to her property, where she used it as a bakery outlet. It is now being used as a wood shed.

David Sampson
David's small store, shown on the right in **Plate 804**, was located at the eastern side of Cletus Touesnard's driveway. The first record of the store was in 1921 under the name of David's son, *Anselm Samson Groceries*, with a business volume less than $2,000. Capt. Anselm opened the store to supplement his fishing income. As he grew older, his daughter Julia helped operate the store. The business was recorded to have a volume of up to $2,000 in 1932. The store was originally a workshop located along the water. Inside were a large counter and bins displaying dry good items such as sugar, flour, barley, rice and wheat. They also stocked canned goods, bulk molasses, baby bottles, nipples and kerosene. Residents recall confectionary goodies such as Cracker Jack popcorn, licorice and hard black candies. David died on April 4, 1920 and Anselm died on March 5, 1938.

Plate 804–Courtesy of Margaret Digout

Lawrence Burke

Lawrence Burke purchased Anselm Samson's store on March 5, 1936 and hauled it to a new location, below his father's (John Burke) property, on March 7, 1936. The purchase price, including all bins, countertop and stock was $40. Lawrence enlarged the store to provide storage space and added a second counter which came from *Catherine Fougere's Ice Cream Parlour*. The store, which sold dry goods and groceries, was listed under the name *Lawrence Burke General Sales* in 1956. He operated the store until 1946 himself, then his sister Mildred operated the store until it closed.

The store was sold to Jeffery Pottie, hauled to Hawker and placed in a field next to George Pottie's where it was used as a wood storage shed. George's house and the shed were burnt by the fire department in July of 1989, since they had become fire hazards. George had earlier moved to Richmond Villa in St. Peter's.

Service Stations

Gerard Touesnard established the community's only service station in 1947 under the *Texaco* umbrella. He opened a canteen for several summers and his wife Cecile and Dorothy Sampson worked there part-time. In 1951, he sold the business to Walter Fougere (1910–1976) who operated it until October 1964. Lawrence (Bucky) Sampson and his wife Anne (LeBrun) purchased it from Walter in 1964 and operate it to this date. Bucky extended the garage to include a body shop.

The earliest businesses to sell gasoline included William LeVesconte, Abraham Beranger, A.J. Boyd and Charlie Pottie. The typical dispenser of the time consisted of a graduated 10-gallon glass cylinder filled from a storage tank using a hand pump. Customers received a measured quantity of gasoline

Plate 805–Taken by Garvie Samson

from the cylinder via a gravity-fed hose. Gasoline was transported to St. Peter's via rail from refineries and pumped into holding tanks. Local deliveries were made by small tankers such as the one operated by Richard MacDonald from St. Peter's who delivered to surrounding communities for *Texaco* for many years. He married Murial Sampson, from the River.

Lavallee

This house was originally owned by Octave Chaisson (see **Plate 805**). He sold it to Joseph and Florence (Landry) Lavallee who established a small store in one of the rooms facing the Number 4 Highway. They sold it to Charlie Fred and Hilda Sampson who sold it to Bill MacLaughlin. The house burnt in 1991.

Nova Scotia Power Corporation

The Power Corporation opened an office and service compound on a site off the Number 4 Highway by the *Tara Lynne Touesnard Community Centre* in 1982. It services communities from Isle Madame to Framboise.

Riverside Industries

This facility was established by Father Samson in an effort to generate employment. It opened in 1953 and specialized in the manufacturing of school furnishings. Early employees included: Gordon Gillis, Bucky (at Caroline's) Sampson, Allen McPhee, Herman McPhee, Sam McPhee and Abraham Burkie from L'Ardoise. John VanMulukom was the teacher/ supervisor. Riverside Industries closed in the late-1970s. Prior to John VanMulukom's death in 1981, he made reproductive vintage furnishings for the Fortress. John's wife, Cecelia (died May 1994), raised purebred dogs for 25 years. She sold the dogs locally and to other dog breeders.

Howard (Howie) Sampson's Groceries

Sampson's store, located on the main highway across from the *River Bourgeois Senior Citizen Apartments*, was opened in the summer of 1970 by Cecile and Vivian Touesnard to sell vegetables grown by Gerard at his Seaview farm. Howard and Vivian opened the present store in 1977. The business found success when a grocery store in nearby St. Peter's closed as a result of a strike. Since then, the store has expanded several times in response to consumer demands. Two of the earliest employees included Cecile Touesnard and Dorothy Sampson. The store was sold to the present owners, Michael and Valerie Fougere, in 1990.

Saint Joseph's Crafts

This business, owned jointly by Arthur Peter Doary and his wife Henrietta, began as an extensive of Arthur's experience as an educator, teaching Technology Education (formerly an Industrial Arts program). His business includes: silk screening, woodworking, trophies, plaques, and stained glass windows. He is presently constructing stained glass windows for the local church designed by Sheila (Sampson) Caissie, daughter of Basil and Virginia Sampson.

Café Bourgeois

This business located across the highway from The River Bourgeois Senior Citizen's Apartments, was built by Paul and Michelle Boudreau and operated between 1975–1980. In 1984, Paul added four apartment units to the café section which he had already converted to an apartment unit. The building is shown in **Plate 806**, taken in 1990.

Plate 806–Courtesy of Ephrem Boudreau

Monique's Beauty Salon
This salon, located off the Number 4 Highway above the ballfield, was operated by Monica Stone from 1962–1983.

MonJoe Fox Ranch
This ranch was operated by Monica and Joe Stone from 1978–1985 at the back of their property. They sold high quality silver fox pelts.

Dog Kennel
Cecelia Anne VanMulukom (d. May 21, 1994) raised purebred dogs at her property below Riverside Industries from the late 1950s until 1994.

Richmond Enterprises Ltd.
Located in River Tillard, Richmond Enterprises is operated by Terry Boudreau who is involved in building construction.

Hughie Samson Auto Body Limited, The Collision Centre
This business was established in 1989 and is located on the main highway above Charlie Burke's property. Hughie is married to Doreen, Charlie and Angela Burke's daughter.

Mrs. Joe D. Burke's Store
Her store was located in their house below the Parish Hall. It was recorded in operation as a grocery store in 1956 and 1960. Joe worked as a plumber.

William Urquhart
This general sales store was located on the North Side across from Ben LeBlanc and close to Jeffery Landry. The store dealt in exporting fish. The business volume is recorded as $20,000–$40,000 in 1882 and $40,000–$75,000, in 1886. This business was not recorded before 1882 nor listed after 1892. William Urquhart lived in Oban and Gerard Touesnard purchased his old house.

Walker's Store
This store was purchase from William Urquhart and Walker continued operating in the same line of business. There are no records available as to when the business closed. The large warehouse was purchased by Archie Morrison.

II River Tillard

Touesnard Kitchen Cabinets Ltd.
Clifford and Anne Louise (Babin) Touesnard began manufacturing specialized, custom-made cabinets in their Grand Gulley shop in the mid-1980s. They sell their made-to-measure oak cabinets throughout Cape Breton. The shop is well-known for it's fine workmanship and customer satisfaction.

Michael Boudreau
Michael operated a very small store which sold cigarette, candies, canned goods and molasses. It was located across the road from Mrs. Mary Young, who operated the Post Office. Michael was Margaret (Thibeau's) second husband; she married Michael after her first husband, Amos Burke, died. When Michael and Alvina (Beranger), John P. Burke's s wife died, Margaret sold the store to Charlie Fred Sampson, and moved to John P.'s to care for the family. Bernard Burke presently owns the property.

Burke Brother's Trucking
The original firm was established in 1967 under the name of *Flynn, Burke Trucking*. It became *Burke Brother's Trucking* in 1979. The firm, initially involved in residential and small commercial projects, has grown at a steady rate and is now involved in larger commercial projects.

III Cannes
Historically, and for the purpose of this chapter, the dividing line between the Lower End and Cannes is considered to be Angus Boyd's Store.

Angus Boyd
This store, located on the lower road east of Boyd's Lane, was one of the oldest and best-known family establishments. Angus Joseph[5] opened the store in 1882 and was selected as an Indian Agent for the Micmac Tribe. The store was first recorded in 1886 as *A.J. Boyd, General Sales*, with a volume of less than $1,000. By 1892, sales had increased to $2,000–$5,000. In 1897, business volume was recorded as being $1,000–$2,000. Following Angus's death at the age of 84 on March 10, 1938, his son William (Willie) Fraser, took over the operation. He operated it until the time of his death in 1955, at which time his son, Blaise Cyril, continued the business. The store closed in 1975 and the property was purchased by Vincent Bourque while Blaise retains the store. See **Plate 807** taken in 1993.

In the 1800s, most of the merchandise was transported by schooner. Boyd's Wharf, with its deep channel and open approaches, was the favourite docking facility for schooners and in later years, for large steamers. Frequently large schooners landed cargo at Boyd's Wharf for other merchants because of the docking facilities. The Province leased the lower level of one of the largest warehouse buildings from Angus Boyd. Merchandise shipped from centres such as Halifax and Boston, arrived at Boyd's Store where it was stored for customers. The upper portion of the warehouse, which was used by the owner, was served by a dumbwaiter from the lower floor. This building remains in relatively good condition.

Plate 807–Courtesy of Raymond Doary

A.J. Boyd sold many of the same products as his biggest competitor, LeVesconte, on Church Point. However Boyd's store carried a stock of bulk merchandise such as flour, bran, grain and wheat. There were a large number of customers from Thibeauville and Scotsmen from the Mountain who shopped here rather than travel to St. Peter's. Alfred Burke recalls that in the lower store there were large bins where items such as potatoes, loose salt and coal were kept. He remembers his father purchasing a ton of coal for $5 and having it delivered to his door. Johnnie (à Bouleau) Sampson delivered coal in a cart for many years, with his little black horse.

There was always something exciting going on around the store or warehouse. On one occasion, Willie discovered the boys, who were always demonstrating their strength, loading the tenth bag of feed on the back of one of the Bourque boys, who was prostrate on the warehouse floor. Lorenzo Pottie recalled how excited the small children in the area were when they erected the *Superior Chain Stores* sign on the store.

A.J. Landry's General Store

Anthony's store was located on the main highway at Boyd's Lane. He sold a variety of items including: groceries, dry goods, suits, hats, shoes, and for a short time, electrical appliances. He also sold Fire Insurance. The store was purchased by the Credit Union in 1973.

Carree, Fortune, MacLean

West of Angus Boyd's store along the lower road, and two houses south of Marshall Digout's residence and Post Office, there was a store listed under the name of Fred E. Carree in 1882 with a sales volume under $2,000. The small general store was listed under the name of John E. Fortune from 1886 to 1892 with a substantial decrease in business volume. It was listed under the name of John's wife, Mary C. Fortune, between 1897–1901.

In 1901, Peter M. MacLean became the new store owner with a sales volume of $500. By 1906, Peter's business volume had increased to $2,000 per year.

Peter was assisted in the business by his son John. When Peter moved to Sydney in the late 1920s, he sold all of his R.B. property to Tom Morrison.

Plate 808–Courtesy of John & Joan MacLean

The family photo, **Plate 808**, includes Peter, John D. and Chink. I had the pleasure of interviewing Peter's grandson, John Gilbert (Chink) and his wife Joan, who advised me that Peter had purchased the store in 1901 following the loss of their homestead by fire. **Plate 809** shows the entrance of MacLean's store. Their farm was located along the Sporting Mountain Road on the way to Dundee. Peter, who could speak French and Gaelic, was originally from Scotland and had married Jessie McIntyre from River Dennis. Jessie's father, Hughie P.J., was in the lumber business there. Peter was first cousins to the *miller* MacLeans from Thibeauville. Across from the store where George and Catherine Boudreau presently reside, there was a barn, shed and a great spring-fed well. This well, believed to be the same used by Caree in 1882, provides ice cold water throughout the year and has never gone dry.

Plate 809–Courtesy of John & Joan MacLean

Tom Morrison
Tom Morrison purchased the MacLean property when Peter and his family moved to Sydney in the late 1920s. Tom did not operate the store but rented the property to D.D. Boyd, who later became his brother-in-law when Tom married his sister, Florence, in 1932 following the death of her first husband, Stanislaus Poirer. D.D. worked for his father, A.J. Boyd, in his store located a short distance down the road. Alfred Burke purchased the property from Tom Morrison in 1943.

The River Grill
This restaurant was located in Cannes on the Number 4 Highway. It was opened in 1947 by Alfred and Maude Burke. Its dining room could accommodate 14 customers. Alfred learned his cooking skills while working with the railway and Ben's Bakery in Halifax. The *River Grill* closed in 1955.

Davidson Auto Body Shop
Estwood operated this shop, located on the main highway a stone's throw from Joe's Brook, between 1962–1988. Everyone knows Estwood for his humour and especially as a premier guitar player with Winston Scotty Fitzgerald and pianist Beattie Wallace.

Charlie Pottie, S.F. Burke and others
This store was located on the Number 4 Highway close to Doctor's Brook, below George and Martha DeRoche's residence. Charlie sold groceries, canned and dry goods and gasoline. Charlie owned one of the earliest cars and stored it in a garage which had double doors at each end. He drove in one end, parked and drove out the other, eliminating backing into or out of the garage. Because of financial difficulties, Charlie had to sell his house and store and Simon F. Burke purchased them for the fire-sale price of $650.

With construction of the new highway in 1932, the store became very popular to motorists with its mid-way location between Antigonish and Sydney. One of Simon Burke's favourite visitors was Dr. J. Clyde Nunn, a respected broadcaster at CJFX in Antigonish. Chink MacLean recalls one occasion at Simon Burke's with his father John MacLean, when a visitor from Quebec dropped by and began speaking to Simon and John in French. The Quebecer asked Simon, *What is it like being a French Canadian living in this part of the country?* Simon replied, *Well I really don't know because I'm a Cape Bretoner myself.* River Bourgeois residents were considered to have a good command of both languages.

Simon Burke sold the store, **Plate 810**, to Amadée Boudreau who operated it for several years. It was sold to Cletus Landry and then to Peter Landry. The store burnt in 1974 and was never rebuilt.

Plate 810–Courtesy of Maude Burke

Christina Dugas' Ice Cream Parlour

This ice cream parlour was located in Dennis Dugas' field across the road from Charlie Pottie. The building was built by Charlie and Dennis for his daughter, Christina. The building included an eating area and the entire storefront was fitted with windows. Material for this building was sawed by Marshall Digout.

When the roadway was constructed in 1931-32, the store had to be relocated. Latimer Construction hauled the parlour above the road to the bottom of Dennis' field, close to Charlie Pottie's house. Christina operated the shop in the late 1920s–early 1930s. When Martha and Sam Dugas retired from the U.S., they used the building as a feed and storage shed. In later years, George DeRoche dismantled the parlour and materials were used to construct a shed and an outhouse.

Grandma's House Bed and Breakfast

The proud owners of this new business which opened in May, 1994 are Tom and Rose (daughter of Amos and Mae Thibeau) Scott, formerly of Dartmouth. The house was initially constructed by Peter MacLean around the turn of the century. Tom and Rose purchased the property, which once belonged to Rose's grandparents, Simon and Laura Burke, in 1993 and began renovations during that winter. They added a turret to the front of the house. This addition, which overlooks the bay, makes a delightful breakfast nook and allows more light into the dining room area. All areas and rooms of the house are tastefully decorated and furnished to create a friendly and relaxing environment. See **Plate 811** taken in 1994.

Plate 811–Taken by Garvie Samson

Charlie Boudreau

Charlie was the son of Capt. Charlie Boudreau who owned several fishing schooners. His small store was first located on the shore road, 100 yards from Doctor's Brook. Following the construction of the new roadway in 1932, the store was hauled to its present location. See **Plate 812** taken in 1990. In later years, Charlie lived in the store and my aunt Martha DeRoche provide him with delicious food for 15 years. He drowned in the River by Doctor's Brook upon his return from Martha's in July 1958. The store was closed after his death.

Plate 812–Taken by Garvie Samson

Charles F. Burke

Charlie's small store was located at the bottom of Isiah Burke's field on the roadway from Doctor's Brook to the Cannes School. It was recorded as a business operation in 1906, with a sales volume less than $500 per annum. The store, which originally had a flat roof, sold dry goods as well as cotton by the pound, molasses, candy, canned goods, vinegar and kerosene. Charlie operated the store until 1922 when he took over the care of his mother. Sam Fougere operated the store between 1923 and 1924 then sold it to Charlie's sisters, Tina and Hattie, who intended to convert it into a house. When they changed their minds, Sam Burke purchased it then sold it to Sam and Martha Dugas. They had it hauled to the lower part of Dennis Dugas's field, which they had purchased, where it was converted into a home.

Robertson's Canteen

William Robertson operated a hot dog stand and sold steamed lobsters in the late 1950s and early 1960s.

Pottie's Drive-In

Peter (Milton) Pottie operated a restaurant at the head of the River from 1967–1971. He sold the business to Pettipas who used the facilities for a summer home.

J & C Take-Out

John and Carmel Doucette purchased the Pettipas property and re-opened the restaurant. They have been operating it successfully to this date.

River View Quick Lunch

This eat-in canteen was operated by Charlie Grimes in Upper Cannes along the Number 4 Highway (see **Plate 813**). Specializing in homemade spruce beer, Charlie operated the business with his wife Genevieve, from 1933 until 1962 when he retired.

Plate 813–Courtesy of Genevieve Grimes

IV Hawker

Meadowlands

This small gift shop is operated by Sally (Baccardax) Landry, a gifted crafts person. She sells natural and dried flowers, baskets, and custom-made gift items.

John Fougere's Meat and Fish Market

Peter (Milton) Pottie recalls the store was in operation in the early 1950s. John used to peddle meat and fish around the River and up Sporting Mountain.

Simon/Leo MacPhee

In 1928, Simon opened a small store from his house, but after one winter's operation, it closed. The following year, Simon's son, Leo and his brother Elias built a store close to the roadway. It remained in operation until the early 1970s.

George Pottie's Canteen

George had a small canteen where he sold fish and chips and hot dogs.

Gogan's Motel

This logged cabin motel, built by Victor Gogan in the early 1950s, was located in Hawker across the road from René Fougere's. Gogan married Melinda Thibeau and Helen Archibald, a highly-respected school teacher in St. Peter's. Elio and Evelina Mancini purchased the business and expanded the facilities to include a dining room where Elio and his wife Evelina cooked for guests and the general public. The motel burned in 1979.

V South River Bourgeois

Victor Burke

In 1945, Victor and Evelyn Burke opened a small store from their home and operated the Post Office. They closed both in 1970 when the Rural Route System was established.

Caree Store

Henry Caree's store is shown in operation until 1886 and can be found on the A.F. Church map. This was the original Lobster Cannery site. Henry was the brother of Fred Caree who operated a store in Cannes.

VI Seaview

Small stores, mostly from their houses, were operated by Colin MacLeod, Jack MacLeod, James Goswell and Mrs. Lionel LeBlanc.

Other Businesses

Other small businesses operating over the years include: *Viscount's Groceries, Rose's Unisex Hair Salon, V & L Electric Ltd.* and *Touesnard's Service Centre.*

VII Travelling Salesmen

In the early 1900s, there were two companies which sold medications such as cough medicine and salves. One of the earliest salesman was Amable Fougere, shown in **Plate 814** who represented W.T. Raleigh Medicine Company. His

Plate 814–Courtesy of Joe Fougere

son Joe advised me that he travelled from one end of the province to the other. He always had a very fast horse and light buggy. He worked with the company until he died in c.1927.

Another Raleigh representative, Patrick Kyte, who lived on the St. Peter's side of the railway tracks, had a River Bourgeois connection in that he was married to Catherine Anastasia Boyd, daughter of Donald and Anastasia O'Toole. Although he was in St. Peter's district, he always attended Sunday service in River Bourgeois. He died in 1920 at the age of 62. One of his four sons, Joseph, continued to work with the same company until his death. Patrick is shown in **Plate 815**.

The other travelling sales representative was Joseph D. Lavallee, who travelled for Watkins (see **Plate 816**). He was always known as Lavallee. Joseph was a great friend of Father Robitaille, perhaps because they were both from Quebec. Lavallee visited clients in the local area, travelling with his horse and wagon and a small bag of oats for fuel. As he grew older, it became more difficult to handle the horse, so he decided to purchase a truck. Attempting to learn how to drive, he had an accident along Grand Gulley Road. While attempting to negotiate a sharp turn, instead of turning the steering wheel he became confused and began pulling on the steering wheel, (with his foot on the accelerator), as he would have on a pair of reins, all the while screaming *woo-back, woo-back*. He wrecked the truck, putting an end to his driving career. Joseph died June 22, 1969 at the age of 87 years.

Endnotes

Plate 815–Courtesy of Sarah Digout

Plate 816–Courtesy of Lillian Smith

1) The A. F. Map was compiled through a Provincial Government program. It shows all property owners and buildings existing in 1888.

2) *The Mercantile Reference Book*, Dunn Wiman & Co.

3) Information (re. McNeil's store) from the Beaton Institute, U. C. C. B.

4) Damien Beranger purchased the parcel of land which was bounded on the south by the Eastern Arm of River Bourgeois, on the east by lands in the possession of Urban and David Sampson, on the north by the rear line of Crown Lease and on the west by lands in possession of Simon Landry, for the sum of $120, on January 18, 1874. Damien was listed as a fisherman at that time. The above parcel of land, containing 60 acres, was sold by the trustees of the late P. D. Beranger to Alexander Beranger on April 15, 1942. On December 23, 1943 the land was sold to Abraham Beranger.

5) Angus Joseph Boyd, 1854-1938, married Mary Fraser (d.1915). They raised 10 children, one of whom was William Fraser 1885-1955. He married Mary Ellen Bourque and they raised 11 children, one of whom was Blaise Cyril, the last son to operate the store.

Chapter IX
Service Personnel

This chapter is dedicated to the Men and Women who sacrificed their lives to preserve the freedom which we all enjoy. In addition to the Service Personnel, the Merchant Mariners are also recognized for their enormous contributions to the War effort. The substantial number who served speaks volumes of the contributions made by this small community. **Plate 900** shows the Monument erected on the Number 4 Highway, in memory of those who **Made The Supreme Sacrifice**.

Plate 900–Taken by Garvie Samson

We also salute the many unselfish men and women who made contributions on the home front. Many moved to Halifax where the women found temporary shelter and comfort from the Sisters of Service. The men worked as stevedores and handled heavy work, while the women worked on teletypes and decoded messages, packed parachutes, made uniforms, (Esquire Shop) knitting, packed bandages, and more. More that one million Canadians fought in the Second World War and 45-thousand lost their lives.

Great War (1914–1918)[1]

Name and Rank	Unit and Branch of Service
Beranger, Capt. Elias	Commander American Transport
Beranger, Lieut.-Com. John G.	U.S. Navy
Bouchie, Joseph D.	Navy
Boudreau, Pte. Peter C.	25th Bn., C.I.
Boudreau, Pte. Simon	Navy
Boudreau, Pte. Wilfred	17th Can. Reserve Bn.
Boucher, Pte. Lawrence	A.E.F.
Bourque, Pte. Douglas D.	**40th and 26th Bns., C.I.**
*Boyd, Sgt. Major George A.	199th Bn., C.I., and 24th Vic. Rifles
Boyd, Pte. Hervey M.	185th Bn., C.I., and C.M.G.C.
*Boyd, Pte. John H.	10th and 8th Siege Batt., C.G.A.
*Boyd, Pte. Russell J.	85th Bn., C.I.
Boyd, Sgt. William F.	C.A.M.C.
Burke, Pte. Edmund J.	165th Bn., C.I., and Field Amb.Corps
Burke, Pte. John C.	17th Can. Reserve Bn.
*Burke, Pte. Placide Elias	165th Inf., A.E.F.
Burke, Master Simon F.	Navy
Cordo, Pte. Moses	106th Bn., C.I.
Fitzgerald, Pte. Clarence	C.A.S.C.
Fougere, Pte. Ephrem	R.C.R, C.E.F.
Fougere, Pte. Peter Anselm	R.N., C.V.R.
LeBlanc, Pte. Henry	10th Siege Batt., C.G.A.
Landry, Pte. Amable	R.N., C.V.R.
Landry, Rte. Bastian	H.M.C.S. Niobe
Landry, Pte. Charles	U.S. Navy
Landry, Mate. Ernest	R.N., C.V.R.
Landry, Gnr. Joseph	10th Siege Batt., C.G.A.
Landry, Gnr. Leo A.	9th Siege Batt., C.G.A.
Landry, Pte. Peter	C.E.
Landry, Pte. Simon	
Landry, Pte. Simon P.	17th Can. Reserve Bn.

Landry, Pte. William E.	C.E.
Landry, Pte. Wilfred D.	94th Reg't., A.E.F.
Morrison, Sgt. Michael	C.A.M.C.
MacNeil, Lt. Charles Herman	**94th Squadron, R.A.F.**
MacNeil, Capt. Frank A.	C.A.M.C.
MacNeil, Lieut. M.G.	100 Winnipeg Grenadiers
*McPhee, Pte. Wilfred L.	115th Bn., C. I.
Pate, Pte. Charles	R.N., C.V.R.
Pate, Pte. Henry	1st Depot Bn.
Pottie, Gnr. Abraham A.	10th Siege Batt., C.G.A., and 2nd Batt., C.G.A.
Richard, Pte. Anselm	C.E.
* Stephens, Pte. William	6th Field Ambulance Corps
Sampson, Pte. Amable	17th Can. Reserve Bn.
Sampson, Pte. Henry	17th Can. Reserve Bn.
Sampson, Pte. Joseph S.	17th Can. Reserve Bn.
Samson, Cpl. Joseph D.	**Killed Nov 1, 1918, 3rd Bde., C.G.A.**
Sampson, Pte. James	C.E.
Sampson, Pte. William	17th Can. Reserve Bn.
Sampson, Henry U.	Merchant Mariner
Thibeau, Bert	Gunner, C.G.A., C.E.F.
Thibeau, Pte. Maurice E.	1st Depot Bn.
Thibeau, Peter A.	
Thibeau, Pte. Terry L.	10th Siege Batt., C.G.A.
Thibeau, Pte. J. Henry	10th Siege Batt., C.G.A.
Thibeau, Sgt. William M.	D.C.M., 106th Bn. and 26th Bn., C.I.
Thibeau, Pte. Robert E.	1st Depot Bn.
Touesnard, Emile	MN

Number enlisted–53; Number killed–3 (in bold); Number wounded–7 (with *)

Ferdinand Digout (Victor Digout's father), fought under Napoleon in the Boer War. He was imprisoned at Melville Cove outside of Halifax and later escaped. He is the forefather of many Digouts in River Bourgeois.

World War II (1939–1945) and the Korean War (1950–1953)

I compiled the following list from interviews and information on tombstones and crosses. It is not intended to be an official list and I sincerely apologize for any errors or omissions.

Name and Rank	Unit and Branch of Service
Barrett, Major T.W.	
Beranger, Alexander	American Merchant Marine
Beranger, Arthur	Army
Beranger, Bert	Army
Beranger, Charles	Navy
Bona, Andrew	R.C.A.F.
Bona, Robert	Navy
Bouchard, Frederick	MN
Boucher, Frederick	**American Marine, Killed in Action**
Bouchie, Frederick	MN
Bouchie, Joseph D.	Navy
Bouchie, Leonard	Navy
Bouchie, Walter	Army
Boudreau, Capt. Charles	Navy
Boudreau, Douglas	Navy
Boudreau, Henry	MN
Boudreau, Peter	MN
Boudreau, Simon	Navy
Bourque, Abraham	**Killed in Action**
Bourque, Adrian	Army
Bourque, Alexander	Navy
Bourque, Aloysis	R.C.A.F.
Bourque, Alpin	American Army and Navy
Bourque, Amable H.	
Bourque, Anselm	MN
Bourque, Anthony	Army
Bourque, Augustine	**Army, Killed in Action**
Bourque, Josime	MN
Bourque, Joseph	Navy
Bourque, Lawrence	MN
Bourque, Michael	American Army and Navy
Bourque, Peter	Navy
Bourque, Raymond	MN
Bourque, Robert	Army
Bourque, Vitas	MN

Bowser, Pte. George P.	Army
Boudreau, Capt. Charles	MN
Boyd, Donald	R.C.A.F.
Boyd, Gerald J.	Air Gunner, R.C.A.F.
Boyd, William F.	Army
Burke, Abraham	Army
Burke, Sgt. Adrian	Army
Burke, Alex	Navy
Burke, Aloysis	R.C.A F.
Burke, Anthony D.	Army
Burke, L/Sto. Anthony Delore	Navy
Burke, Anthony P.	Army
Burke, Augustine	
Burke, Douglas	Navy
Burke, Harry	MN
Burke, Capt. Howard	MN
Burke, Lawrence	MN
Burke, Michael	82nd U.S. Navy Construction Bn.
Burke, Philip	Army
Burke, Raymond	MN and Army
Burke, Robert	Paratrooper
Burke, Simon F.	MN
Burke, Sam	MN, fireman on *Excapart*
Burke, Victor	Army
Burke, Vitas	MN
Chamberlin, Pte. Catherine	C.W.A., C.A.
Chaisson, John Paul	MN
Deveau, Charlie	MN
Digout, Andrew	Army
Digout, Bernard	Army
Digout, Danny	MN
Digout, Charlie (Son of Victor)	Navy
Digout, Charlie (Son of Tranquil)	MN
Digout, Ferdinand	Army
Digout, Pte. G.A.	Canadian Infantry Corps
Digout, Marshall	R.C.A.F.
Digout, Vincent	Paratrooper, Army
Digout, Vincent Cornielus	Navy
Doary, Chief Officer Peter Wilfred	MN and R.C.N. (R)
Fougere, Sgt. Amable Henry	Army
Fougere, Anselm	MN

Fougere, Edward Leo	MN
Fougere, Ephrem	Army, Vimy Ridge
Fougere, Herman	Army
Fougere, John	American Army and Navy
Fougere, Joseph	Navy
Fougere, Peter	MN
Fougere, Simon A.	MN
Fougere, W. Anthony	
Fougere, William Henry	Army
Fougere, Wilfred Anthony (Ginger)	Army
Gillen, (Madden) Laura	R.N., R.C.A.F.
Goyetche, Henry (Elmer)	American Army and Navy
Grimes, Charlie	American Secret Service
Grimes, Paul	American Army and Navy
Holland, Thomas W.	Gunner, R.C.A.
Kehoe, Jack	Army
Kehoe, Neil	Army
Kyte, Charlie	Lead Hand, R.C.N.V.R.
Landry, Albert	MN
Landry, Albert	Army
Landry, Amable	MN
Landry, Bastian	Navy
Landry, Bertie	Army
Landry, Charles P.	Bosun Mate, Cdn MN
Landry, Cletus	Army
Landry, Ernest	MN
Landry, Fabian	MN
Landry, Fabian	Navy
Landry, Gervase	Army
Landry, Hector	Army
Landry, John B.	Sapper, R.C.E., Army
Landry, John L.	Army
Landry, Leo	MN
Landry, Mark	Army
Landry, Vincent	R.C.A.F.
LeBlanc, ??	Halifax Rifles, Army
LeBlanc, Clifford	**MN, Boat rammed, Hfx Hbr. – Killed**
LeBlanc, Douglas	Army
LeBlanc, Edgar	WWII and Korean War, Army
LeBlanc, Fred	Army
LeBlanc, Hilary	Army

MacIsaac, Edmond	Army
Madden, Jack	Army
Martin, William	Navy
McPhee, Elias	Army
McPhee, Herman	Army
McPhee, Joseph	Army
Morrison, Bernard	Navy
Morrison, Charles Hilary	LAC R.C.A.F.
Morrison, George	Army
Morrison, Herman William	Firefighter, R.C.A.F.
Morrison, Patrick	American Merchant Marine
O'Connell, Daniel Stewart	Able Seaman, R.C.N., V.R.
Pottie, Abraham A.	Army
Pottie, Euseph	Navy
Pottie, Hyacinthe	Navy
Pottie, Louie	Army
Paté, Anselm	Army
Paté, Joseph	Army
Paté, Louis	Army
Paté, Malcolm	American Army and Navy
Paté, Samuel	**Killed in Action, Army**
Paté, Walter	Army
Paté, Pte. Walter Clifford	**Carleton York Reg, ArmyKilled in Action in Italy, Sept. 1944**
Richard, Albert	**MN**
Richard, Alfred	MN
Richard, Charlie	MN
Richard, Clarence	MN
Richard, Egbert	Navy
Richard, Fabian	MN
Richard, Isaac W.	MN
Richard, James	Army
Richard, Joseph	MN
Richard, Pte. Leo	C.A.M.C.
Richard, Martin	MN
Richard, William	MN
Robertson, Raymond	Army
Robertson, William Matthew	Navy
Sampson, Albert	R.C.A.F.
Sampson, Corp. Anselm Henry	Unit 60 R of C Dept.
Sampson, Corp. Anthony G.	Army

Sampson, Anthony	Army
Sampson, Clarence Anthony	Artillary, Army
Sampson, Charles P.	MN
Sampson, Charles Lawrence	MN
Sampson, George H.	MN
Sampson, Cnr. Gilbert	C.B. 87 Can. Med (Bty) R.C.A.
Sampson, Gus (Elias's son)	MN
Sampson, Henry L.	Able Seaman, R.C.N., V.R.
Sampson, James	MN
Sampson, James A.	MN
Sampson, Joseph	MN
Sampson, Lawrence Charles	MN
Sampson, Mark F.	Artillary, Army
Sampson, Michel G.	**R.C.N.R.A. 871 Stoker Killed October 26, 1944**
Sampson, Peter David	Infantry, Army
Sampson, Simon	Infantry, Army
Sampson, Thomas	MN
Sampson, Vincent	Army
Sampson, Whitney	Artillary, Army
Sampson, Wilfred	**MN, Drowned off Freighter**
Samson, Cyril J.	MN
Samson, Edmund	**Army, Killed in Action**
Samson, Mark A.	**Army, Killed in Action**
Samson, Martin	**Drowned, MN**
Samson, Paul	American Merchant Marine
Thibeau, C. J.	Gunner, Army
Thibeau, Edgar	Army
Thibeau, Louis	Army
Touesnard, Alain Gustave	MN
Touesnard, Emile	MN
Touesnard, Ernest	Army
Touesnard, F/T Joseph Peter	MN
Touesnard, Richard	Army
Trueman, Roy	MN
Wedge, Bennie	Navy
White, Charles	MN

War Stories [2]

Learn Two More Dead

Though the news of Victory in Europe was receive here with joy, it was tempered with sadness as a few days before word came that two more of our boys had given their lives for their country. First, Mrs. Paul Samson received official word that their son, Edmund, had been *Killed in Action*.

Edmund, who was one of the first local boys to join up, enlisted in the *Hussars* in Montreal in May 1941, and after three months in Canada was sent overseas. He fought in France, Belgium, Holland, and was in Germany when he was killed. He was 30-years-old and is survived by his mother and father, two brothers, Simon and Louis in the United States; also one sister, Mary at home.

Another brother, Mark, was officially reported missing shortly after D-Day and though a returning soldier from Shubenacadie wrote that he was with Mark in a German prison camp in July last, no other word has been received from him since he was reported missing.

On the following day, Mrs. Firmin Bourque received word that her only living son, Abraham, had been *Killed in Action*. Abraham, who was only 24-years-old when he was killed, had enlisted in July, 1941. He fought in France, Belgium, Holland and was in Germany when he died. He is survived by his father and mother, two sisters, Mrs. Charles Fougere at home, and Mrs. Carl Swift of Halifax. Funeral services for both boys were held at St. John the Baptist Church at River Bourgeois, Father Robitaille officiating.

Anthony D. (Delore) Burke sailed on the *HMCS Moosejaw*, with a compliment of 75 men. The *Moosejaw* was the first Canadian battleship to sink a German submarine. On September 10, 1941, it had to ram an attacking German U-Boat to sink it since they were surrounded by other U-Boats. The captain and crew showed their humanitarianism despite the obvious danger, rescuing 37 German survivors.

Chief Petty Officer Peter Wilfred Doary, R.C.N.(R) official no. A-978, was cited in a dispatch for distinguished service in the *Canadian Gazette*, dated January 1, 1946, *For outstanding zeal, efficiency and devotion to duty.* The dispatch was signed by Naval Secretary, A. Johnson.

Joseph (Camille) Bouchie, a Merchant Mariner, was torpedoed twice.

L.A.C. Aloysis Bourque was torpedoed on the *Caribou*, crossing from Sydney to Newfoundland on October 14, 1942. He swam for an hour before finding a raft on which he spent another five hours while being fired on by machine gun.

Peter Bourque, R.C.N.–Torpedoed on *Charlottetown*.

Patrick Morrison–Killed while on board a Beam Trawler in the American Merchant Marine.

Fred Boucher–Killed while serving in American Marines.

Edward Fougere–Torpedoed on August 25, 1942 on *Spind*. Spent 5 hours in lifeboat, was machine-gunned in arm and leg. Picked up and taken to Gibralter where he spent two months in hospital. Left for Liverpool, England on a Norwegian boat. Was torpedoed again on his way to England and landed in Newfoundland. Sailed back to England, returned to Newfoundland, thence to Halifax where he joined the *Lady Holsn*. He sailed to the south and was torpedoed again at St. Lucia, near the wharf. While jumping into a lifeboat, he broke his leg, spent some time in hospital then returned home.

Endnotes

1) *Antigonish and Great War*, page 137.

2) Press Report, River Bourgeois, May 28, 1944.

Chapter X
Landmarks and Buildings Recycled

Lighthouse

In River Bourgeois, the lighthouse was second in significance only to the Catholic church. Because of the numerous comments I have received concerning its loss, a photograph of the original building has been used on the book cover. The lighthouse was identified in the *List of Lights, Atlantic Coast* as *Bourgeois Inlet Lighthouse No. 598.* It was constructed in 1903 on land and right-of-way purchased from William LeVesconte. The original building[1] was modified several times until its final demise and replacement by a Skeleton Tower. The Department of Transport felt the lighthouse structure was too costly to maintain and burned it on May 25, 1989.

Lighthouse-keepers

During its long and useful service, the light was attended by a lighthouse-keeper. There is no official record of the hiring of the first light-keeper, however records show a Martin Burke was dismissed on May 1, 1912. He was succeeded by Daniel Sampson, Charlie à Doll's father, who was born in River Bourgeois.

Sampson was appointed light-keeper on April 12, 1912, and assumed his duties until September 1, 1939, a term of 27 years. Sampson is listed as Roman Catholic, French, British-born, with no military service and four dependents. His salary was $90/year to start and was reclassified in 1916. By 1929, he was earning $120/year and at the time of his retirement in 1939, at the age of 76, he earned $150/year.

William P. Bouchie was Sampson's successor; he was 60 years of age at the time of his appointment. He was born in River Bourgeois on October 2, 1879, a Roman Catholic Frenchman, British-born with no military service. His salary began at $120/year but increased to $150/yr on October 1, 1940, pursuant to reclassification. His salary increased until October 1948, at which time it was $315/year. Bouchie attended the lighthouse until June 1949, when he reached the age of 70. He was succeeded by Frederick A. LeBlanc (born November 28, 1912), who assumed his duties on June 16, 1949. He was Roman Catholic, French, and born in River Bourgeois. He served full-time until March 1966, upon the electrification[2] of the lighthouse. He then worked part-time until February 1, 1967. He provided dedicated service for 18 years.

Modifications

The following is a summary of events surrounding the Lighthouse. **Plate 1000** shows Peter Tapper holding a typical lense used in the lighthouse. Detailed information has been included in **Appendix 8.**

Plate 1000–Courtesy of the Canadian Coast Guard

1) Constructed in 1903.
2) Operation changed from oil-burning to electricity on December 7, 1966. Lighthouse unstaffed as of February 1, 1967.
3) In 1970, tower removed, light's identification changed in List of Lights from #598 to #732, and lighting changed to mercury vapour (see **Plate 1001**).
4) May 28, 1989, lighthouse burned and replaced by Skeleton Tower.
5) August 8, 1989, Tower completed, white fixed light changed to red fixed light.
6) October 12, 1989, Bourgeois Inlet renamed to River Bourgeois Lighthouse.

Plate 1001–Taken by Garvie Samson

Quetique Lighthouse

This lighthouse, situated outside the harbour entrance in Lennox Passage, served as an integral part of the Lighthouse System and was often staffed by local residents. Records show the first light-keeper as Cyril Sampson who served until 1907, followed by Fred A. Burke (1907–1929), Abraham Pottie (1929–1947), and Hyacinthe Pottie (July 10, 1947–Sept. 15, 1947). Abel Joseph LeBlanc and his wife Melinda of Petit de Grat operated the light from Dec. 1, 1948–Dec. 1, 1955, at which time they were transferred to

Jerseyman Island. They were succeeded by René Terrio from West Arichat who attended the lighthouse until July 1, 1956. He was succeeded by Edward Leo Landry and his wife Eileen Francis of Petit de Grat who served until October 1, 1956.

Noteworthy Residences

LeVesconte House

William Isaac LeVesconte[3] and Ethel Mary Shaw moved into their new home in River Bourgeois between Nov.–Dec. 1904. While their house was being constructed, William set up temporary residence in a building on the premises, later called the *Dairy* by family and servants because it was subsequently used as a dairy, dry goods and general storage building.

The beautiful home shown in **Plate 1002** was constructed and designed by Désiré Terriot from the Magdalen Islands who acted as general contractor. The house cost $6,000. Peter Beaton from Bras d'Or constructed the cornices, mouldings and fancy woodwork. Terriot, who was also involved in the church renovations, used the old Communion rail on an exterior veranda.

When William began building his house, he intended to accommodate his parents as well as his servants, but his mother would not live in the same quarters as the servants, so he began building servant quarters next to the house. William's fiancée, Ethel Shaw, issued the ultimatum; *the servants live with us or I won't marry you.* The interior of the servant quarters was never finished.

Plate 1002–Courtesy of Jack and Ada LeVesconte

(l to r) Kenneth and John LeVesconte pose in front of their house

The main residence contained six bedrooms, a large living room, drawing room, dining room, kitchen, and a study located on the northeast corner facing the entrance driveway. The drawing room featured a fireplace with a glazed tile hearth and marble mantle. The fireplaces and masonry work were completed by a Mr. McRae from Grand Anse. His son was known throughout the area as *John the Bull.*

The house was plastered and featured wanes coating, plastered mouldings at the ceiling, a concrete basement, and double-cladded exterior walls. Claire Landry[4], Caroline LeVesconte's daughter, remembers looking through the stained-glass windows in the drawing room as a child. She was intrigued by the different colours and reflections created as the light shone through. Stained-glass windows were rarely seen, except in churches.

The attic, which contained three finished rooms, served as a great play area for the children and as classrooms where Caroline taught her siblings before they went to regular schools. Eva (LeVesconte) Clare[5], one of William's daughters, recalls one room was called the *blanket room*. There were several cubbie-holes which served as great hiding places and storage areas for extra beds.

The LeVesconte family always had servants. Mary Emma Landry worked for them, and they treated her as one of the family. When she married Victor Digout, they had their wedding reception at the house.

Sister Lola Burke recalls how Ethel LeVesconte always invite her to sleep-over on Good Fridays, although they were not Catholic; it never made any difference.

Jack and Ada LeVesconte lived in the old homestead between 1938 and 1944. They sold the property to Simone Samson, a hairdresser from the U.S.A married to one of Paul Samson's sons. Her intention was to establish a small summer hotel for tourists, but she did not proceed with the project because of illness and the expense of renovations. Allen Touesnard purchased the property from Simone in 1946 and used the fields for farming. He sold the property to his son Alfred and Ann in 1957. They found the roof was quite rotten and realized the house was too large for their use so they removed the upper 1–1/2 stories of the house. The lower portion formed a very cosy house with a spectacular view and property. George DeRoche, Fred LeBlanc and Paul Burke worked on the renovations.

Bissett Residence
This distinguished house, located immediately above the Government Wharf, was originally owned by George Henry Bissett and Virginia Lee (Boudreau) of D'Escousse. Other owners were Ernest Landry (Docité Landry's son), and Joe (Camille) Bouchie. See **Plate 1003**.

The Bissetts were very well-to-do as merchants and property owners. They were strong supporters of the Church, and offered one of their warehouse buildings for social functions such as fairs, dances and meetings. I interviewed Laura Gillen[6] in St. Peter's; she was caring for Hazel Bissett, whose grandfather was George H. Bissett. Laura showed me some of the spectacular photo albums belonging to the Bissetts. George Henry's son, George, was married to Mary Jane Boyd. Their children were Clarence, Clara, Marjorie and Hazel.

Plate 1003–Courtesy of Lenova Sampson

Some of the servants who worked for the Bissetts included: Ida (Sampson) Bourque, Mary Emma (Landry) Digout, and Tina Bourque. The house was dismantled in 1970.

Deslaurier Residence
Joseph Deslaurier (1847–1927) came to River Bourgeois from Tracadie with Father Martell who was the Parish priest there. He purchased property in the early 1800s and married Philisité (1867–1952) Samson. The Deslauriers were very religious and opened their home to priests. Florence Touesnard showed me some of the many religious articles used by these priests. James Richard, who boarded there in 1939, recalls the mantle used by the priests during their morning mass. Following Joseph's death, Allen Touesnard obtained the property and Philisité lived there until her death. She is remembered as a loving and caring person.

A kitchen[7] was added to the house by Philisité's father, David, my great-grandfather. The rafters used in the construction were hand-hewn and imported, likely brought from Boston for ballasts in the vessels. Each is identified with Roman numerals carved into the wood.

Digout Residence
The Cannes residence of Victor and Mary Emma Digout (**Plate 1004**) is believed to be one of the oldest standing buildings in the area. It was originally constructed as a

Plate 1004–Taken by Garvie Samson

log house and the original logs are still concealed within the framework. It is presently owned by Germaine (Digout) Mombourquette and is believed to be 150 years old.

Another house which some believe is just as old, is located on Roderick Burke's property on the South Side. This house was owned by Docité Landry's parents.

MacLean Residence
The original house owned by Hugh MacLean, located in Thibeauville close to the Post Road, was constructed in 1880 and contained 14 rooms. Following the deaths of most of the MacLean family[8], Anthony Rousseau and his sister Todie obtained possession of the house in 1956. They sold it to Wilfred LeBlanc who sold it to Clarence and Elsie LeBlanc on August 17, 1968. Clarence and Elsie showed the premises to George DeRoche and me on August 13, 1991.

Some of the materials used in construction of the house, such as the douglas fur boards measuring 1–1/2 inches thick and 18 inches wide, were imported. Clarence was told the house was used by stagecoach drivers and passengers as a stop-over on their way from Sydney to Antigonish. It was also used as a boarding house during the construction of the railroad, and by school teachers such as Marie Boyd, teaching in Balmoral.

Milling Frolics were frequently held at the house as Clarence could attest, with the long kitchen table in place when he purchased the property. A Post Office also operated from here. One of the artifacts Clarence found in the attic was a musket with a powder-splint drift. The musket could propel a steel shot 5/8 inches in diameter 150 feet. Apparently Maggie MacLean was not fond of guns so her brother, Hector, hid the musket in the attic.

River Bourgeois Senior Citizens Apartments
Located off the Number 4 Highway in River Bourgeois, this 10-unit apartment complex was constructed by Terry Boudreau, a quality builder, for the Dept. of Housing and Consumer Affaires. It opened in 1986.

Recycled Buildings

Many early buildings in River Bourgeois were relocated, or parts were removed, *hauled* and used for other purposes, such as starter homes or sheds. The best time for a *hauling* was on a Sunday afternoon in the winter, when the ground and harbour were frozen and covered with a light dusting of snow. The Pastor announced the event at Sunday Service and after lunch the owner could be assured of a large and enthusiastic crowd. The building would be fitted with runners, a few skids, and a long, strong rope. The following properties are examples of this recycling.

Plate 1005–Courtesy of Sarah Digout

Henry LeBlanc/Whitney McPhee's House
Henry LeBlanc began constructing a house next to Capt. Charlie Boudreau's property, west of Doctor's Brook in Cannes. The structure progressed to the point where the roof and walls were boarded in, then it was sold to Henry Boudreau who shingled the roof, then sold it to Whitney McPhee. Whitney had it hauled over the ice to his property above Stewart O'Connell's, where it was finished. **Plate 1005** shows the community assisting in the haul.

Whitney, his wife Nellie, and their son Stanley lived in the house until January 27, 1941, when on a cold and windy day while Whitney was working in the woods and Nellie was teaching school, the house caught fire and burned to the ground.

Damien Beranger's House
Damien Beranger's house was located in the Lower End of the River, west of his store. The main house included a kitchen and parlour. As was customary when the children grew up and left home, parents found they no longer required a large house. The kitchen could normally be accommodated in some other room so it was detached and hauled to another property where it served as a temporary home. Frequently, as additions were made to it, it became a kitchen again.

In this case, the kitchen was sold to Whitney Sampson and hauled across the harbour to the east end of Charlie P. Sampson's field, adjacent to the roadway. It was then purchased by Bessie Bona and relocated to Grand Gulley Road above Michael Owens' property.

Plate 1006–Taken by Garvie Samson

The remaining part of the house was purchased by Roderick Touesnard in 1942 and hauled to the Jib field, located across the road from Rita Sampson, next to the late Richard Touesnard's house. It was purchased by Johannes Peppercamp and hauled by James A. Sampson with a bulldozer, to a small field across from Bernard and Lenova Sampson. See **Plate 1006** taken in August 1990.

Alex (à Noré) Bouchie's Kitchen

Alex and Agnes (Landry) Bouchie's house was originally owned by M.J.T. McNeil, a school principal who moved to Halifax in the early 1900s. The kitchen was purchased by George Pottie and hauled to Hawker where it became his home. George moved into the Senior Citizen Home in St. Peter's and the house was left vacant. The Fire Department burnt the house in 1989, since it had become a fire hazard.

Charles P. Sampson's Porch

This porch was sold to their son Mark then to Gertie (Sam's wife) Boudreau and hauled to the field below the Senior Citizens Apartments. The main part of the house remained in its original location and was purchased by Lloyd Stone. He completed extensive renovations to the house in 1992, including the installation of a new foundation wall, septic tank, bathroom and artesian well.

Cannes School

Following construction of the River Bourgeois Consolidated School in 1954, the Cannes School was left empty. It was sold to Adrian Bourque in 1955 who in-turn sold it to Alzear Samson from Petit de Grat. Alzear dismantled it and constructed a house there from the materials.

Urquhart/ Walker Store
Urquhart's Store, which later became Walker's Store, was located next to a field called *Le Parc à Walker* (Walker's Field), below Paul Sampson's house. The building was sold to Archie Morrison, a former councillor, who hauled it across the ice to John Doucette's lane, down Grand Gulley, and along the Grand Gulley Road to his field, where it was converted into a barn. When Farley Mowat purchased the property, he refurbished the building and it remains in excellent condition.

Bissett's Buildings
The last of the three Bissett warehouses, located just west of the present Government Wharf, was torn down in the early 1940s by Freeman Bouchie. As it was dismantled, many shingles fell over a floor opening and Freeman fell through, causing serious injury to his shoulder. Materials from this building such as joists, rafters and boards, were used in the construction of the storage shed presently located adjacent to the Government Wharf.

Valerie Goyetche's House
In 1949, Valerie Goyetche was working in Halifax and wished to return to the River to care for her ailing mother, Julia. She was unable to find an affordable house close to the main road so she asked her brother, Clifford, to keep an eye-open for a building which could be used to start a house. She purchased Alex Sampson's Post Office for $35 and a piece of land from her nephew Simon Sampson for $65. Clifford took pictures of the building as it lay in her field, and updated her as to the construction progress. D.A. Sampson undertook most of the carpentry work and Alex Bouchie built the chimney. During her 34 years in the house, she had 25 people staying with her and some, such as Jane Samson, died and were waked there. Financing to complete her modest house was raised through Pantry Sales, sewing, and caring for the elderly.

Charlie Robertson's House
Charlie purchased property and a storage shed from Peter LeVesconte in the mid-1940s when Peter was living in Arichat. He renovated and extended the LeVesconte cold storage building. Claude Bourque recalls working on it when the roof was raised and other modifications were made. The Robertson family moved into their home in 1951.

Hilaire and Ida Bourque's House
This house was originally located next to Amable A. Burke's property. Hilaire's barn, which belonged to Amable Landry, was torn down in 1989 when it was 150 years old. It was constructed from hand-hewn lumber and secured with wood dowels.

Ernie Bourque's House
Ernie and Margaret Bourque's house was constructed from a building located close to the lane next to Charlie Landry's house.

Plate 1007–Courtesy of Hilda Burke

Anthony (Delore) Burke's House
Delore Burke built a small house in the lower end of his father's field on the South Side where his cousin, Nora (Mrs. George Cameron), presently lives. The house, shown in **Plate 1007**, measured 8 feet x 16 feet and was built by Clifford LeBlanc. Anthony Landry recalls working on it. Delore had earned the $300 it cost to build the house by cutting a car load of props.

Plate 1008–Courtesy of Hilda Burke

The small house was towed to Church Point by D.A. Sampson and his horse, along the ice. Alex (à Noré) Bouchie used materials from this small building to construct the house shown in **Plate 1008**. Delore and Hilda sold the house to Louis and Lillian Smith.

Leo and Frances Digout's House
The original house, originally located on the South Side hill close to where the Tanner family lives, was hauled across the ice to its present location.

Post Office/Store
When Delore Burke took over the Post Office from Alex Sampson in 1943, he constructed a building from a shed he obtained from his father, Amable F.

Burke. The store was purchased by Walter Bouchie, and his sister, Helen, attended the store and Post Office. Under Walter's ownership, the store was expanded using a section of Alfred and Maude Burke's restaurant in Cannes. Delore and Hilda eventually re-purchased the store and had it hauled to where Louis and Lillian Smith presently live. It continued to operate as a store and Post Office until Delore's new house was completed in 1964, then the businesses were relocated to his basement. The store was purchased by the ball club and hauled across the ice to Memorial Field.

Touesnard House

Gerard and Cecile Touesnard purchased Amable (à Noré) Burke's house on the North Side and relocated it to Oban.

James and Caroline Sampson's House

For a starter house in the late 1930s, James and Caroline Sampson bought the small LeVesconte store located across from the main store, from Peter LeVesconte for $35. The building was hauled by James A. Sampson in 1938. To raise money for their new house, Caroline sold her cooking at *Box Socials* in the early 1940s. The Sampsons raised their family here, and in 1955 they moved into their existing home. (Caroline recalls scrubbing down the Glebe House after Fr. Robitaille died, in anticipation of Father Samson's arrival.)

Andrew Boudreau's Barn

Mary Emma (Landry) Digout recalls that her old house (Amos Landry's from the South Side), was hauled down to Andrew Boudreau's and used to construct a barn. She remembers that the kitchen was painted pink, and each time she is in River Tillard, she goes into the barn to see the pink walls.

LeVesconte's Boat Storage/Workshop

This building was purchased by Jim Bouchie and Leo Digout to salvage the 2 inch x 6 inch flooring which they used to construct a 30-foot boat in the late-1930s. The building measured 40 feet x 24 feet, had a workbench along the full length of one side, large doors at the water side, and many windows at the perimeter. (See building at left of the schooner on the cover of this book.)

Plate 1009–Taken by Garvie Samson

Bucky's Apartments

Following construction of the new parish glebe in 1955, the old glebe became obsolete. It was purchased by Bucky (Lawrence) and Ann Sampson and hauled to property originally owned by Touma Samson in November 1968. The building was converted into three rental units shown in **Plate 1009**, October 1994.

Davie and Gladys Touesnard's House

Davie and Gladys (Thibeau) Touesnard purchased William Urquhart's home in Seaview, dismantled it and used some of the materials to construct their present house in River Bourgeois.

John and Annie Sampson's House

Annie and the late John Sampson's house belonged to Patrick Fitzgerald who lived in Grand Gulley, where Ervin and Janice Touesnard currently live. The house is now owned by George and Laurie Grinnell.

Lavallee's Storage Shed

This small building, located in Lavallee's field, was originally Anselm Samson's salt shed, located across the road from Cletus and Mary Touesnard. Lavallee used it to store his wagon.

Joe DeRoche's House

In 1932, Joe DeRoche constructed his house from a storage building originally located across the road from George Boudreau's, in Cannes. The building was floated up the River to Joe's Brook on oil barrels and puncheons. From there it was hauled to its present location above the Number 4 Highway where Joe, an accomplished carpenter, fashioned a comfortable house from the original framework.

Richard and LeBlanc Houses

Margaret (Digout) and Alfred Richard's house was constructed from the main portion of Peter MacLean's house. Alfred purchased the MacLean property from Tom Morrison in 1943 and lived there for a couple of years. In 1946, he separated the kitchen from the main house and had the main section hauled to the Highway. Because of the steep embankment close to the house, it was necessary to raise the house on cribwork before it could be hauled. A bulldozer operated by Mark (à Sousie's) Landry did the hauling which lasted all night, according to Alfred Burke.

The kitchen portion of the MacLean house was purchased by Hilary LeBlanc and relocated to its present location on the Number 4 Highway, where it was finished into a cozy little home.

Endnotes

1) The original lighthouse foundation is of stone and mortar and measures 12 feet, 8 inches x 12 feet, 8 inches x 1 foot thick. It is located 12 feet north of the new 10 feet x 10 feet x 1 foot poured concrete base of the Skeleton Tower. The lighthouse was painted red from the railing up.

2) Information was obtained from Canadian Cost Guard files at the Dartmouth Office. Excellent co-operation from Yves Leclerc, Maureen Trudeau and Peter Tapper.

3) William Isaac LeVesconte was born at D'Escousse, July 18, 1862. His fiancée, Ethel Mary Shaw, was born at Lockside, Richmond County, June 19, 1886 and they were married in Lockside on November 8, 1904, by Rev. Edward A. Ansell. William died on March 31, 1942, at the age of 80 and Ethel died October 29, 1959, at the age of 73.

4) I had the pleasure of interviewing Eva and her husband Douglas Landry in 1993 and 1994. They were most helpful in providing information and pictures relating to the LeVesconte family.

5) Eva (Levesconte) Clare was interviewed on October 20, 1990, and died one week later, on October 27, 1990. She was most enthusiastic about this book and was looking forward to another interview.

6) Laura Gillen, from St. Peter's, was interviewed on separate occasions and was most helpful in providing information on the Bissett family and events which occurred in River Bourgeois.

7) Information from Cletus Touesnard whose father, Allen, obtained the house after Joseph Deslaurier died.

8) Hugh and Mary MacLean raised eight children including four daughters; Sarah Ann, Margaret (Maggie, 1876–1959), Cassie and Christie, and four sons; John (Jack, 1873–1956), Hector (December 27, 1877–April 6, 1955), Charlie and Stewart (April 7, 1882–Sept. 2, 1954). Many of the MacLeans, including Hugh and Mary, were buried in the cemetery east of the Caledonia Hall, which was built by Anthony Rousseau.

Chapter XI
Gales and Fires

Gales

One of the earliest documented storms in the area was recorded by Dr. J.W. MacDonald[1] in 1811. He described the hurricane in the Antigonish region as *the severest gale within the memory of living man. The storm began on October 1. It up-rooted the houses, and the brands blown from hearths set fire to the buildings. Large elms bent before it to the ground like hay before the mower's scythe.*

Bishop Plessis[2] recorded in his diary on July 26, 1812, during his voyage by boat from Cheticamp to Port Hood, that *a hurricane, which passed the coast on September 30, 1811, blew down part of the woods, so that now there are as many trees flat on the ground as there are standing.* During his visit to St. Peter's on the first of July, he recorded that Lawrence Kavanagh's substantial residence, located close to the water's edge, *was destroyed in a heavy storm in the autumn of 1811, so the family had to stay in the out-buildings, which had been used as a kitchen and lodging for their servants. A most spacious house is under construction in a safer and better location than the former one.*

The *Saxby Gale*[3], so named because it was predicted two years earlier by an English admiral bearing this name, caused significant destruction in the Maritimes. The storm occurred on October 4, 1869, (the same year the St. Peter's Canal was opened and River Bourgeois received it's first priest). New Brunswick experienced considerable damage especially in the Fredericton area where 40–50 houses and barns were destroyed. Yarmouth was heavily affected with tides rising four feet above normal. The tail-end of the storm damaged wharves, vessels, roadways and buildings in River Bourgeois.

The next significant storm to hit the province was called the *August Gale*. It occurred on August 23–24, 1873. It first struck the southwestern part of the province, reaching Cape Breton Island on August 24. Hurricane winds were accompanied by equally heavy rain and high tides washed away wharves and bridges. The gale blew houses off their foundations and removed roofs from others. In addition to the destruction of property, a considerable number of lives were lost. On Isle Madame alone, the heads of 68 families drowned, and 200 buildings were destroyed.

Capt. David A. McLeod[4] described the storm as he experienced it upon his schooner:

It was about ten o'clock and blowing a living gale with a blinding rainstorm... Away blows the main mizzen, lower and upper topsails all to pieces, followed soon after by everything on the fore but the foresail that was on deck. About then the deck load broke loose and went over starboard side carrying away bulwarks and stanchions. This was the first fear I felt and although we had not a bit to eat, I did not feel hungry...

On Sunday morning, January 29, 1911, a heavy Northerly gale lifted several local barns off their foundations. The unfortunate owners were John Bouchard, Charles D. Burke, and Ferman Bouchie.

Quake

On the afternoon of November 18, 1929, an earthquake with it's epic centre in the Gulf of St. Lawrence, rumbled through Cape Breton for approximately two minutes. Damage from the quake was most severe in Sydney where an 8-foot tidal wave hit the shores, flooding the lower streets.

Damage occurred across Cape Breton; cracks formed in the roadways and minor landslides occurred. One of the heaviest capital losses was on Isle Madame where the bridge crossing Lennox Passage was destroyed.

Hurricane Damages Church

In August, 1955, Hurricane Hazel hit the area, removing the uppermost portion of the steeple from St. John the Baptist Church. The steeple was repaired at a reduced height where it remains today.

Forest Fires

The earliest recorded fires[5] on Isle Madame were those which burned during the summer of 1829. Those fires consumed a number of small bridges, culverts and roadways over swamp areas where brush and trees were used to form the road base. The biggest loss was the wooden bridge at Lennox Passage. In addition, considerable acreage of prime timber forest, which was vital to the booming shipbuilding industry, was destroyed.

While surveying a new route from Hugh McLean's mill to River Tilliard in the same year, John Luce[6] made note of *an extensive fire that had laid waste nearly the whole extent of forest from the 7th mile to the bridge at River Tilliard. What was previously densely populated forest is now barren land.*

Recent Forest Fires

The spring and summer of 1947 were particularly hot and dry, so the forests and hay fields were very vulnerable to fire. In addition, firefighting equipment was not available to confront or control any major outbreaks.

Between April 15–October 15, 1947, there were five fires[7] in Richmond County causing damage to 5,644 acres of property. The fires also destroyed or caused severe damage to: 700 acres of marsh and bog land, 4,332 acres of woodland containing trees up to 30 feet in height, and 612 acres of barren land. Two fires in June destroyed 4,131 acres, while other fires destroyed 25 acres in July, 1,500 acres in August, and 12 acres in September. Leo and Mae McPhee provided me with information regarding the losses in Thibeauville.

The most destructive fire to hit the community began in Thibeauville, and within a couple of hours it had reached Hawker. Allegedly, the fire was started by a cigarette dropped on the platform of a well in Charlie Thibeau's field.

Sam McPhee and his brother Whitney were working in L'Ardoise at the time, and when they saw the flames, they hurried back to the River. Upon their arrival, Sam found his house and belongings completetely engulfed in smoke, without hope of saving anything.

Jeffery Pottie's house was located a short distance away and he was working in Sydney. When he heard of the fire, he bundled his belongings and headed back home. In the excitement, he grabbed the wrong boots, size 11 instead of his size 9. His wife, staying at the River, stuffed her best dresses in a suitcase and made her way to Murdock Fougere's house. She laid the suitcase in the field, since there appeared to be no danger of fire, but upon her return a short time later, she found her suitcase in flames. The Potties lost their house, including out-buildings and chickens, and all their personal belongings.

Alexander MacDonald was fighting the fire in Thibeauville. Returning home, he found his house and outbuildings consumed by flames. Alexander had just butchered four pigs for Allan Touesnard, which were hanging in the shed. The pigs, his poultry and some livestock were destroyed by the fire. The family lost everything. Alexander died a short time after the fire.

Fire on the South Side

While the Thibeauville fire was raging, another fire began on the South Side in Victor Burke's barn. Victor informed me that workmen had just placed the mowing machine and family sled in the barn and they had left the doors open. A spark from the kitchen stove flew into the barn and set the dry hay on fire. (Others reported that the fire was started by a cigarette.)

Fred LeBlanc, who lives a quarter mile from Victor, credits the fire trucks from Port Hawkesbury and St. Peter's for saving his property. High winds from the northwest were blowing cinders onto his property and the firefighters kept putting them out. The Thibeauville fire and the South Side fire burned until they almost met at Richard's Pond. There were no homes lost on the South Side. Amable Burke lost several cords of pulp, however he did not suffer any monetory loss since the pulp company had already paid for the wood.

When sparks from the South Side began to fly across the harbour towards the Church, Fr. Robitaille brought the Blessed Sacrament to LeVesconte's shore. Shortly after, the wind changed direction and the church was safe.

Martha DeRoche recalls the fire very well as her first husband Sam Dugas, who died a year after the fire, used to bring firefighters home to lunch and she brought them numerous baskets of food.

Domestic Fires

Allegedly, the main cause of these fires, which usually happened in the winter, was overheating of stoves and chimneys. Stoves were stoked until the tops were red hot in an attempt to keep the fires burning throughout the night. Insulation was not a serious consideration during construction of these houses. Indeed, men used to boast as to how much firewood they burned during the year. Chimneys were generally placed too close to walls, and exposed chimneys and walls were frequently papered for decoration. Since firefighting equipment was not readily available, most fires resulted in total losses. Chimney fires were a regular occurrence so every home had a ladder on the roof and alongside the house. Salt was often used to kill chimney fires.

Residences Destroyed by Fire

- **John J. (the diver) Sampson's** residence burned to the ground in January of 1942. The simple chimney fire resulted in tragedy. John was bedridden and had to be carried from the house on a mattress. Simon Landry (Simon à Simon), who lived next to Andrew Robertson's in Grand Gulley and whose wife was the former Mary Burke, was visiting Charlie Sampson next door when the fire started. He ran over to offer assistance. The sleigh in which they were to place John did not have a platform, so Simon found one and lifted it upon the sleigh by himself. The lift and excitement proved too much for Simon. Upon their arrival at Charlie's, he dropped dead. John J. Sampson died in June of the same year. His son, Vincent, constructed his new house on the same foundation.

- **Camille Boucher and Pauline Bond's** house, left vacant for several years, was becoming a safety hazard as some children were breaking into the boarded house and smoking. It was burned by the Fire Department in 1981.

- **Willie and Mary (Boudreau) Robertson's** house was burned in 1987 by the Fire Department. It was occupied by John McPhail at the time of the fire.
- **Amable (à Touma) Samson's** house was burned by the Fire Department on November 7, 1968 at 8pm. The Convent was hauled to this property in late November, 1968.
- **Albany (Beni) Samson's** house was burned by the Fire Department.
- **Joe and Elizabeth (Stone) Touesnard's** house, originally built by Sutton Boudreau, accidentally burned. It was occupied by Willie (à Millina) Sampson at the time of the fire.
- **Simon and Katie Landry's** house, located above the Lower End School, burned on February 20, 1972. It was owned by Frank Hamm from Halifax and occupied by Anna Martin at the time of the fire.
- **Obeline Burke's** shed, located below the Senior Citizen's Apartment Complex, burned on May 24, 1990.
- **John** (Charlie R.'s father) **Burke's** house located below Howie Samson's Body Shop, was burned by the Fire Department on September 29, 1987.
- **Jane Bowser's** 1-1/2 story barn was burned by the Fire Department in April, 1987 upon request.
- **Whitney McPhee's** house burned on January 27, 1941 at 10:30am, during high winds and very cold temperatures. Whitney was working in the woods and there was no one around to fight the fire. Their son Stanley was in school at the time. The elderly Frazine Bouchard (Peter Bouchard's wife) and Amable Burke who were living in the house, escaped the fire but the house was completely destroyed.

  Following the fire, the McPhees lived in Amable and Charlotte Burke's old home. Following Amable's death, Nellie and Whitney built a new home.
- **Bernie (Ben) LeBlanc's** barn located close to Paul Samson's on the lower road, a short distance from Willie Boyd's store, burned on October 30, 1982. Arson was suspected.
- **Paul and Bella Samson's** old homestead, located on the sharp turn between Jeffrey Landry's and Willie Boyd's store, burned to the ground on October 31, 1982. It was owned by their daughter Mary Samson, who lived in the Richmond Villa at the time. This was the second building to burn in two days and arson was suspected in both fires.

- **Stella Nelson's** house, located below Aloysis L. Burke's, burned in 1990.
- **William Boyd's** first house burned down one Sunday while the family was at church. They returned to find the house totally consumed in fire and the only thing they could salvage was a crucifix. As William approached the scene he exclaimed *What did I do God?* Mary Emma Digout used to go there to care for Cecilia Boyd when she was a child. A second house burned in 1925.
- **Peter and Jessie (MacIntyre) MacLean's** house in Sporting Mountain was struck by lightening and burned to the ground in 1901. Following the fire they moved to River Bourgeois.
- **Maurice Fougere** burned to death in a fire at his camp on Sporting Mountain Road in 1954.
- **Isiah (Zie) and Lettie Burke's** old house was burned for public safety by the Fire Department on May 3, 1990. It was owned by Ruth Shupe at the time.
- **Marie Richard's** shed, located at Bernie McPhee's in Hawker, burned on April 14, 1984.
- **Charlie Pottie's** 1-1/2 story house and woodshed, which was originally Anselm Samson's Store in the Lower End, burned on July 17, 1989. It was recorded under the name Terrance Pottie at the time of the fire.
- **Albert Richard's** mobile home, located behind Joe McPhee's store, burned on April 13, 1980.
- A cabin on the South Side owned by **Donnie Landry** of Halifax, burned in July, 1983.
- **Jack (John Francis) Madden's** home in Thibeauville burned on April 8, 1961. He died in the fire.
- **Tom Morrison's** barn in Sporting Mountain burned down in July, 1943.

Businesses Destroyed by Fire

- **Lavallee's house/store**, vacant for several years and in poor condition, burned as a result of spontaneous combustion (materials stored in a cardboad box) on August 12, 1991. It was owned by Bill MacLaughlan at the time of the fire.
- **Charlie Pottie's** store burned in the spring of 1974. It was owned by Peter LeBlanc at the time of the fire.

- The **Department of Transportation Garage**, a major complex in St. Peter's, was completely consumed by fire on April 9, 1989.
- The **Richmond Motel**, owned by Elio Mancini of St. Peter's, included 10 units and a large dining room. It burned to the ground in 1979.

River Bourgeois School

One of the early schools burned in August 1887. Suspicion of arson was recorded by Inspector M.J.T. McNeil in his report for the year ending October 31, 1988. See the chapter on *Education* for details.

St. Peter's Church

This church burned on May 9, 1942. The sod-turning for the new church was on May 14, 1952 and the new church opened on May 18, 1953.

L'Ardoise Church

On April 11, 1972, fire completely destroyed **L'Eglise des Sainte-Agnes Gardines**. A new church was completed and blessed in December 1976.

Endnotes

1) Dr. J.W. MacDonald wrote of the early history of Antigonish. His essay of 1876 speaks of the early churches.
2) Bishop Plessis left Quebec on May 20, 1812 for a tour of Cheticamp and surrounding areas.
3) Scientific Services, Halifax, Mr. Frank Amirault.
4) Captain McLeod's memoirs are recounted in *Cape Breton Captain* edited by Roland Caplain, December 1992.
5) Department of Lands and Forest , Shubenacadie, Neil Wilcox, Nov. 18, 1991.
6) Reported by Dr. Madden from Arichat in his correspondance to William Hill, September 10, 1829. PANS, 7/6/78.
7) John Luce to James Turnbull, PANS, 7/5/162.

*** I wish to thank Blair Stone and Raymond Ferguson of the St. Peter's Fire Department for assisting me with information regarding some of the domestic fires reported in this chapter. The St. Peter's Fire Department was established in 1964.

Chapter XII
Sports

Baseball

Baseball was certainly the most important sport in the community. It is difficult to confirm when the game was first played at the River, however photographs provided by Mimi Fougere, dated 1915, show players wearing baseball gloves at that time, and by their wearing apparel, it appears they were members of an organized league (see **Plates 1200 to 1205**). Players included: Charlie Boudreau, John James Fougere, Bill LeBlanc, Joe Digout and Jim Boyd. Other early photos, provided by George Digout, were dated 1931 and 1932 (see **Plates 1206-1207**). These photos were of games played in River Bourgeois and St. Peter's against the Micmac Indians from Barra Head, who always had a strong team.

On August 14, 1991, I interviewed Marshall Bourinot[1] whose family published the Richmond County Record from Arichat, between 1900–1972 and covered every baseball game. He related the following story concerning one of the early River Bourgeois baseball teams.

The President of the Arichat Baseball Association was a Mort Binet, a World War I veteran. He was a close friend of my father, and asked him if he could get the R.B. boys interested in coming to Arichat for a game some time. Now the boys from Arichat had the idea that they had the best team in Cape Breton, so the next time Hervey Boyd came over my father asked, 'Hervey, the Arichat boys want to play you fellows in a baseball game.' Hervey laughed and replied, 'Ok, that's great, we'll come over.' The game was arranged and the R.B. team came into Arichat harbour in a small sailing vessel.

I remember it very clearly. They were big, fine looking men from the River. Arichat had a ball field on High Street. I went up with my father who said, after watching them warm up, 'You know these River boys are pretty damn good', to which I replied, 'Well dad we'll find out today.' There was a Digout fellow, pitcher or catcher, I forget which, he was damn good. The first three men at bat from the River hit home runs. Oh my gee could they play ball. They beat Arichat handily. The River had good teams for a good many years.

Lorenzo Pottie told me that when he was pitching, between 1930–1937 the league included: Barra Head, L'Ardoise, St. Peter's, Louisdale, Arichat, Petit de Grat, Port Hawkesbury and River Bourgeois. Locally there were two teams, one from the Lower End lead by Jim Bouchie, and a team from Cannes

Plate 1200–Jim Boyd

Plate 1201–Joe Digout

Plate 1202–Bill LeBlanc

Plate 1203–Charlie Boudreau

Plate 1204–John James Fougere

Plate 1205–Bill LeBlanc

Plates 1200–1205 courtesy of Mimi Fougere

lead by John Boyd. The teams played against each other for practice but pooled their resources for important games and rarely lost. When the Sydney Steel Kings came to the River for an exhibition game in 1929, the game was played in Tom Morrison's field in Sporting Mountain. The River team beat them soundly.

River Bourgeois hosts Halifax

On July 15, 1932, the Maple Leaf Cardinals from Halifax played River Bourgeois in Thibeauville, about three miles from the Cannes Post Office. Steve Smith and Bob Restin, who later became R.B. residents, were taking

Plate 1206–Courtesy of George Digout

Plate 1207–Courtesy of George Digout

the Halifax team to Sydney for an exhibition game and decided to have a warm-up game with R.B. on their way.

There was a baseball field in River Bourgeois at that time, but nothing compared to Henry Thibeau's lovely field in Thibeauville. With considerable persuasion, he allowed the team to play one game in his field, since the hay crop had already been harvested. According to Leo McPhee, it must have been a "tall order", because no one went through *that* field. There was considerable interest in this game, and the River rallied support for its team.

The game began and one of the Cardinal players made it to first base but in his attempt to steal second, James (at Gommie's) Sampson, who had a tremendous fastball, accidently hit him and broke his jaw. The game continued, with River Bourgeois beating the Cardinals 2–0. The Halifax team wanted to avenge their loss and stayed to play a second game. Once again, with the strong pitching of James Sampson, they were defeated. During this game, James hurt his arm and never pitched effectively again. After the second loss, the Halifax team returned home rather than proceeding to Sydney for their scheduled game.

River players included: Jim Bouchie, Walter Fougere, James Sampson, John Burke, John Landry, Joseph Digout, Cameron Boyd, Wilfred Dugas, and Johnny (at Gommie's) Sampson.

Leo McPhee remembers when the Micmac Indians used to play in Cameron Boyd's field. There was one Micmac with only one arm, Ben Johnson. He was their favourite pitcher. He would catch the ball, toss his glove in the air and then throw the ball. He could really hit the ball as well, and was something to watch.

Formation of Baseball League

During the Second World War, there weren't many men around to play baseball, so it wasn't until 1945, when the veterans returned, that interest in the sport was revived. Steve Smith was interviewed on two occasions and he provided details regarding the formation of the League.

In 1947, Steve and his friend Robert Restin moved to R.B. and established a small woodworking shop. They met with Walter Fougere and Arthur Digout and decided to explore the possibilities of forming a League. One of the major problems related to when the games could be played. Sunday was the logical day to play, however since most of the teams were from Catholic parishes and playing baseball on Sundays was frowned upon, they had a problem. The parish priest in R.B. was Father Pierre Robitaille. He was very well-known and highly respected by the parishioners and clergy. A meeting was arranged with Father and the proposal was put before him. After considerable thought, he gave his approval and remarked, *This would probably be a good medium for the parishioners to get to know each other better.*

With his endorsement, approval from other parish priests was obtained. It was just a matter of mentioning that Father Robitaille had agreed and they followed suite. Armed with support from the clergy and parishioners, the Richmond County Baseball League was formed in the summer of 1948.

Baseball Teams

The River Bourgeois Red Sweaters won a considerable number of Baseball Championships. The first win was recorded by James Mombourquette, a reporter for *The Richmond County Record.*

> *Rockdale, October 3*
>
> *Behind their ace pitcher, Fred Digout, and sparked by Fraser Boyd's timely hitting, River Bourgeois ended the 1948 version of the Richmond County Baseball League by pounding out a 16-8 decision over St. Peter's on their home diamond.*

The St. Peter's team included: Billie MacEwen (1st), Charlie Carter (centre field), Keats Williamson (3rd), Francis Burke (pitcher and 2nd), Lloyd Pottie (left field), Todd Wambolt (catcher), Blair Ross (short stop), Bill Pearo (2nd), and Peter Burke (right field).

River Bourgeois reached the finals with St. Peter's by virtue of a 13-5 victory over the Petit de Grat Red Caps on September 19, 1948 in a game played at the Louisdale diamond (see **Plate 1208**).

ARICHAT, CAPE BRETON, CANADA, OCTOBER 16, 1948

County Baseball Champions

Plate 1208–The River team included: upper row from left to right: Bob Reston (manager), Alfred Burke (2nd), Hervey Boyd (3rd), Mark Landry (pitcher), Peter Boyd (left field), Fred Digout (pitcher), Fraser Boyd (1st), Stanley McPhee (left field).
Lower front left to right: Walter Fougere (catcher), Arthur Digout (short stop), Steve Smith (catcher), John Boyd (coach), Steve Landry (centre field), Gerard Boyd (right field), George Digout (mascot).

Members of the Petit de Grat team included: Adolphe Boudreau (1st), Henry Fortune (3rd), Arthur Boudreau (short stop), Peter Boudreau (left field), Josslyn Landry (centre field), Cletus Boudreau (catcher), Louis Samson (pitcher and short stop), Roy Boudreau (right field), George Jollimore (2nd).

The Richmond County Record trophy was presented to the winners by M.J. Bourinot, honourary guest, and editor of the *Record*. F.A. Thurgood, LLB, President of the League, acted as master of ceremonies during a banquet at the Cosy Corner Restaurant. Walter Fougere received the trophy on behalf of his team. The League included teams from Petit de Grat, St. Peter's, L'Ardoise and River Bourgeois.

Several baseball photos (**Plates 1209–1220**) of River Bourgeois teams and activities have been included in the following pages. They are courtesy of Russell Fougere unless otherwise noted.

Baseball Revived

From 1964–1968, Richmond County Baseball League was basically inoperative, except for the occasional exhibition game. Fr. James Mombourquette from L'Ardoise attempted to revive the League, however the original fields were in poor condition and the teams didn't have any money. In 1969, Gerald Robertson returned to the River and with the support of Jim Boucher and players such as Kenneth Boucher and Bucky Sampson, he decided to work toward reviving the League.

Plate 1209–1949 Team
Front–Earl Landry, Art Digout, John Boyd (coach)
Middle–Steve Smith, Anthony Burke, Gerard Boyd, Steve Landry, Donald Landry
Back–Lawrence Pottie, Fraser Boyd, Walter Fougere, Hervey Boyd, Fred Digout, Stan McPhee

Plate 1210–1950 Team (Courtesy of Maude Burke)
Front–Lawrence Pottie, Steve Landry, Anthony (Tony) Burke, Arthur Digout, Steve Smith (coach), Earl Landry
Back–Stanley McPhee, Gerard Boyd, Hervey Boyd, Fred Digout, John Boyd, Fraser Boyd

Plate 1211–1953 River Bourgeois Tigers
Front–P. Pottie, P. Bourque, L. Pottie, B. MacPhee
Back–S. Smith (coach), J. Boyd, C. Boyd, G. Digout, R. Fougere, C.W. Boyd (manager)

In early 1969, an Executive Committee was formed which included: Royal Bank manager, Bill Smith, from St. Peter's–President; Mimi Fougere–Vice President and Gerald Robertson–Business Manager. Gerald remarked that if it had not been for the untiring efforts of Mimi Fougere and Jim Bouchie and the support and interest of Bill Smith, the League would have been dormant for several more years. During this same year, the RABA (Richmond Amateur Baseball Association) was formed which included teams from Petit de Grat, Louisdale and River Bourgeois. Alderney, D'Escousse, L'Ardoise, River Inhabitants and St. Peter's joined the League in the following years.

Some of the workers who helped organize their own teams included: Richie and Robert Mann from St. Peter's, two of the best players in the league at

Plate 1212–1955 River Bourgeois Tigers (Champs)
Front–A. Burke (batboy), S. Smith (coach), P. Burke, A. Digout (captain), B. MacPhee, R. Fougere
Middle–G. Robertson, G. Samson, C. Boyd, F. Boyd, S. McPhee
Back–P. Pottie, J. Boyd, G. Digout

Plate 1213–1958 River Bourgeois Tigers
Front–Ken Boucher, Irving Burke, Stan Digout, Bucky Sampson, Eddie Fougere
Back–Peter Robertson, Garvie Samson, Leo Sampson, Jim Boucher (coach), Maynard Boyd, George Boyd, Russell Fougere

Plate 1214–1959 R.B. Tigers (Champs)
Front–G. Robertson, G. Samson, J. Boucher (manager), G. Boyd, E. Fougere
Back–B Sampson, P. Robertson, R. Fougere, K. Boucher, M. Boyd, A. Burke

Plate 1215–1961 Champs (Courtesy Garvie Samson)
Gerald Robertson and Garvie Samson show off their championship trophy

Plate 1216–Steve Smith and Charlie Robertson put the score on the board at Tom Morrison's Field in Sporting Mountain. The scoreboard was constructed by Charlie Robertson.

Plate 1217–1965 River Bourgeois Tigers
Front–Maynard Boyd, Norman MacPhee, Charlie (Bucky) Sampson, John Burke, Ken Boucher, Bobby Smith
Back–Lawrence (Bucky) Sampson, Bobby Boucher, Leo King, Louis Digout, Russell Fougere, George Robertson, Patrick Goyetche

Plate 1218–Mixed team from Cannes Front–Stan Digout, Gerry Fougere, Aurthur Digout, Maynard Boyd, Hubert Fougere

Back–Germaine Digout, Mimi Fougere, Eddie Fougere

Plate 1219–1951 R.B. Little Leaguers Front–K. Boucher, D. Richard, B. Smith, P. Robertson, G. Boucher

Back–B. Gordon, E. Fougere, G. Robertson, M. Boyd

Plate 1220–Walter Fougere (r) presenting Jim Bouchie (l) with an autographed baseball on the event of his retirement from coaching.

that time, Melvin Burt from Louisdale who had the backing of the Landry Brothers, and Pat McCarthy, Charlie and Alex King for the Riverdale (Lower River Inhabitants) team.

During the 1970s, there were Government Grants available to construct baseball fields and purchase equipment. All League teams took advantage of this opportunity to improve their facilities. Community interest in the sport rebounded and during the mid-1970s, the calibre of play was as good as it had been in the mid-1950s. Many players from the RABA went on to play ball for high calibre college teams.

Senior Championships

R.B. Tigers won Senior championships in 1948, 1953–55, 1958, 59 & 61. The Tigers name changed to Moosehead Schooners who were champions in 1970.

Richmond All–Stars

The All–Stars won the Nova Scotia Intermediate **C** Championship and went on to win the Maritime Championship in 1961. Teams players included: Gerald Robertson, Bucky Sampson, Garvie Samson and Elmer King from Port Hawkesbury.

Maritime Midget Champions

In 1954, several players from River Bourgeois were selected by Coach John Bourinot of Port Hawkesbury to play on an All–Star Team which comprised of players from Port Hawkesbury, Point Tupper and Mulgrave. Three players from the River Bourgeois Tigers were selected: Russell Fougere (short stop), Gerald Robertson (3rd base) and myself, Garvie Samson (left field and pitcher). Our team, the Port Hawkesbury Hawks, competed and won against Inverness, Sydney Northside Arrows, Halifax Monarchs, Louisville Cubs of New Brunswick and were awarded a win against PEI (by default). The team's success was significant as it was the first time a Cape Breton team had won *The Maritime Midget Baseball Championship*.

On November 19–20, 1982, celebrations were held in Port Hawkesbury at the Sheiling Motor Motel in Port Hastings, and continued for two days in Port Hawkesbury. It was a dual occasion, a Reunion of the 1954 Maritime Midget Baseball Champions and a tribute to the Port Hawkesbury Colonial Hawks, winners of the *1982 Atlantic Bantam B Championship*. Addresses to team members, wives and guests were given by Johnny Bourinot, Billy Joe MacLean (MLA for Inverness South), Freeman Roach (town councillor), and coach Dan Willie MacDonald. The Hawks players and wives were treated like royalty by the Town of Port Hawkesbury as well. For two days, they signed baseballs and autographs at the local shopping centre. Ironically, one of my golfing partners in Dartmouth, Elmer King, was a player with Port Hawkesbury in later years.

The 1954 Midget Championship team is shown in **Plate 1221**. Team members, 28 years later are shown in Plate 1222 while their lovely wives are shown in **Plate 1223**.

Plate 1221–Courtesy of A. Walker

Front (L to R)–Gordie Embree, Pete MacIntyre, Francie McNamara, Robert MacDonald, Gerald Robertson, Darrell Meagher, Jackie MacDonnell.
Back–Coach John Bourinot, Douglas Baker, Arnold Cameron, Francis Kelly, Garvie Samson, Russell Fougere.

Plate 1222–Courtesy of Garvie Samson

(L to R)–Russ Fougere, Peter MacIntyre, Doug Baker, Robert MacDonald, Garvie Samson, John Bourinot, Frank MacNamara, Jack MacDonnell, Arnold Cameron, Darryl Meagher, Gordie Embree.

Plate 1223–Taken by Garvie Samson

Players in Big Four League

Russell Fougere and Georgie Boyd played in the Big 4 Senior Baseball League. Georgie played with the Halifax Cardinals in 1961 and 1962. Russell played with the the Halifax Cardinals in 1962–1963 and with the Dartmouth Indians from 1964–66. Georgie hit some of the longest balls ever seen at the Wanderers Grounds in Halifax. Russell was voted to the League All-Star Team in 1966.

Richmond County Midget All–Star Team

In 1971, an All–Star team was selected from teams in the RABA to play in the *Cape Breton Summer Games*. After winning in Cape Breton, they played and won against Kentville and Antigonish to reach the finals against Halifax. The Richmond team, which had never played a game in competition together before the series, beat Halifax, who had only one loss in 37 previous games, to win the Championship. Team members included: Felix Sampson, Allen Gibson, Gerald Landry, Morris Boudreau, Terry Sampson, James Sampson, Richie Mann, Billie Digout, Robert Robertson, Barry Burke, Lloyd George and Sandy Burns. The team's coach and manager was Stan Pashkoski, assistants Richie Cotton and Guy Boyd and batboy, Jimmie Pashkoski.

Moosehead Schooners were the 1978 Provincial and Atlantic Champions.

Playing Field

When Father Samson became pastor of the parish in 1950, following the death of Father Robitaille in 1949, he immediately realized that the parish was in great need of recreational facilities. Construction of a centrally-located baseball field was a priority.

Whitney and Nellie McPhee were very interested in the welfare of the community and agreed to sell a parcel of land, including a storage shed, to the parish. The land transaction was completed on July 19, 1955. Acreage included a bog and a hill which contained good fill material. James Sampson, my father, who was superintendent with Martell's Construction, negotiated a deal with Jim Martell whereby the parish could have the free use of a bulldozer if they provided an operator and paid the fuel costs. My father operated the machine gratis and within three weeks, the work of pushing the bog aside and filling it with material from the adjacent hill was completed. A Parish baseball field, later to be named *The River Bourgeois Memorial Field*, became a reality.

Equipment for the field and players was purchased by the parish whose revenue was generated through bingos in the Parish Hall. (See **Plate 1224** and **Plate 1225** of the Parish Hall as it was being expanded.) Upon completion of the playing field, another extension was added to the hall to accommodate a kitchen and to increase the seating capacity for bingo games. The CWL provided assistance on numerous occasions and held fundraising events for equipment. With the support of Father Samson and volunteers such as Jim Bouchie, Walter Fougere, Cameron Boyd, John Boyd, Steve Smith, Adrian Burke, Gerard Touesnard, James Richard and Whitney McPhee, baseball prospered and the entire community benefited.

Workers and Coaches

Several individuals made contributions to construct Memorial Field, worked to maintain it, coached, or worked behind the scenes to keep baseball alive throughout the years. These individuals include: Cameron Boyd who took

Plate 1224–Courtesy of Hilda Burke

Plate 1225–Courtesy of Hilda Burke

great pride in preparing the field for games, Rev. Flavien Samson who was instrumental in the construction of the new field, James A. Sampson who constructed it, Marie Boyd, Nellie McPhee, Hilda Burke, Robert Restin and Steve Smith who began the League in 1948, John Boyd, organizers of the RABA, Mimi Fougere, Bill Smith, Gerald Robertson, Glen Gibson, Jim Bouchie, Peter Pottie, Conrad Fougere and Gilbert Bouchie.

1994 Teams

Teams in the RABA include: Petit de Grat, Little Anse, Louisdale, Port Hawkesbury, St. Peter's, Lower River Inhabitants and Inverness. Unfortunately, River Bourgeois has not had a team for the last few years.

Little League

For several years, Bob Pettigrew, John Burke and Bobby Smith used to organize games among the young players. In 1969, the juniors showed interest in getting involved in baseball on an organized level and a Little League was formed. Sylvia Pottie, Conrad Fougere and Stanley McPhee were the leaders in organizing the Little League which began operating the same year, although it wasn't officially registered until 1972. Conrad was involved in the League until 1989. During the last number of years, there weren't enough players to form a team so local players joined the St. Peter's team.

Initially the League included teams from, Petit de Grat, Arichat, D'Escousse, Louisdale and River Bourgeois. Later, teams from St. Peter's, Little Anse, L'Ardoise, Chapel Island and Lower River Inhabitants, joined. Teams categories included Mosquito (8-11 years), Beavers (12–13 years) and Bantam (14–15 years).

Little League Winning Teams

In 1971, before the League was officially registered, River Bourgeois won the Little League Championship. Other winning teams include: Mosquito in

Plate 1226–1983 Richmond Mosquito Champs (Courtesy of Marie and Conrad Fougere)
Front (L to R)–Dennis Pottie, Blaine MacPhail, Mark Fougere (bat boy), Paul King, Mark Burke, Junior Bouchie, Lorne MacPhail.
Middle–M. MacPhee, Trevor Brown, Tony Burke, Billie Bouchie, Tim Allen, Leon Sampson, Kevin Fougere, Charlie Clow
Back–Conrad Fougere, Gus Burke, John Allen

Plate 1227–River Bourgeois Beavers, League Champs (Courtesy of Marie and Conrad Fougere)
Front (L to R)–Russell Burke, Donnie McPhee, Bradley Bouchie, Donnie Gibson, Donnie Sampson, Stephen Burke
Middle–Glen Pottie, Kevin Landry, Mike McPhee, Peter Touesnard, Fraser McPhee, Bruce Boudreau, Rodney Burke, Brian Viscount
Back–Coaches Conrad Fougere, Stanley McPhee and Raymond Doary

1983 (**Plate 1226**), Beaver in 1972 (**Plate 1227**), 1981 and 1987, Bantam in 1983. **Plate 1228** shows the 1989 champs.

Plate 1228–Courtesy of Marie and Conrad Fougere

Little League Coaches

Little League coaches over the years included: Conrad Fougere, Tony, David and Patrick Konning, Leo MacNeil, Charlie Williamson, Sr., Bucky Sampson, John Allen, Gus Burke, René Fougere, Allie Digout, David Digout, Terry Boudreau, Gordie Fougere, Kenneth LeBlanc, Raymond Doary, Stanley McPhee.

Edwin's Field

During the late 1970s, a controversy erupted over children playing at the parish baseball field. Edwin Bona decided to construct a field so all the children could play freely. With assistance from his large family (14 in all) and most of the children in the community, and by wheeling and dealing, he managed to construct a field for softball and lob-ball with dug-outs on property owned by the parish, close to the Tara Lynne Community Centre.

Plate 1229–Courtesy of Ethel Stone

The *Edwin Bona Community Softball Field*, (**Plate 1229**) dedicated on July 26, 1988, although not large enough for baseball, has been a great asset to the children and the community during the last number of years. There is every hope that difficulties surrounding the main baseball field will be resolved soon, as there is a growing number of young players in need of larger facilities to develop their skills such as the youth of earlier generations enjoyed.

Edwin, his wife Mary, and their children, were recognized for outstanding volunteer service to the community in 1988 when Edwin was awarded Air Canada's prestigious *Heart of Gold Award*. Edwin was one of only 12 Canadians to receive the national award for community involvement. The number of complimentary songs and poems written by his children are testimonials of the admiration and respect family and friends had for him. Edwin died in August 1990.

Lob-Ball

Edwin began coaching lob-ball in the late 1970s. Children played in Henry U. Samson's field and John à Willie's field eventually moving to the Edwin Bona Community Softball Field. Upon completion of Edwin's field, local teams were organized which played against other Richmond County teams. Each year, a major tournament is played during *River Bourgeois Heritage Days* during which entries from all over Nova Scotia participate.

Hockey

With the abundance of salt water coves and fresh water ponds, there was never a shortage of ice surfaces when the weather co-operated. After a heavy snowstorm, everyone teamed together to clear a playing surface. The snow around the rink served to stop stray pucks. In the early 1950s, heavy timbers were used to enclose the ice surface. I recall several games played in a rink below Willie Boyd's wharf. Fraser Boyd, a great athlete, was one of the best players. **Plate 1230** shows Walter Fougere in full hockey dress in 1935.

Plate 1230–Courtesy of Russell Fougere

Enclosed Outdoor Rink

Playing hockey on the river and lakes was fun, however it was impossible to organize and schedule games because of the unpredictability of the weather and the uncertainty of suitable ice. Jim Bouchie, who was a thinker and a doer, decided to constructed an outdoor rink which could be flooded and maintained.

He constructed a rink in the lower section of his field beside the roadway with the assistance of Gerard, Kevin and Maynard Boyd and his sons Kenneth and Gilbert. The walls were four feet in height and electric lights were strung across the rink to provide adequate lighting for hockey games, practice and public skating. The rink was close to his workshop where he installed a hot water boiler to provide adequate hot water to flood the ice surface. With such a facility, establishing games was possible and hockey and skating improved considerably. Teams which regularly played at this rink during the 1960–70s included St. Peters, French Cove, Louisdale and Port Hawkesbury. In 1964, an indoor rink was constructed in Port Hawkesbury and hockey at the outdoor rink was reduced considerably until its closure.

Local Players

One of the many players who benefited from this rink was Mike McPhee who made it to the professional ranks. He is featured in the *Personalities* chapter.

Several other players had success in this sport including: Russell Fougere who played with Antigonish Junior, Intermediate and Senior Bulldogs and varsity hockey with N.S. Tech (now TUNS), Georgie (Dr. George) Boyd who played with Dalhousie University, and I played with the Junior Bulldogs for two years while attending St.FX.

Track and Field

There were always track and field meets between the schools in the area. One of the earliest members of the St.FX varsity track and field team was Dr. Murdock Sampson. I was a member as well, however not nearly as fast as Russell Fougere who held the record in the 220-yard dash at the Highland Games which stood for several years. He also had the Nova Scotia Juvenile record in the 100-yard dash and was a silver medalist in the 220-yard dash at the 1957 Maritime Intercollegiate track meet.

Golf

Unfortunately, there weren't any golf courses close to the River until Dundee Golf Course opened nine holes in July of 1977, then expanded to 18 holes in 1983. One of the older gentlemen from the River who plays there several time per week is Anthony Landry. Billy Sampson and Kenneth Bouchie play regularly and now Russell Fougere is caught with the bug. I was fortunate enough to win the Senior Championship at Brightwood in 1993 and was runner-up in 1994.

Tennis

In 1977, Howard and Vivian (Touesnard) Sampson began their grocery business in River Bourgeois. Their son, Blair, began playing tennis at the small tennis courts in front of the main entrance to the school. He didn't have a coach or a mentor, he just seemed to be a natural at the game. He began playing serious tennis out of Port Hawkesbury and with the Nova Scotia Tennis Club out of Halifax. He travelled throughout Canada playing at various competitions including the Canada Summer Games where he did very well.

Blair attended Saint Mary's University in Halifax where he earned a Bachelor of Commerce degree. During two summers, he was the tennis pro at St. George's Tennis Club in Dartmouth and gave lessons at the Burnside Tennis Club in the same city.

Families in sports

With so many athletes from the River, it was inevitable that some of their children would be active in sports. My daughter, Susan Samson, was a competitive swimmer and rower and my son, John Samson, was active in karate, rowing, running and dirt biking.

Russell and Rita Fougere's six children have all been competitive athletes– Marie ran track, competed in figure skating, played ringette and soccer; Walter played baseball, hockey, ran track and cycled; Blaise raced motorcycles, ran track, paddled, played soccer, baseball and hockey and now races jet skis; Claudine played soccer, paddled and cycled; Tina paddled, ran track and played soccer; and their youngest daughter Robin is a competitive swimmer (with the Dartmouth Crusaders for 8 years and now with U.N.B.), competes in track and field, paddles and plays soccer. All have competed at the national level in at least one of their sports.

Mike and Bruce Fougere of Dartmouth, sons of Hubert and Marguerite from the River, are accomplished hockey and lacrosse players. Mike played with Prince Andrew High School when they won the Provincial Championships from 1984–86. He also played lacrosse with Bruce when they represented Nova Scotia in the 1985 Canada Games in Saint John, N.B. Bruce played Pee Wee AA for the Nova Scotia Selects when they represented Nova Scotia at an International Hockey Tournament in Quebec, in 1981. He played AAA Midget with the Halifax MacDonald's and Halifax Junior (A) Lions. Bruce was recruited by Colby College, Waterville, Maine in 1987, where he played varsity hockey and goalie for the lacrosse team.

Brian King, son of Charlie King and the late Florence Goyetche of the River, is a strapping 6 foot-5 inch hockey defenceman. He played with the

Dartmouth Fuel Kids as a junior and with the Dartmouth Moosehead Mounties Senior team when they won the Hardy Cup (Canadian championship). He played with UCCB and is now playing very strong hockey with the Dalhousie Tigers. His older sister, Brenda Lee, was a competitive figure skater while his younger sister, Barbara, was a top level swimmer and volleyball player.

Endnotes

1) Interviewed Marshall Burinot (May 25, 1904–November 25, 1991), and his wife, Ina on August 14, 1991, in Arichat. During the interview, Marshall related stories regarding baseball in Richmond County.

Chapter XIII
Personalities

During my interviews, the names of certain individuals and families were mentioned often, either because of their direct contributions to the community, or because of the prestige they brought to it while pursuing careers in other parts of the country. Selecting individuals to profile wasn't easy, as the community produces so much talent, but in the following paragraphs I profile a few.

Touesnard Sisters

The talented Touesnard sisters, Rhonda (Mrs. Dennis Lanctot), Tara Lynne (deceased) and Krista, are the daughters of Adrian and Tina (Mombourquette). (**Plate 1300**, l to r–Tara Lynne, Rhonda and Krista.) I interviewed Tina and Krista on April 18, 1993; Tina related how her daughters became involved in fiddling, singing and dancing.

Plate 1300–Courtesy of Tina Touesnard

In 1978, Mrs. Winnie Chafe (PhD–Music) held a meeting in Port Hawkesbury to find out if there were any children interested in taking violin lessons. Adrian attended the meeting because Rhonda had expressed an interest in the fiddle. The next day, Tina and Adrian ordered a fiddle from Antigonish and had it sent to the River via Acadian Lines. Immediately, Tara Lynne wanted to play. She would have to wait, however, because she was only six-years-old and Winnie wanted her students to spend a couple of years in school before they enrolled in her course.

Tara Lynne began fiddle classes the next September and Tina drove the two girls to Port Hawkesbury once a week for the next two years. Classes closed in Port Hawkesbury, so the two girls continued their lessons in Sydney. Younger sister, Krista, began to express a keen interest in taking fiddle lessons as well. For the next two years, a family member drove the girls to lessons in Sydney twice a week, since Krista was only six and in a different class from Rhonda and Tara Lynne. Krista caught up to her sisters in another two years and the three girls travelled to Sydney together once a week for the next 8 years.

Plate 1301–Taken by Garvie Samson

The first contest that Rhonda and Tara Lynne entered was at the Pictou Exhibition. The girls had never played *Old Time Music* before so they purchased a sheet music book by Don Messer, selected a waltz, gig and reel, practiced the tunes entirely on their own, and entered the contest. Both girls did extremely well in what was to prove the beginning of their illustrious careers. In addition to their fiddling skills, the girls step-danced and sang. **Plate 1301** shows some of their winnings. I am told there are more packed in boxes.

Accident takes a talented musician

On April 25, 1994, the entire community was shocked with the sudden news of Tara Lynne's death in an automobile accident, on her way to perform on ASN's *Breakfast Television*. The esteem in which the 21-year-old was held by all, was demonstrated by the number of admirers who came to pay their respects during the following two days. St. John the Baptist Church was filled to capacity an hour before her funeral mass began. Under the able direction of Winnie Chafe, 80 fiddlers and musicians came from great distances to play a selection of Tara Lynne's favorite tunes.

Tara Lynne's awards include: 1989 *Atlantic Junior Citizen of the Year*; the 1990 *Terry Fox Humanitarian Award*; 1990 *Phi Delta Kappa International Scholarship Grant*; 1990 and 1991 *Alumni Music Awards* from Acadia University; and the 1991 *Curtis Chipman Award* from Acadia University. She appeared on the YTV program entitled *Canada's Best* as a follow-up to receiving the YTV *Terry Fox Achievement Award* in November, 1990. In 1991, she was awarded a *Cultural Life Award* by the Cultural Federation of Nova Scotia which recognized and honoured her exceptional leadership, commitment and dedication to the cultural life of the province. In June 1992, she won first prize, nationwide, in the traditional category of *Give Me a Song Contest*, sponsored by *Today's Generation Magazine* and Roland Canada. She was also named *Queen of the Fair* at the 1991 Eastern Nova Scotian Exhibition where she won the talent competition.

Among other activities, Tara Lynne was a member of the Nova Scotia Youth Orchestra and the Cape Breton Summertime Revue. River Bourgeois renamed its parish hall *The Tara Lynne Community Centre* during the summer of 1994 in honor of her contribution to the community. At the time of her death, she was pursuing a degree in music at Acadia University in Wolfville, Nova Scotia. She is remembered as a loving, caring person.

Mike McPhee

Mike McPhee was born in Sydney on July 14, 1960 to Stanley and Monique (Bourque) of River Bourgeois. His siblings are: Fraser, Donald, Germaine, Gerald and Veronica. Mike attended the River Bourgeois school and graduated from St. Peter's High School at the top of his class.

He began his illustrious career playing pond hockey at the outdoor rink constructed by Jim Bouchie on the Church Point. When Mike was seven, Edon Carruthers of Port Hawkesbury asked Stanley if Mike could play Atom **A** Hockey in Port Hawkesbury. Later he played with St. Peter's High School and the Strait Pirates, a Junior **B** team. Mike's coach, Scott Grady of St. Peter's, was always very pleased with Mike's performance.

When the Strait Pirates played a tournament in Boston, Mike was scouted by three college teams. He chose RPI (Rensselaer Polytechnical Institute) in Troy, New York, because the college offered an excellent engineering program. In addition to proving himself a high calibre hockey player, Mike graduated in high scholastic standing with a civil engineering degree.

Drafted

Mike was drafted in 1980 by the *Montreal Canadiens* (124th overall, the 8th pick in the 6th round) while he was playing with RPI. He played with their farm team, the Nova Scotia Voyageurs, for two years before joining the parent club. His first Canadiens goal was scored against Andy Moog while he was playing on a line with Guy LeFleur and John Chabot. One of his greatest accomplishments was winning the Stanley Cup in 1986 with the *Montreal Canadiens* where he spent 8 successful seasons. In October 1992, he was traded to the *Minnesota North Stars* and in 1993 the team moved to Dallas, changing its name to the *Dallas Stars*. Mike has continued as a steady, reliable player. He is considered on of the NHL's top defensive forwards. **Plate 1302** shows Mike in his *Stars* uniform with a summary of his hockey career until 1992.

#17

Mike McPhee

position: *left wing*
shoots: *left*
height: *6'1"*
weight: *203*
born: *Sydney, Nova Scotia (July 14, 1960)*

Career Scoring

			Regular Season					Playoffs				
Season	Club	Lge	GP	G	A	Pts	PIM	GP	G	A	Pts	PIM
1980-81	RPI	ECAC	29	28	18	46	22	-	-	-	-	-
1981-82	RPI	ECAC	6	0	3	3	4	-	-	-	-	-
1982-83	Nova Scotia	AHL	42	10	15	25	29	7	1	1	2	14
1983-84	Montreal	NHL	14	5	2	7	41	15	1	0	1	31
	Nova Scotia	AHL	67	22	33	55	101	-	-	-	-	-
1984-85	Montreal	NHL	70	17	22	39	120	12	4	1	5	32
1985-86	Montreal	NHL	70	19	21	40	69	20	3	4	7	45
1986-87	Montreal	NHL	79	18	21	39	58	17	7	2	9	13
1987-88	Montreal	NHL	77	23	20	43	53	11	4	3	7	8
1988-89	Montreal	NHL	73	19	22	41	74	20	4	7	11	30
1989-90	Montreal	NHL	56	23	18	41	47	9	1	1	2	16
1990-91	Montreal	NHL	64	22	21	43	56	13	1	7	8	12
1991-92	Montreal	NHL	78	16	15	31	63	8	1	1	2	4
NHL TOTALS			**581**	**162**	**162**	**324**	**581**	**125**	**26**	**26**	**52**	**191**

Member of the 1986 Stanley Cup Champion Montreal team ... Has three career hat tricks, including one against the North Stars ... A three-time winner of the Habs Jacques-Beauchamp Trophy as the team's unsung hero ... Acquired August 17, 1992 from Montreal in exchange for a fifth-round pick.

Plate 1302–Courtesy of Stanley McPhee

In addition to his successful hockey career, Mike always finds time to support charitable organizations such as the Montreal Children's Hospital, the Danny Gallivan Cystic Fibrosis Golf Tournaments, and the Nova Scotia Special Olympics. Mike married his high school sweetheart, Jane Ann (Hicks) from St. Peter's and they have two children, Adam and Allison.

I had the pleasure of playing several games of golf in Dartmouth with Mike, his brother Fraser and Billy Sampson, at my home course, Brightwood Golf and Country Club. We are proud of the manner in which Mike conducts himself, on and off the ice.

Gordon Gillis

Gordon Gillis moved to Halifax from River Bourgeois in 1959 to begin an apprentice program in cooking. He has been very successful and I consider it noteworthy to record the progress of his career.

1960–62 Cook on *C.G.S. Baffin* in the North Atlantic and Arctic Circle.

1962–76	Chef for the RCMP in Halifax and Toronto.
1976–84	Chef Supervisor at Camp Hill Hospital in Halifax.
1984–present	Executive Chef at Government House in Halifax. He is responsible for preparing and presenting all dishes for the Lieutenant Governor and Dignitaries such as: the Royal Family, the Governor General, and all visiting Lieutenant Governors in Canada.

Awards earned in Culinary Competitions

1979	Gold medal for making a violin from gum paste (icing sugar, cornstarch and water)
1980	Silver medals (2) for dessert and violin made of gum paste
1981	Gold medal for *Last Supper* display made out of shortening
1981	Silver medal and Bronze medals (3) at culinary art shows in Halifax for ice sculptures
1983	Silver medal for centrepiece at Art show
1983	Gold medal and Bronze medals (3) for seafood and two ice sculptures
1986	Passed exam for certification in *Canadian Program for Chefs* (C.C.C.)
1989	Nova Scotia *Chef of the Month* for March
1989	Gold medal for violin made out of gum paste
1989	*Citation Award* from the Clover Group for years of outstanding effort in accelerating the growth and quality of the food service industry
1991	Voted Nova Scotia *Chef of the Year* by his peers
1992	Silver medal in Boston for violin made out of chocolate
1992–93	Received plaques from UNICEF for volunteer work
1993	Designed Pastilage centrepiece for Team Nova Scotia at the Culinary Art Show in Boston

In acknowledgement of his excellent work, Gordon has been awarded honorary memberships in various associations such as the RCMP **O** Division of the Sargeant's Mess in Toronto and named an Associate Member of the Royal Canadian Mounted Police Veterans Association.

Gordon is currently a member of the Nova Scotia Chefs Association, the

Plate 1303–Courtesy of Gordon Gillis

Plate 1304–Courtesy of Gordon Gillis

Maritime Association of Chefs de Cuisine, the Canadian Federation of Chefs de Cuisine and the American Culinary Federation, Inc. **Plate 1303** shows one of his competitive displays and in **Plate 1304**, Gordon meets Princess Ann.

Excellent work, Gordon! You've *cooked up* a great career!

John J. Sampson (1861–1942)

Johnny was the son of Catherine (Langley) and Charles Sampson from the Lower End. His residence burned in 1942 and his son Vincent later built his present house on the same foundation. John died in June of 1942 at the age of 81 years. See **Plate 1305** of Johnny and his wife, Josephine Beranger.

Plate 1305–Courtesy of Vincent Sampson

As a Diver

He was known as *Johnny the Diver* because of the nature of his profession and to distinguish him from several other John Sampsons. He learned his trade from James Sampson (Charlie at Anti Minnie's father), who was also a diver. Johnny worked in Sydney Harbour, Liverpool, N.S., off the coast of Newfoundland and at the St. Peter's Canal, where damaged vessels came to receive temporary repairs. His diving suit, including a steel helmet, gloves, lead-weighted belt, lead-weighted boots, and the vital air pump, were on display at the River Bourgeois Museum last year.

Operating the air pump required skill, an understanding of rope signals and absolute reliability. If the diver didn't receive proper quantities of air, he could be left helpless at the bottom, since he could not surface without help. Charlie Fred Sampson, who had learned his trade while working with the *Foundation Company of Canada* in Halifax, was his reliable attendant for many years. My father, James, operated the pump on occasion. Johnny was a pioneer in using dynamite underwater.

Plate 1306–Taken Garvie Samson

His skill in repairing damaged vessels was well known. One assignment was recognized by the commander of a Russian warship, which had suffered damages to it's hull and sank in Sydney Harbour. Johnny welded a large patch to the damaged hull, allowing the vessel to sail into New York, where it was placed in a dry-dock. Upon its arrival, the Russian commander sent Johnny a *Waltham Watch*, **Plate 1306**. The watch is inscribed as follows: *Little thanks to best diver John G. Sampson, from Commander of Russian Navy, Mgorpenev, Commander R.N.* (The initial G. should have been J.)

Locally, John was always called upon to repair or resurface sunken vessels in the harbour such as the dredge which was grounded in the Lower End in the 1930s and Sam Fougere's boat in Cannes, which suspiciously sank overnight while at anchor close to the shore.

Telephony Company President
John was the first President of the *River Bourgeois Mutual Telephone Company*, founded in 1916. He was a most ardent supporter of the system and served as its President until 1942, when he retired because of illness. He personally laid out the location of all the telephone poles at the River.

Sawer
Johnny operated a cross-cut saw powered by a stationary engine. He went from door-to-door cutting firewood at a minimum cost to residents. Following

his death, Vincent operated the saw for a short time. The last time was in 1943 at the MacDonald Hotel in St. Peter's. The customer paid $1/hour for the equipment while the operator was responsible for transporting the saw-jack and all the labour required to load the jack and remove the sawed wood. Apparently Simon Fougere had the same type of apparatus, except that his engine was mounted on a dedicated wagon. After operating the saw for one year, loading and unloading the heavy motor from the wagon, Vincent understood how his father was injured.

Other equipment
Johnny owned and operated two other pieces of equipment. One was the *stump puller*, the other a set of *jack screws*. The former was widely used during land clearing and construction of the main highway in 1931. The latter was used to raise buildings for the installation of new basement walls.

Juste Francois (Franco) Paté

Franco (**Plate 1307**) was born in Rockdale outside of L'Ardoise. He moved to the U.S.A. where he found employment with the *Stetson Hat Co.* and upon his retirement, he purchased a house in Cannes from Daniel Fougere, across the road from the late John Landry. The house is presently owned by Alex (at Joe P.) Burke. Franco lived many years at the River and made a number of significant contributions before he moved to Rockdale where he lived with one of his brothers, then Jim Taylor for two years before he died.

Plate 1307–Courtesy of Alfred and Maude Burke

Photography
When River Bourgeois residents went to the U.S.A. to find work, they required passport papers with photographs which Franco took. He also photographed families, buildings, vessels and scenes. Unfortunately, trunks filled with glass negatives were discarded when he moved to Rockdale, as they were considered worthless. The late Marie Boyd was fortunate to salvage some of his photographs and they were a real asset in my work. Franco had his own darkroom and developed and enlarged his own film. To make coloured photographs, he placed a piece of cellophane in front of the camera lens.

Innovator
Franco made numerous gadgets, such as weather barometers and a boat

designed especially for hunting birds (see **Plate 1308**). The canoe-shaped boat was propelled by paddlewheels, driven by foot pedals and a chain and sprocket mechanism from a discarded bicycle. The hunter, covered by a tarpaulin which contained openings for visibility and the muzzle barrel, could paddle unsuspectingly within close proximity to a gaggle of ducks, and shoot from very close range.

Plate 1308–Courtesy of Alfred and Maude Burke

Gunsmith, Clocksmith, Taxidermist, Cyclist

Franco repaired guns and clocks and made all his own parts. Anthony Landry, who lived close by, recalls seeing dozens of *flint* guns which Franco was always taking apart and repairing. He had a number of stuffed birds, as he was an avid bird hunter.

Mary Emma Digout recalls Franco visiting them and saying, *By the sounds of your clock, it isn't working properly*. He took the clock off the wall and repaired it on-the-spot. Vincent Richards and Lorenzo Pottie recall Franco's bicycle. It had a huge front wheel where the cranks were attached, and a small rear wheel. The bicycle had solid rubber tires and a steel frame. *It must have weighed 100 pounds. He always kept it in riding condition.*

Nero François Jellico

During his time at the River, Franco's special friend and companion was his huge dog *Nero*. Ada LeVesconte recalls the animal's name because it was so unusual. Franco taught Nero to perform many tricks, one of which was ringing the Angelus by tugging on a rope attached to a bell in the attic. He constructed a wagon from bicycle wheels and trained the dog to haul wood and hay in the summer. In the winter, he hitched him to a sled. Franco frequently sent Nero to A.J. Boyd's store with a basket and note for small grocery items. Residents recall seeing the dog sitting in a chair, upright like a human with a gun in his paws, posing for a picture. According to Gerard Touesnard, Franco could teach the dog to do anything.

Actor, Composer

Some of Franco's many activities included: composing poetry and songs, acting, dancing and performing skits and plays. Sister Lola Burke recalls going to Franco's performances as a child. *Everyone would sit outdoors where he would entertain them with his own compositions of songs and plays. His home was a real place of entertainment. He was an excellent singer and could dance so effortlessly. One of the young men he taught to sing was Mark Samson who was killed in the Second World War.*

It is because of his songs, which relate to situations and events in the community, that Franco will be best-remembered. Some of his compositions included: *Le Heron de la Prairie*, about a heron that did not migrate and spent the winter in a swamp behind John Landry's house; a song concerning the *Old Age Pension*; another regarding politicians *Constructing a Bridge from the North Side to the Church Point*; and one relating a *Journey to D'Escousse by car*. He composed a number of other songs which I will attempt to record in the near future.

Plate 1309–Taken by Garvie Samson

Some of the individuals who assisted me in gathering the lyrics and melodies of Franco's songs are: Anthony Landry, Lorenzo Pottie, Evelyn Fougere and Gerald and Jim Taylor from L'Ardoise. The Taylors were able to recall some of Franco's songs from 40 years ago, when Franco lived with Jim Taylor before he died. The elderly Jim Taylor is shown in **Plate 1309**.

Amos Thibeau (1904–1992)

Amos (**Plate 1310**) was born in Thibeauville, the son of Peter and Justine (Larade) from Cheticamp. His siblings include: Robbie, Burt, Whitney, Rita, Mary and Rachel. Amos and his wife, Eva Mae, raised two daughters, Shirley and Rose.

I had the privilege of interviewing Eva Mae (Burke) and Amos Thibeau on two separate occasions. During the first interview in January 1990, Amos was 86 and bedridden as a result of a fall he took while repairing siding on his summer home in River Bourgeois. I interviewed Mae and Amos again in February 1991, at the Acadia Square Lodge in Halifax. Amos was having difficulty with his left shoulder, but stilled managed to play fiddle as smoothly as he always did.

Plate 1310–Courtesy of Starrla Thorne

Amos began playing fiddle at the age of nine and was playing at dances one year later. He always used steel strings and tuned the "G" string to any key desired, a system called the *scotch base*. He also played the accordion. His father, Peter, and his brothers all played fiddle.

When Amos was working in Halifax during the Depression, he played for dances on a regular basis. There was a dance almost every night and step-dancing on Sundays. He recalled that people of every race and colour attended and everyone had a great time. In the early 1930s, he earned his living playing at dances. At that time, a clean room in Halifax rented for $1.50 per week and 25 cents could buy a good hot meal anywhere. On Sundays, he would earn $3 and during the week from $2–$3 per evening. Since the hourly wage was 25 cent/hour, this was a lot of money.

Amos and Hank Snow

In 1933, Amos had the opportunity to play fiddle for Hank Snow while Hank was on tour in Halifax, and the two became very good friends. Hank asked Amos to leave Halifax and become one of his musicians, but Amos did not want to move away from the city.

Hank never forgot him and sent Amos and Mae congratulation on their 50th wedding anniversary. In his congratulatory letter, Hank referred to their playing together in the *starvation years* and considered Amos to be equal to musicians such as Don Messer and Ned Landry. In the mid-1980s Amos met Hank in Sydney and they had a great time talking about the good old days. Hank, as usual, was very nice and they had a very enjoyable evening reminiscent about the old days.

Marie Boyd

Marie Anastasia Boyd (Nov. 3, 1903–December 15, 1989), daughter of William S. and Annie (Hureau), devoted her entire lifetime to teaching, organizing and participating in community activities.

Plate 1311–Courtesy of Russell Fougere

Marie (**Plate 1311**) earned her Teacher's Licence from the Provincial Normal College in Truro in 1922 and taught school until 1940, when she had to resign because of poor eyesight. However this impediment did not prevent her from tutoring high school students, who surely would not have made the grade without her assistance.

Her benevolence of time, money and energy was well known and appreciated, particularly by the service personnel during the Second World War. Knowing of the terrible conditions in which troops found themselves, many of whom were barely 18 years of age and away from home for the first time, Marie organized community groups to collect and pack *Care Packages*, which were mailed Overseas. She kept the service personnel informed as to community events by publishing a monthly newsletter. The first edition in 1942 was called the *Bourgeois Bulletin*. The name was later changed to the *River Bourgeois Round Up*. In appreciation of her work, she was showered with letters by all who received a gift or read a newsletter. The *Round Up* was discontinued at the end of the War.

In 1954, concerned that the troops who had died were not being properly recognized, she began re-publishing the *Round Up* to raise money for the erection of a cenotaph. The result of her efforts is the Monument erected at the ballfield seen in **Plate 900**. (The community ballfield area was appropriately named, *Memorial Playground*.)

Some of her community contributions included: Chairperson for the C.N.I.B. and collecting door-to-door donations, Chairperson for the March of Dimes, and Chairperson of the local Canadian Red Cross. She was tireless in her efforts to have a Seniors Residential Complex constructed in the community.

Marie spent innumerable years working with the C.W.L. in different capacities including serving as its President. In 1979, she was a recipients of the *Special Service Pin* for her devotion beyond the call of duty.

She was the first female board member, Secretary of the *River Bourgeois*

Mutual Telephone Company and served in this capacities for 20 years.

Her support for community projects, particularly the youth, was evident as she rarely missed a baseball game or any sporting activity. She kept team records for decades, and was one of their most loyal supporters. She also supported organizations such as the 4-H Club, the garden club, and Community Days.

Marie loved her community and realized the importance of recording its history. In this regard, she collected and saved innumerable documents and photos, many of which have been helpful in completing this chronicle. She never forgot the church and made provisions in her Will to have a crest erected showing the date of its establishment. (This crest was designed, constructed and erected by Anselm Sampson following her death).

James Richard, with the community's support, submitted appropriate documentation for her Appointment to the *Order Of Canada* in the early 1970s. His submission was never acknowledged. The community feels she is more than deserving of appropriate recognition.

Sister Ann Samson

I had the pleasure of interviewing Sister Ann on December 11, 1991 at which time she was 100 years, 10 months old. She was very alert with all her faculties. According to Sr. Lola, this lady was incredible, and during our interview in Moncton, she confirmed it.

Sister Ann, daughter to Philomen (Bourque) and Thomas Samson who was a mail courier and servant at LeVesconte's for many years, taught school before entering the religious order and continued to teach for 24 years after, in Arichat. She became ill in Arichat and was transferred to Trois Rivières, Quebec. They told her she could not be cured, but did not mention the cause of her illness (many would like to have this illness and live so long).

Plate 1312–CTaken by Garvie Samson

Her siblings include: Catherine, Sophia, Victoria and Charlie. He mother was a Bourque from the Lake.

Sister Ann (in **Plate 1312**) used to sing in the River Bourgeois Choir. She began composing poetry when her nephew,

Joe Bouchard from St. Catharine's, Ontario, was in the war on the front lines, guarding England from the German bombardments. She used to respond to his letters in verse which he really enjoyed.

Birthday Celebrations
Sister Ann talked about the celebration they had for her 100th birthday in 1991. Everything was very quiet so she said, *This is no way to celebrate a birthday*! and began singing.

She composed many poems which I may record in another book at a later date. I have taken the liberty to include an exerpt of the poem she wrote for Father Samson on September 26, 1991, when she was 100 years and 7 months of age. A truly remarkable lady who is now approaching 104 years young.

In Memory of Father Samson

Dear Father Samson
What did Peter say
When you knocked on his door
Late at night that Thursday

- Peter -

For God's faithful servant
No time is kept here
A knock is sufficient
No worries grow here

- Father -

So I entered and sat
Quite close to the rock
Wondering who would be
The next one to knock

- Peter -

It is a great distance
From worries to bliss
Your compass was steady
Your way could not miss

Now tell me the story
Of your priesthood career
Tedious but fruitful
My signs that appear

- Father -

O dear Lord's doorkeeper
I worked not for show
I'd rather keep silent
Let my past doings go

- Peter -

We have from the River a number of souls
You counselled and formed and escaped the coals
I shall call them to come with palms to greet you
Heaven's door is well-locked, no one can see through

It's to meet my approval
You do not consent
The good ladies of R.B. (River Bourgeois)
Will soon have it sent

- Peter phones -

Good gentle ladies
Would you kindly phone up
Your little master's works
So he can climb up...

Chapter XIV
Social Activities and Handicrafts

The Social Side

Residents of all ages enjoyed a very active social life, which helped develop a strong sense of community along with passing the time. Later generations inherited some of the talents of their forefathers. A few River Bourgeois offspring and their accomplishments are mentioned in this chapter.

Card Games

Playing cards is still one activity enjoyed by many residents. Everyone owns a deck of cards and a cribbage board. Initially forbidden by certain of the clergy, this activity is now a very important one, especially for the elderly who are confined to their homes.

There are stories of serious poker games where the stakes were very high. High stake players included: Joe Kyte, Richard MacDonald and Linda Sampson's father, Wallace Preshang (Linda was married to Lawrence Sampson). According to Linda, during one poker game her father lost his horse. More stories are found in the chapter **Anecdotes**.

Bingo

Bingo was started by Father Samson in the early 1950s as a means of raising money to support community social activities, such as baseball. It continues to be the favourite entertainment for many parishioners who also have an opportunity to socialize at games.

Silent Movies

The earliest movies shown at the River were played at Bissett's last warehouse, next to the Government Wharf, and at the Lower End School which had a large auditorium on the second floor. The school also featured a stage for concerts, plays, public gatherings and fairs. Since the movies did not have sound, a piano player added the sound written for that particular movie which added immensely to the entertainment.

Anthony Landry recalls that Allain Touesnard had a silent movie projector which he used to show movies in Bissett's building. To earn money for the 10-cent admission charge, Anthony sold tickets on a free razor. Victor Gogan, who came to the River from New Brunswick and married Melinda Thibeau, travelled to different areas including Cannes School and The River Grill, showing movies in the late 1940–50s. When Father Samson came to the River in 1950, he purchased a movie projector and showed movies on Friday and Sunday nights in the Parish Hall, located above Whitney McPhee's property.

Radio and TV

Amable Pottie (Cannes), was possibly the first to have a radio in the community. His radio was powered by a battery called a *full-pack*, and carried the *Victor* trademark. Alfred Burke, who later owned the same model, recalls going to Amable's to listen to the radio and especially to hear Amos Thibeau playing with the *Merrymakers*. Sarah Digout recalls other popular radio shows including: *The Gillens, The Shadow, Amos and Andy, Pepper Young's Family, The Road of Happiness, The Happy Gang, Charlie McCarthy* and *The Lone Ranger*. On Church Point, Sarah Digout recalls that Daniel Sampson had one of the earliest radios.

Kitchen Rackets and Musicians

At the turn of the century, these get-togethers which included music, dancing and the occasional bottle of liquor, were not supported by parish priests and many parishioners believed it was a sin to dance except at special occasions such as weddings. Should news of a house party reach the ears of the parish priest, the congregation could expect a sermon from the pulpit the following Sunday.

Thibeau Family

Amos Thibeau played for many dances and house parties, especially in later years when restrictions on parties decreased. He recalls going to D'Escousse to play all night; it was hard work. Sometimes his brother Johnny, who was a very good player, would go along and give him a hand. He played in places such as Cheticamp and St. Peter's where fiddlers such as Carl MacKenzie, a great Scottish Cape Breton fiddler, remarked about his *smooth playing*.

The Thibeaus' were considered to be the premier dancers and musicians in the area, and if anyone was a good dancer, it was remarked that *they had the Thibeau in them*. Old Susie, Charlie's mother, was another Thibeau. She would get up and step-dance when she was almost 100 years old. All of the children were also great dancers.

It appears that the Thibeau musical ability continues to spread from one generation to the next. Billie Sampson, whose mother was Virginia Thibeau, played in a musical group called *Friends of the Family* for 10 years in the Halifax-Dartmouth area. Now his son, Aaron, plays in the famous semi-rock group *ICU*. Billie's brothers Arnold, Gary and Wayne, are fine musicians and Arnold has composed some 100 songs.

Delore Burke is also a decendant of the Thibeau family. Delore and Hilda fostered and supported music in their home on Friday nights in the 1950s. There was always a *jam session* and youngsters such as Billy, Gary and Wayne Sampson, C.J. Richard, Delore's son Irvin, William (Bunter) MacEwen from St. Peter's, and myself used to have wonderful sessions. Hilda (Delore's wife), was always gracious with a huge lunch served at the end of the evening. During the winters, Claude Bourque, Leo Bouchie and Delore used to have *jam sessions* at the post office while awaiting the mail's arrival. Isiah Bourque, Delore's uncle (shown in **Plate 1400**), was always ready to play at a party. He was a wonderful entertainer. Charlie P. Sampson (Minnie's husband), was a lovely singer and dancer, and played the mouth organ. Murdock Sampson, another Thibeau descendent who loved music, had a wonderful time scratching on the fiddle and playing the guitar.

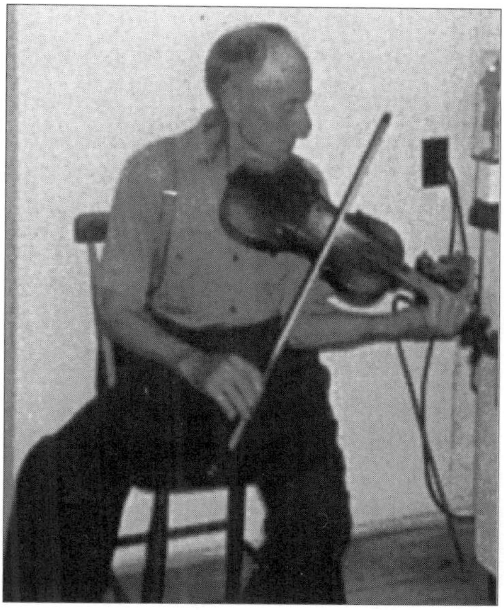

Plate 1400–Courtesy of Maude Burke

Richard Family

The Richard family from the South Side was also very musical, with each playing either the guitar or the fiddle. They included: Isaac, Edward, Gerald, Joseph, Richard and Amable. They played at dances in St. Peter's, Dundee and Black River in the 1940–50s. Raymond Pottie usually played guitar for them.

Others at the River

John P. Burke played the mouth organ and the accordion while Charlie (à Doll) Sampson played the accordion. Alfred Richard plays the accordion and a mean mouth organ; he even made a private tape recording. One of his favourite tunes, *Jerome's Farewell*, was composed by Danny Digout (Josephine Digout's brother), a fisherman who loved to play the mouth organ. Lillian (Robertson) Morrow played the accordion and her son, Carl, played the guitar. Peter (Milton) Pottie, son of Peter (Lorenzo) and Margaret from Cannes, plays the fiddle and accompanies many singers and violinists with his guitar on the program *Cape Breton Ceilidh* aired on Dartmouth Cable TV.

Music Alive and Well

The musical talent emerging in this new generation from children whose parents are originally from the River is astounding. In addition to the famous Touesnard sisters who are featured under *Personalities* and up-and-coming guitarist Ervin Touesnard, the Bonas have a big musical family with eight sons and six daughters. They include choir members Ethel, Joan, and Betty while Wayne is a guitarist and composer of many songs. Louis and Anne Bona, who live in Sackville, have three talented musicians in their family with Louanne singing in local musical groups, and her sister Karen singing in various choirs. I understand they are outstanding vocalists, particularly as a duet. Their brother, Tom, works professionally as a percussionist with various bands throughout the Halifax Dartmouth area. He worked on the recently released CD, *Fire Rooster*. I would be remiss if I didn't mention Russell and Rita Fougere's daughter Tina and my daughter Susan, two talented vocalists.

The *Richmond Fiddlers*, a group of talented musicians which includes several members from River Bourgeois, began playing in 1986 for their own pleasure and for charitable events. They practice weekly at the Bonnie Brae in St. Peter's. Members of this group include: Gordon Coady, Joe MacNeil, Mr. Martell, Marline LeVesconte, Wallace Gillis, Wayne Bona, Harvey McEwan and Ervin Touesnard. Rounding out the group is Estwood Davidson who played with Winston Scottie Fitzgerald for 26 years and at the age of 80 is still one of the premier guitarists in Nova Scotia. His son, Harold, is a fine bass player with a musical group from Halifax. Other local musicians and vocalists include: Michael and Joan Owens, singer and composer Susan Walsh, Robert and Betty Park, Donald MacRae, Henrietta Doary, church organist, and Delore Burke, an all around talent.

Other musicians with roots in the River

In 1988, the Dartmouth group *ICU* which includes Aaron Sampson, David Lee Waugh, Jeff Nearing, Blaine Touesnard, Darryl Gaines and Michael Fougere, won the *Battle of the Bands Contest*, including a recording contract with *A&M Records* and a $25,000 cash prize. Three of the band members have roots in River Bourgeois: Aaron, son of Billie and Beverly Sampson; Blaine, son of Emile and Carol Touesnard, and Michael, son of Hubert and Marguerite Fougere. *ICU* continues to play to audiences throughout the province after releasing their first CD, *Stand On Your Own.*

Amable and Ida Fougere's Family

Amable H. Fougere, his wife Ida, and their eight children lived on Church Point in the early 1960s. Ida was a school teacher and played the piano. Her daughter, Marianne, married to former Dartmouth School Board member and teacher Thomas Rissesco, is a music teacher who plays piano, organ and fiddle. Their son, Anthony, is an accomplished classical violinist.

Although classically trained, Anthony has won numerous fiddling competitions including: the 1992 and 1994 *New Brunswick Fiddling Championships;* first place finishes in competitions at Sackville, New Brunswick, Belle River, Ontario and New Carisle, Quebec. He also placed third in the prestigious *Canadian Open* in Shelburne, Ontario in 1990, the first Nova Scotian since Johnny Mooring to place in the top three. He won the Sackville, N.S. *Down-East Fiddle Competition* on several occasions and has numerous top place finishes at the *Dartmouth Old-Time Fiddling Championships.*

In addition to these accomplishments, he has won vocal competitions such as the Gilbert and Sullivan class in the *Kiwanis Music Festival* three years in a row and was a member of *Nova Scotia Songbook* which represented Canada in Toyama, Japan, where they won top awards. Anthony, who is pursuing a career in music, is currently teaching violin in Halifax and is a member of the band, *Black Pool.*

Anthony Woods

Anthony Woods, son of Dartmouth Alderman John and Barbara Woods and grandson of Charlie and Agnes Sampson from Church Point, is an accomplished violinist. He played with the *Nova Scotia Youth Orchestra* for eight years, *Acadia University Symphony Orchestra, Dalhousie Quartet, Chebucto Orchestra, Symphony Nova Scotia* and the *Dartmouth Senior Strings,* which won a Gold Medal at the *International Music Festival* in London, England. Anthony is pursuing a career in medicine at Dalhousie University in Halifax.

Jim and Valerie Boyd's Family

The family of Valerie (Landry) and the late Jim Boyd is also a very musical one. Their two daughters, Ann Cooke and Sue Boyd are proficient on piano, accordion, organ, flute and several other instruments. Ann and Wally Cooke's children are also very musical. Their eldest son, Peter, was heavily involved with the *John H. Gillis High School Stage Band* in Antigonish on guitar and saxophone, while his younger siblings–Valerie, Susan, Jane and John–are members of the *Antigonish Highland Society Pipe and Drum Band.*

Valerie won the highest amateur award in Nova Scotia piping in 1992, the *Grade I Champion Supreme Award.* She was the Nova Scotia Champion in Grades II, III and IV during the previous three years. She is now Pipe Major of the AHS Band and also plays with the world famous *Halifax Police Pipes and Drums.*

Caledonia Hall

Plate 1401–Courtesy of Hilda Burke

Caledonia Hall, located between Hawker and Louisdale, was constructed in the late-1950s by Anthony Rousseau. It was a very popular place of entertainment especially on Saturday nights. Bands playing there included Joe Murphy and Winston Scottie Fitzgerald; both very popular entertainers in the 1960s. The hall is now operated by the Canadian Legion.

Ice Skating

Ice skating was as popular for the ladies as the men though priests frowned on girls skating with boys. The favourite winter activity was a skating party around a bonfire. When the River had a keen sheet of ice, Friday and Saturday nights were spent outdoors skating and singing around fires made of brush or car tires. Since the opportunity was so great and it was free, one needed but a pair of skates. They were easy to obtain since one of the largest skate manufacturers in the world, *The Starr Manufacturing Co.*, was located in Dartmouth, but times were tough and people had very little cash. Those who

Plate 1402–Courtesy of Hilda Burke

Plate 1403–Courtesy of Hilda Burke

Plate 1404–Courtesy of Deidre Boyd

had a pair of skates shared with others, regardless of the size. It was common to see ladies wearing men's skates; the important thing was to be skating (see **Plate 1401**).

Swimming

Although there was plenty of salt water around, it was always very cold. There were only a few weeks of half-comfortable swimming in the summer, but this did not discourage some of the hardier ones. **Plates 1402** and **1403** show typical early vintage swimming apparel. One of the most famous beaches in the area is located at Point Michaud, below L'Ardoise. The most popular location for swimming and diving off a wharf was at A.J. Boyd's in Cannes (**Plate 1404**).

Weiner Roasts and Clam Boils

During the summer, weiner roasts and clam boils were very popular. In the early-1950s, Sunday evening was the best time to have a get-together. I recall on many occasions bringing musical instruments to River Bourgeois with Billy Sampson and C.J. Richard, to have a sing-along. Uncontaminated clams were available in abundance and supposedly best and healthier during the months which contained the letter "R". Mussels could be found by the ton on the shores. Only the seagulls ate them, if there wasn't any other food.

Weddings

Everyone enjoyed a wedding, especially since it was the only real opportunity to legitimately enjoy a dance. It seems that the cold weather and snow were not an impediment to travelling to weddings outside of River Bourgeois. One gentlemen told me that typically seven or eight men would leave for a wedding in D'Escousse for instance, via Louisdale, a distance of 10 miles. The lead man would have a couple of bottles of rum in his pockets. He would go for a distance, take a swig, then stick the bottle in the snow for the next in line, and so on. The last man had to finish the bottle, no matter what condition he was in. By the time they arrived at their destination, they were ready for a party.

Fun on the Slopes

With the abundance of hills and more than enough adventurous youngsters to test them, sledding has been a very popular sport. Homemade bobsleds, with capacities of up to 10 people, were very popular and a tremendous amount of fun. There was no shortage of artisans to build the sleds as fisherman were skilled in making ribs for boats which were not unlike the curves of the sleigh-runners. The same could be said regarding skis, which were simply boards with one end steamed into a curve and a couple of strings to secure them to ones boots. For those who required ready-made skis, a couple of barrel staves were the answer.

Pie Socials and Bean Suppers

During the early days of education, each community had to financially support its school. Residents generated some income through events such as Pie Socials. For the occasion, girls baked pies or cakes which were placed out for auction. The highest bidder, hopefully a favourite young lad, would have the opportunity to walk the lassie home and share the tasty pie along the way. These Socials were very popular and many resulted in lasting relationships.

Bean Suppers were fundraising events held at the schools and proceeds were used to purchase school supplies and fuel. These events were understandably less exciting than Pie Socials.

River Bourgeois Community Days

Community Days are an annual social event which began in 1978 as a Homecoming. The celebrations held on Labour Day Weekend include: beauty pageants, baseball, lob-ball and softball games, tennis competitions, a parade of floats and a gala concert at closing. Supporters of the event who provide trophies include: the River Bourgeois Credit Union, Eddie's Backhoe Service, Richmond Repairs–Louisdale; Burke Bros., St. Peter's Drug Store, McBouche Tavern and Grill, and Arthur Doary. The event is becoming bigger and better, attracting more visitors every year.

Horse Racing

For the most part, horses were used for farming and were often too heavy and muscular for racing. But, since the mode of transportation was horse and buggy, there were a considerable number of people who used their horses more for transportation than farming. Those who owned these horses showed them with great pride.

Horse races were held on the R.B. harbour, usually from Boyd's Wharf to the Lower End return. Some of the racers included: George H. Bissett and John Henry Jackson from St. Peter's, Henry LeBlanc from the South Side with *Victor*, a horse he had purchased from Alexander O'Donnell, and Amable F. Bourque from Church Point. Gerard Touesnard, who was always fond of animals, recalls one Sunday afternoon's race when Amable Bourque's mare, which had been purchased from a Mr. MacInnis from West Bay, had shown her speed with my father, James, at the reins. The other racers weren't pleased when he won the race handily because he was a novice driver and they considered themselves experts. People used to line the lower road to watch this Sunday afternoon event.

It is interesting to note that one of the local residents was called Gold Dust, although his real name was Willie Sampson. He was a professional horse driver in the U.S.A. and was given the name because he kept his horses so clean and polished.

During harness racing on ice, horses were sometimes fitted with shoe-corks affixed to the normal horse shoe to improve their footing.

Handicrafts

The number of talent people engaged in crafts is varied and extraordinary. Following are some of the most frequently mentioned during my interviews.

Plate 1405–Courtesy of Madeleine Cook

Quilts

Many older residents have been making quilts for years, however with the aging population, there was some fear that this art would be lost. One former residents who has helped revive this activity is Madeleine (Sampson-Beranger) Cook. Madeleine began quilt-making in Halifax 12 years ago and is now providing free lessons at her home. She is more than qualified to teach, as her work has won numerous awards. The quilt shown in Plate 1405, named the *Olympic Quilt*, placed 2nd at *Quilts of the Island* in Sydney. Her quilts have placed in the top four in each of the last four years at the annual competition in Sydney. She won numerous awards at competitions while residing in Halifax. One of her students, Sylvia Allen, recently placed 1st in the Novice category in Sydney.

Charlotte LeBlanc from the South Side, has been making quilts and sewing all her life. She sews extremely fast and makes some very interesting designs.

Woodworking

A considerable number of men have taken up woodworking as a hobby. One of the families which has passed the tradition on is the Richard family. **Plate 1406** shows Charlie Richard and some of his model boats. In

Plate 1406–Courtesy of Fabian Richard

Plate 1407, his son Alfred, who also builds model schooners, is shown with some of his very finely detailed decoys. Alfred is currently teaching George Digout, who is retired at the River, some *tricks of the trade.* Three of Charlie's other sons, Fabian, Clarence and John, have inherited his skills in making fine objects out of wood; their work includes lawn ornaments.

Plate 1407–Taken by Garvie Samson

Ernie Bourque, an accomplished finishing carpenter previously mentioned for his contributions to the church, has constructed 15 fiddles (see **Plate 1408**). He has also constructed sail boats and ice boats such as that shown in **Plate 1401**. Billie Sampson, son of Basil and Virginia, built two violins and two mandolins of very high quality. One mandolin was purchased by Robbie Steiniger, a guitarist with singer Sue Medley.

Plate 1408–Taken by Garvie Samson

Arthur Doary has been mentioned for the varied work he has done for the church in woodwork and stained glass windows. He is also involved in silk screening, crest designs and trophies.

Gordon Gillis fashioned five violins from pastry, one of which is shown with his profile in the **Personalities** chapter. His medal-winning pastry presentations were made hollow, like wooden violins, including the strings (see **Plate 1303**). They are real masterpieces.

Chapter XV
Organizations and Associations

Agricultural Society

One of the first organizations to be formed in the community was the *The River Bourgeois Agriculture Society*. The organization, initiated by Father Pierre Robitaille, PP, was in operation by 1917 and included: Fr. Robitaille, Andrew Robertson, Marcel Digout, William S. Boyd, William Sampson, Emile Touesnard, Joseph Deslaurier, Alex Landry, Henry Bouchie, William Bouchie, J.P. Burke and Albany (Beni) Samson. The intention of the Society was to assist farmers in learning more about improved farm practices, and to obtain financial assistance.

The importance of agriculture and proof of the Society's growth is reflected in a Petition dated 1918 requesting an increase in Government grants to the Society from $15,000 to $20,000 per year. The Society expanded, with its new membership including: J.D. Burke (President), P.D. Beranger, Felix Bona, John Bona, A.R. Bouchie, Freeman Bouchie, Louis Bouchie, Marshall Bouchie, A.J. Boyd, D.D. Boyd, Alex Burke, Amable G. Burke, Amable H. Burke, Cyperein Burke, Mrs. John Burke, John L. Burke, A.A. Fougere, Simon Goyetche, Anselm Landry, William MacDonald, Wm H. Robertson, Alex Sampson, Anselm Sampson, Daniel Sampson, David Sampson, Desiria Sampson, Isaiah Landry, Norman Sampson, Paul Sampson, Paul A. Sampson, Thomas Sampson, and Alex Young.

Because of its large membership and varied personalities, the local Society had a very strong voice. In 1918, for example, members of *The River Bourgeois Agriculture Society* recommended that Agriculture Societies who changed from one breed to another without consulting the Department of Agriculture, should suffer a penalty of losing their claim to shares of the grant for the aid of agriculture. The petition further requested that the Government amend the Act to embody this idea.

Father Robitaille, an expert farmer and strong leader, was of considerable help to local residents during his years as parish priest from 1909–1949 when he died.

Historical Society

The formation of the *Cape Breton Historical Society* was initiated by Father Robitaille in the early 1920s to encourage and support research into the French origins of Cape Breton, and to promote and manifest these origins.

Credit Union

The establishment of the local Credit Union began with the signing of a *Memorandum of Association* on April 27, 1938, with 11 subscribers and 16 shares issued. The subscribers included: Allen Touesnard (farmer), James H. Bourque (poultryman), Sam Fougere (farmer), Clarence Landry (fisherman), Charles LeVesconte (teacher), John L. Landry (farmer), Abraham Beranger (merchant), Peter LeVesconte (collector), Alex P. Bouchie (carpenter), Ernst B. Touesnard (farmer) and James H. Sampson (farmer). Each subscriber had one or two shares except for Peter LeVesconte who had three shares. The signatures were witnessed by A.W. Rankin from St. Peter's who was Agriculture Representative.

The first report from the Supervisory Committee (W.F. Boyd and A. Beranger), dated October 23, 1939, showed dividend earnings of $10.36 for 47 active members. It was suggested that this amount be given to the treasurer to entice him to continue his very important duties in the organization.

During the war years, business was slow, since there was very little money in circulation. Following the war, many service personnel returned home with money to invest. In 1951, members of the community took the initiative to re-organize the Credit Union as a community service since there was no banking institution in the community. Officers participating in the re-organization included: James T. Richard–President; Marie Boyd–Secretary, Nellie McPhee–Treasurer, Walter Fougere–Credit, John Landry and Charlie Fred Sampson on Service Committee and members Alex Bouchie, Mary V. Sampson and Abraham Beranger.

From the early 1950s, the business grew steadily and Marie Boyd was in many ways responsible for much of the growth. She walked from door-to-door collecting deposits from 5 to 25 cents toward accounts. In 1973, the Credit Union purchased A.J. Landry's General Store, located at the corner of Boyd's Lane and the Number 4 Highway. The business now boasts a savings volume of $4-million. Staff includes Mimi Fougere–Manager, an employee of 16 years, Joan (Sampson) Burke–Assistant Manager, and Marilyn Boudreau.

The first Credit Union Office is shown in **Plate 1500** with (l to r) Virginia Burke, Mary Robertson and Ethel Bowser. This building was originally Lamond Landry's house which had been hauled from the South Side. It was used by Joe D. Burke's family while their present house, now owned by Hilda, was being remodelled. At the time the Credit Union purchased the building, it was being used as a barn. Hilda Burke recalled that the preferred business day was Saturday, when residents would make deposits or draw

Pate 1500–Courtesy of Hilda Burke

funds from their accounts. On occasion, *River Bourgeois Mutual Telephone Company* meetings were held in this building.

Catholic Women's League of Canada (C.W.L.)

In 1953, the River Bourgeois C.W.L. Chapter was formed by Rev. George J. MacLean with 52 members. Executive Charter members included: Father Flavian Samson, P.P., Lillian (Mrs. Cameron) Boyd–President, and Evelyn (Mrs. Victor) Burke–Secretary. Individuals serving as president throughout the years include: Lillian Boyd, Evelyn Burke (two terms), Marie Boyd, Stell Bourque, Rita Landry, Thérese Pottie, Deirdre Boyd (two terms), Thérese Digout, Margaret O'Connell and Ann Clow, presently serving her second term. Fr. Bernard MacDonald acts as spiritual director. In 1979, the C.W.L. presented 25-year pins to 16 of its original members and special Service Pins were presented to Hilda Burke, Marie Boyd and Rita Landry. Membership now numbers 100.

Contributions made by the C.W.L. throughout the years include: the church chimes, equipment for early baseball teams, furnishings and appurtances for the old and new church halls and glebes, catechism books, student bursaries, Altar albs and church supplies. Contributions to the social life of the community include: catering for church functions, weddings, and various celebrations. Members play a vital role in humanitarian and religious work such as visiting the sick and providing Christmas baskets to the elderly and shut-ins. They assist the clergy by providing catechism teachers, representatives to recite the rosary at funerals, and lay readers for Sunday service.

The C.W.L. has not limited its assistance to worthy causes within the community;

it reaches out beyond these boundaries to assist organizations such as: the Children's Aid Society, Development and Peace, the Terry Fox Marathon of Hope, Strait/Richmond Hospital, Christmas Daddies, and in 1980, adopting a refugee family. The work and deeds of this Association are truly representative of the nature of the people who reside in the community.

Youth Organization

Between 1945–1947, James T. Richard initiated and acted as the first President of a local Youth Organization. He was supported in this work by Angus Rankin from St. Peter's. Angus was the local Agricultural Representative and, in addition to his own work, taught agriculture at the high schools, judged at fairs, assisted with the organization of community groups, and was a community worker extraordinaire. James recalls the Lower End youth playing baseball on the Island in the late 1940s; they rowed across the river from Jimmy Henry Sampson's. Father Samson initiated the construction of a River Bourgeois ballfield in the early 1950s.

St. Peter's Sea Cadets

This organization was established in 1957 by James T. Richard who was selected as Commanding Officer, a post he held until 1963. Other officers included: Fred Doary (2nd in Command), John Landry, Ernst Digout (French Cove), Fr. Paul MacNeil, Chaplain, and Doctor Digout, Medical Officer. When James retired, Justin MacKenzie was selected Commanding Officer.

Cadets included: Cyril William (Billie) Babin, Bernard Burke, Kenneth Boucher, Everett Doary, Donnie Richard, Peter Robertson, Leo Sampson, Douglas MacDonald, Leo Burke, Linus Sampson (French Cove) and Raymond Landry (L'Ardoise). In total, there were 27 Cadets in the first year.

Leo Sampson recalls that most of the indoor training was done in the old St. Peter's Hall, where they had to practice marching with their sleeves and pants rolled-up, until they achieved some semblance of organization. A target range was set up behind the large hill at Memorial Field. Their rifles were British Enfields' converted to 22 calibres. He never forgot the difficulty ironing his uniform, particularly pressing the seven pleats in the trouser legs, which represented the Seven Seas.

Richmond 4-H

The River Bourgeois Club was established in 1981 by Glenda Sampson who volunteered as General Leader, a position she held for two years. Stella Doutaz is the acting General Leader.

The objective of the Club is to provide students with an opportunity to participate in many of the activities they will become involved in as adults. Selected activities include: woodworking, sewing, food preparation, fisheries, cake decorating, dog obedience, photography, outdoorsman, showmanship, livestock, crafts and heritage collection.

To encourage students to do their best work, there are local, County, and Provincial competitions. Camp Rankin, located in Cape George, provides excellent facilities to hold competitions and meetings.

Junior Achievers

Junior Achievers provides high school students with an opportunity to learn the intricacies of owning and operating their own company. As members of their own company, they are responsible for: selecting officers, preparing shareholder reports, selling shares, selecting and marketing a product, and reporting on all related activities. Each May, they have the option to liquidate the company, continue its operation the next year, or have it operate as a commercial enterprise. Companies compete against each other locally and finalists compete at the Mayflower Mall Trade Show in Sydney.

St. Peter's Junior Achievers, which includes students from River Bourgeois, won top place in Canada during the last two years of competition, which speaks highly for the students and their teachers. In 1993, Amy Touesnard, from the River, won the $1,000 first prize in Canada for her essay, *Free Trade, Is it Opportunity or Nightmare?*

River Bourgeois 50+ Club

This club was formed in March of 1993. The intention of the Club is to involve seniors in various social activities.

The Museum Building, located next to the Tara Lynne Community Centre, has been obtained by the Club and is currently being renovated by seniors. It is expected to be open by Christmas and will serve as an excellent facility for members to congregate, play cards, darts, bingos, knit, and hook rugs.

River Bourgeois Community Services Society

This Society was formed in 1978 to organize and administer financing for the construction of a new Community Hall. The old Parish Hall was a financial burden on the Parish. It was in constant need of repair, posed health problems as septic tanks could not be installed, was expensive to insure, and parking was inadequate and unsafe. Charter members of the Society included: Terry Boudreau, Arthur Doary, Leda Konning, Edwin Bona and Leo Fougere.

A new Community Hall was recommended and constructed in 1978 at a cost of $60,000. Financing was obtained through a variety of Government Grants, and pledges from the parishioners totalling $20,000. The new hall and surrounding facilities are owned by the Community and the Parish rents the facility on a user-fee basis. This greatly reduces the financial burden on the Parish. The initial building was constructed by Leo Fougere and the expansion, which occurred four years later, was completed by Clifford Touesnard.

This Society continues to serve a very important role in the community, acting as an umbrella under which projects such as the museum, the Edwin Bona Ballfield, the professional standard tennis courts, and the funeral home, were undertaken.

Home and School Association

This Association has always played an important role in supporting and assisting the local school teachers in their role as educators, and financially by providing extras not included within the education budget. A few of the many items the Association provided by raising money through bake sales, selling raffle tickets, and bingos, include: tape recorders, computer software, curtains and games. Recently, the Home and School was instrumental in obtaining the school playground equipment, and had it installed at the Community Playground. Henrietta Doary was President of the Association during the last two years.

Chapter XVI
Anecdotes

This chapter contains stories of events which occurred in River Bourgeois and the surrounding area back to the mid-1800s. Some are factual, while others are hearsay. None are intended to be offensive or derogatory.

Cross of Repentance

Plate 1600–Courtesy of Joseph Fougere

Playing cards was one of the most common forms of entertainment, and occasionally religious rules were bent to accommodate a game. During one particular poker game on a Good Friday (at the home of either Jimmy Henry Sampson or Amable Fougere), everyone's cards turned black. Some may suggest that the participants were just seeing things, but something scared these full-grown men enough to make them want to atone for their transgressions.

Shortly after the incident, following consultation with the parish priest, the men decided to erect a cross close to the area of the occurrence. Some of the card players erected a cross on the corner of Amable Fougere's field, where it remained until the 1930s (see background of **Plate 1600**). The cross was constructed of 6-inch x 8-inch wood stock and measured 8-feet in height. It was imbedded in concrete and surrounded by a hexagonal slab of concrete where people often came to pray. The incident was considered serious enough to warrant the priest's blessing of the cross.

Armless Man

Bernard Sampson remembers returning from Abraham Beranger's store when he was little and coming around the turn by Amable Fougere's house, he met a man with only one arm. When he arrived home, he related the story to his mother, who said, *I don't believe there's anyone around here with only one arm.* In truth, Amable had been fitted with a prostate hook in his left arm, however he had died many years before this incident occurred.

Headless Man

Stella Hinds, John P. Burke's step-daughter, relates the story of Charles Sampson walking home from the brook by the old River Bourgeois school wearing oil-clothes. Charlie walked into his house and said *I walked home with a man without a head*. His sister was dying with T.B. so his mother told him not to tell anyone about the man, believing it would bring bad luck. The next day, one of their cousins drowned.

Cascaret Island Logs

Charlie Richard purchased Cascaret Island[1] as a source of firewood and lumber. During the mid-1940s, Charlie and his sons cut a number of logs on the island and placed them close to the shore, in preparation for their conveyance to the River.

One calm Sunday morning, as the Richard family was preparing to leave their South Side home for Mass, Joe Richard from Richard's Pond came racing down the gravel road on his bicycle. He informed Charlie that by the sounds he could hear through the heavy fog, someone was stealing his logs.

Off went the Sunday clothing and onto the tractor and bicycles went the Richards, with Fabian carrying a shotgun. They loaded themselves into the work-boat at Richard's Pond and rowed toward the scene of the crime. Upon their arrival, they were amazed to find all their logs in a boom, ready for the short trip to D'Escousse. On this day, the rustlers would be denied *the fruits of their labour*. Brandishing the shotgun, the Richards were very convincing and without too much fuss, into River Bourgeois steamed the motor boat, with boom in tow, while the Richards shouted directions.

Show and Tell

Parishioners at St. John the Baptist Church were very frugal, particularly so when it came to using woven fabrics such as those contained in flour bags. These bags were used as pillowcases, handkerchiefs, quilting and underclothing. Manufacturer labels and instructions were normally removed by soaking in bleach.

Sunday's church services were generally very well-attended, and it was on such occasions that children often demonstrated their acting and crying abilities. And so it was, at this Sunday morning service, without warning a certain two-year-old lad leapt from his mother's arms and headed toward the altar rail. He was followed in hot pursuit by his mother, whom I understand was of considerable proportions. As she approached her son, he immediately fell to the floor, kicking and screaming to assure he would get everyone's undivided attention. He lay prostrate on the floor, requiring his mother to lean forward to grasp him. In the process, her dress rose appreciably at the rear, fully exposing her undergarments to the curious congregation who were "taking it all in". A roar was heard, particularly from those in the front seats, for what reason the priest never knew, when the label *Robin Hood Brand* and the instructions *OPEN HERE*, were fully exposed.

Fearless Frenchman

There are many tales as to the feats of the modest Hilaire Bourque and his brother Maurice. They included: jumping into and out of apple barrels with their hands held behind their backs, or kicking the ceiling with both feet simultaneously, starting from a standing position.

When Hilaire (c.1878-1967) was a young man, he used to go pogie fishing in the Boston area and frequented the pubs on the weekend. Bernard Sampson, who also fished from the same port, came to visit the same pubs Hilaire did 20 years earlier. Bernard was intrigued when he saw the name *Hilaire Bourque* inscribed on a Life Preserver Ring hanging on the wall, and upon inquiring was advised it was a Frenchman from Nova Scotia.

The bartender recounted the events of a Friday evening while Hilaire was relaxing at this water-side pub after a week on the pogie boat. Apparently a certain burly Irishman, who had more than his share of whisky, questioned the bartender while gesturing toward Hilaire, as to why he allowed children to drink in a man's pub. Hilaire was used to such remarks and normally ignored them, however when the Irishman persisted in questioning his French heritage, it was more than he could tolerate. Before the intimidator knew what had happened, he and his friend were outside, either thrown out the door or the window. Those friends remaining in the pub lay groaning on the floor. The pub's owners had never heard of such a single-handed exhibition and decided to hanging the Life Preserver Ring in his memory.

Treasure in Richard's Pond

The story is told that on one occasion in the early 1800s, the inhabitants of Les Etanges (close to Richard's Pond on the South Side) heard that they were about to be raided. They took all their valuable French coins and artifacts and placed them in a strongbox, then lowered it into Richard's Pond for safekeeping.

Apparently, three boys from D'Escousse heard about the treasure and went to visit Elie Richard, who lived at the Pond. They were well-prepared with quantities of black rum and after many drinks and much persuasion, Elie disclosed the location of the treasure.

Within two weeks, on a damp and foggy night, the threesome rowed to Richard's Pond, set-up a tripod above the strongbox, raised it from the muddy bottom then scampered back to D'Escousse unnoticed. Within the month they left Isle Madame for France, returning several years later lavishing sums of money on elaborate new homes and building a sawmill. Victor Burke recalls the story of Pierre Richard, who had only one leg, going to Richard's Pond with his spear, attempting to find the treasure.

Brickery Treasure

Willie Boudreau (Andrew Boudreau's father), related to Frances Digout's aunt, Mary Young, that he had once seen a strange ship anchored at the Brickery outside of Bury Head. While walking along the shore, he had spoken to a man, a woman, three children, and several crew members from the ship. They told him they had come into the area for shelter from a recent storm, but he was suspicious.

Willie returned to the site several days after their departure and discovered they had excavated a deep hole to unearth a large box. Evidence confirms the story of a hidden treasure. Allegedly, the box contained precious artifacts from a chapel at Louisbourg.

Barn Doors

There are some interesting stories concerning the *miller*[2] family. To say the MacLeans were strong-willed would be an understatement. Following the purchase of a black 1948 Dodge sedan, they decided to construct a garage to protect it from the elements. Time came to install the doors and a heated discussion erupted as to how the doors should be mounted. Stewart wanted a single door which would swing upward, Hector wanted two swinging doors and Jack wanted a sliding door. The dispute was settled in the kitchen one rainy afternoon when Maggie held straws in her hand and each brother selected one. Stewart selected the shortest straw and the vertically-operating door was installed.

Removing the car from the garage was quite an operation. Stewart drove the car while Hector and Jack hoisted the door open.

Articulating Lights

Thibeauville roads were windy; indeed, they were mere *paths for horse and buggies*. The MacLeans owned one of the first vehicles to ply these serpentine roads. Stewart was never happy driving the car at night; he felt the car's headlights should point in the direction of steering to provide better visibility while negotiating the sharp turns. Ironically, car manufacturers later incorporated this feature on some models.

Peanut Farm

Joe DeRoche planted potatoes on a small piece of land he owned at the end of the lane leading to Nick MacPhee's house. During one harvest, Joe came down the road with a load of potatoes that were very small, according to anyone's standards. Joe's brother said, *Where did you get those potatoes, on a Peanut Farm?* The name remains to this date.

The Cast Iron Pot

The Bissetts were very successful merchants and exercised strict discipline on their vessels. Apparently, upon the return of a seven-crewmember vessel from the fishing grounds, one cast iron pot was found missing from the galley.

Following interrogation of each of the crew members, none would claim responsibility for the missing pot, so G.H. Bissett decided to deduct the value of seven cast iron pots from each of the crew member's earnings; a severe penalty intended to discourage any further losses on his vessels.

Short-Lived Winning

In the fall of 1932, when Route 4 construction was being completed, a raffle was held on one of the Clydesdale horses used during construction. Tickets were 25 cents each. Sam Dugas (Martha DeRoche's first husband who died at the age of 50), won the raffle. In the evening, he placed his prize in the stable and gave the horse a large quantity of oats. The next morning, much to Sam's surprise, the horse lay dead in the stable.

Power at City Hall

For several months in 1992, the fair City of Dartmouth was virtually controlled by River Bourgeois Blood. We had, sitting in the Mayor's Chair (when Dr. John Savage decided to run for provincial politics), Deputy Mayor John Woods, son of Clinton and Kay Woods of Halifax. Kay was the daughter of Charlie and Agnes Sampson from Church Point. Holding the purse strings was City Administrator John Burke, whose parents are Charlie and Angela Burke from the North Side. Heading Engineering and Works we have Russell Fougere, whose parents were Cecilia and Warden Walter Fougere from the South Side, and finally Gerald Boyd, Construction Manager in Engineering, whose parents were Donald and Leona Boyd. He is the grandson of D.D. Boyd. Not a bad roster coming from one small community!

Speeding

John P. Burke was a councillor and great orator. He held high profile jobs in various locations and always owned a respectable car. (Being such a huge man, he wasn't inclined to walk great distances.)

On one occasion, he was returning from Sydney in his 1929 *Durant*, with John Henry Thibeau at the wheel. In Irish Cove, John Henry failed to negotiate a turn, went over an embankment, and totalled the car. The pair made their way back to Sydney where John P. purchased a new 1930 Pontiac. Returning to the River, John P. was queried as to the cause of the accident and he exclaimed, *No wonder we went off the road, John Henry was going 25 miles per hour!*

A Short Courtship

Frances Digout recalls when Jane Sampson's mother, Catherine, was married for the second time. Catherine had just finished her latest job as housekeeper for a priest in Main à Dieu, and returned to live with Jane at Church Point. Her first husband had died several years earlier.

Mr. Doyle from Whiteside, who was looking for a wife, appeared at Jane's door early in the week. He had a short conversation with Catherine in the kitchen, while Jane busied herself in another part of the house. Following his departure, Catherine was smiling and Jane asked her mother why. She replied, *I'm getting married next week.*

Jane went over to Ida Bourque's the next day and told them of the good news and asked if Frances, who was then 17-years-old, would be bridesmaid. Frances was delighted, as she could sport her newly purchased coat.

Chewing Tobacco

Alfred Burke remembers going fishing for sculpin with Bill Sampson (at Charles) to get bait for his lobster pots. He used tea leaves wrapped in brown paper to imitate chewing tobacco since a can of twelve plugs cost $1.10 at that time. Now one plug of chewing tobacco costs $3.68, plus tax!

Operation

Dr. Jack MacDonald performed a mastoidectomy on Gerald Boyd as he lay on his kitchen table.

Longevity

- Fred Doary's grandmother, Judic (Ranson) Doary from Janvrin's Harbour, died at the age of 107. At that time, she was one of the oldest people in Cape Breton. Fred and Jeline recall that when they were married at St. Thomas Aquinas Church in Halifax, Judic came for breakfast. She was 104 at that time.

- Suzanne Sampson died at the age of 103 and 10 months.

- Sister Ann Samson, whom I interviewed at the age of 100, is still alive in Moncton, New Brunswick. She is almost 104 years young.

- Joe Bouchard's mother was born on December 8, 1869 and died on December 8, 1969; she was exactly one century old. Arthur Doary, who was also born on December 8, used to celebrate his birthday with her.

Logs Float Truck

During the winter of 1944, David Touesnard was hauling a load of firewood on Lindloff (Hatchery) Lake when suddenly the rear end of the truck broke through the ice and David's passengers, William and Clifford Landry, found themselves staring at the sky. The front wheels of the truck remained on firm ice while the rear of the truck remained afloat by the buoyancy of the logs chained to the truck's platform. A group of 50 people from the River walked down to the lake and towed the truck to safety. Gerard Touesnard hauled the logs to the hatchery by horse and sleigh.

Seaview Poet

Lloyd MacRae, whom Gerard Touesnard confirms was a very funny fellow, was very shy and bashful as a child. At one school concert he ventured on stage, after considerable prodding from his teacher, and recited the following poem[3], believed to be his own composition. *Here I am upon the stage, just a pretty little figure. If the girls don't like me now, they will when I get bigger.*

Gifts Remembered and Special Birthdays

- Martha DeRoche, her mother Tillie Bourque, and Hattie and Tina Burke, were always known for their generosity to the sick and to organizations such as the Scarborough Missions.

- On July 12, 1994, Martha and George DeRoche received a letter and plaque from Allister Marshall, Councillor for the Micmac Indians in Barra Head, thanking them for their generosity in helping the Indians with clothing over a 20-year period, beginning in the 1950s. It was a fitting and timely gift, as my dear godmother was 89 years young on July 15, 1994.

- Residing close to the DeRoche residence, one of the Maritime's finest musicians, Estwood Davidson, celebrated his 80th birthday in 1994.

North East

The most tragic single incident to occur in the community surrounds the sinking of the *North East*[4], a 32-ton fishing schooner, on May 21, 1866. The following is an account of the incident taken from the Parish Registry, dated May 28, 1866, as recorded by Rev. J. Courteau.

Father reports that a burial service was held for Martial Dugas (aged 64 years), husband of Suzanne LeJeune, and of his four children, Isaac (aged 24 years), husband to Marie Bourq, Firman (aged 22 years), Martial (aged 19 years), Simon (aged 14 years), of Henrie McPhee (aged 36 years), married to Sophie Landry and of Donald MacLean. All were drowned in the Strait of Canso close to La Pointe à la Croix, their vessel having capsized under sail.

This information was supplied by Tranquil Digout, the sole survivor who was rescued by another vessel within one-half hour of the shipwreck, on May 21, 1866.

Dr. Joseph and Peter Digout, Marshall Dugas' grandchildren, were told of the tragedy[5] as children. Joe relates that the *North East* was built in R.B. in 1865 and that her captain was Marcel Dugas. She sailed with a compliment of eight men. Logs for the vessel were hauled by an ox called *Northeast*, purchased from a man from Hill's Lake. She capsized during a squall from the northeast on May 21, 1866 and sank close to Creignish at Pointe à la Croix. The vessel was seen by onlookers, including the pastor from Creignish who gave the crew Conditional Absolution.

All crewmen died except Tranquil Digout, who survived by holding on to one of the ship's hatches, until he was rescued by a Glauchester fishing schooner, captained by a Mr. Boye or Buoye. He was put ashore in Port Hawkesbury and walked all the way home, a distance of 30 miles, to convey the devastating news to the families. Henry McPhee, who was married to Suffica (Pierro), was also rescued but died later of exposure.

Endnotes

1) Cascaret Island is located 500 yards south of Richard's Pond, in Lennox Passage, and includes 50 acres of woodland. It was the original home of Jean Baptiste Pertus who moved to South Carolina with his wife where they had a son, John, born in 1843. The family moved to Cascaret Island in the spring of 1844. While on the Island, two more children were born, namely Arthur and Delvina. The family lived on the Island until 1865 when they moved to Poulamond, on Isle Madame. Cascaret Island is presently owned by two Americans. Until recently, the remnants of the original foundations remained visible.

2) Name frequently used in reference to the MacLeans who operated the Carding and Sawmills in Thibeauville.

3) Information from Gerard and Cecile Touesnard.

4) The *North East* is listed as being built in River Bourgeois in 1866 and being a schooner of 32-tons according to John P. Parker, M.B.E., in his book, *Cape Breton Ships and Men*.

5) Dr. Joe's notes were made available to me by his daughter, Claire.

Appendix 1

Lobster Canning

The following operations were included in the canning process:

a) Steaming
b) Cracking
c) Canning
e) Labelling and storage

a) Steaming

Lobsters were placed in a large metal tank or caldron, measuring 4-feet wide, 4-feet high and 8-feet long. The boiler was fitted with a hinged metal lid which was raise by a rope and pulley attached to the ceiling. Each batch of lobsters included two hand-barrels or approximately 150 pounds. The lobsters were cooked in salt water. The huge tank was supported by three brick walls, two and one-half feet in height, built on a concrete slab. Two walls ran parallel to the boiler and one along the back forming the firebox.

When the lobster batch was cooked it was removed from the boiler with the assistance of a large scoop, with a metal hoop, cotton netting and a wooden handle. The lobsters were placed on racks to cool.

Firewood was often collected along the shore and purchased locally. Leo McPhee relates that on one occasion Paddie Burns arrived at the factory, on a Sunday, with a row-boat loaded with firewood. Apparently he did not realize what day it was. Rather than have him return to False Bay with the wood, they decided to stretch the rules and accepted the load.

b) Cracking

This process involved breaking open the claws and tails and discarding the bodies and legs. Robbie Thibeau and Amos Thibeau performed this work for a few years. Amos told me that they had a large flat chopping block upon which the lobster were opened using a large cleaver. The severed parts were carried to a table where a woman removed the meat and place it into baskets. The men yielding the cleavers were called "Crackers."

c) Canning

Lobster meat was packed in cans of one pound and one and one-half pound tins lined with wax paper. Tails were packed on the bottom, white and red meat from the claws was place around the perimeter and tamale was placed on top for decoration. The cans were carefully weighed to assure the customer received the proper amount. The cans were brought to another area of the plant where covers were fitted by hand soldering.

Ned Thibeau soldered the tops on the cans. To speed the process he used two soldering irons. Following soldering, cans were boiled in fresh water for some twenty minutes and allowed to cool. The cover was then punctured to allow steam to escape then re-soldered. By the time the plant closed, sophisticated sealing machines had replaced the soldering irons.

e) Labelling and Storage

Canned lobster was packed in 24-can crates and transported to the Cannery located across the road. Here cans were washed, polished, labelled and packed for shipment to destinations such as Halifax and Boston. On an average day, the factory could produce ten cases of lobster meat.

Cannery

This red building was 50-feet x 30-feet and two and one-half stories in height. The first floor was used for canning and storage and had a pair of double doors facing the processing plant and several windows. The second floor contained sleeping quarters for those who lived in Thibeauville and other remote areas, a kitchen and dining area. The chimney was located at the mid-point on the west side of the building close to the stairs. The third floor had a relatively low ceiling and was mostly used for storage.

Sandwich Spread

In the early 1920s, a new product called Sandwich Spread became popular. It made use of the meat in the small legs along with tamale and roe. Meat from the legs were extracted using a roller device resembling a clothes ringer.

Lobster Prices and Wages

Many source confirm that lobster sold for three cents a pound. John Burke told his son Charlie that he recalled when a one-pound lobster sold for one cent. Lobster prices were low and so were wages, they varied from 10–15 cents per hour when the factory closed in 1928.

Appendix 2

Some Vessels Built in River Bourgeois 1810–1840

Year	Name	Builder/Owner	Tons
1810	Morning Star	Lewis Bouchie	52'- 8",62
1810	Justin	Martin Sampson & Concord Bouchie	
1811	Mary	Micky Burke	41' - 3"
1812		Anselm Landry	

1813		Anselm Landry	
1813	Nancy	Joseph & Peter Bourque	40'- 6"
1814	Dolphin		52'- 0"
1814	Swallow	Built in R. B. by Anselm Landry	
1814	Morning Star		
1814	Two Brothers	Martin & John Samson	
1814		Louis Boudreau	
1815	Dolphin	Louis Bouchie	41'-1" 36
1816	Mary	Micky Burke	
1816	Sophia Landrie	owned by Joseph Bissett	27
1817	Dommitil	Joseph Bouchie	
1818		Anselm Landry	
1818	Lively	Simon Fougere	
1818	Dolphin	Basil Bouchie	
1819		M. Dugat	
1821	Sir James Kempt	John Landris	62'x20'x11'
		(Brigantine 94	
1823	Canso		42'- 8"
1824	Martha		28
1824	Martha		24
1824	Dolphin		52'-0"
1824	Janocsin	Louis Bouchie	42'- 0"

The following were registered in Arichat after 1824

Year	**Name**	**Builder/Owner**	**Tons**
1824		John Samson	
1825		built in R. B. in 1811	
1825		John Landris	
1826	Nancy	Built by Abraham Sampson	
1826	Nancy	Simon Fougere, New owner	
1829	George the Fourth	Built in R. B.,launched May 22	
1830	Polly	Andrew Dugas	
1830	Hope	Andrew & Cypren Landry	
1830	Louise	Built in R. B., July	
1831	Martha	George Edward Bissett	
1832	Margaret	John Sampson	50'- 8"
1832	Hope	John Sampson	
1832	Maria	Abraham, Simon and Fabian Fougere	
1833	Martha	Sale	
1834	Melinda	George Edward Bissett	

Year	Name	Builder/Owner	Tons
1834	NIP	Michael Fougere	52
1834	John Burke	Built and owned by John Burke	
1836		George Henry, Peter Landries	50
1837	Snape	John Francis Wilson, Arichat, owner	37
1837	Celentian	Marsaites & Bastian Dugas	14
1837	Morning Star	Basil & Bernadim Bouchie	15
1838	Charles&Elizabeth	Built by Abraham Fougere	30 tons
1838	Two Brothers	Built/Owned Andrew& Matthew Dugas	19
1839	Gander	Built in R.B. by Peter Bourque	48
1839	Maria	built by Joseph Samson	32
1839	Henrietta	Built in R.B. by George Edward Bissett	18
1840	Flying Fish	Built in R. B., 12 May	20
1840	Maria	Built in R. B., Owners John & Gilbert Bourque	30
1840	Susan	Built in R. B., owner Joseph Bourque	32
1840	Louis Janvrin	Built in R. B., July 6. Also 1830	23
1840	Julique	Built in R. B. by Richard @Placide Dugas	23
1840	Sophia	Maurice, Annie, Lucien, Edward, Peter Bourque	30

CHECK OUT THE FOLLOWING TAKEN FROM CAPE BRETON SHIPS AND MEN

Year	Name	Builder/Owner	Tons
1842	Temperance	I. and W. LeVesconte	16
1843	Mary	Basil Boucher	24
1844	Esperence	C. Landry and others	25
1853	Friend		84
1856	Elizabeth	Basil Boucher	17
1858	Annie	Donald Boyd	25
1859	Adelade	Charlie Landry	18
1859	Charlotte	Fabien Fougere	27
1859	Bright Star	Urban & David Sampson	19
1859	Sophia	Placide & Desire Bourque	19
1861	Philomel		26
1861	Philomene	Placide Dugas	22
1861	Morning Star	Euseleus Boudroit and others	25
1861	Maria	Abraham Fougere/Roderick McKenzie/ Charles McFadden	28
1862	Express	G. H. Bissett	31
1862	Martha	James MacLean	25
1863		James MacLean	28

1865	Elizabeth	William Urquhart	30
1865	Minnie	James McLean	52
1865	Elizabeth	Gilbert Bourque	18
1865	Union	G. H. Bissett	25
1865	Partners	Celestin, Aime and Andrew Dugas	25
1865	Hector	George Walker	35
1866	North East	Marcial and Isiah Dugas Lost May 21 1866 in the Strait of Canso.	32
1866	Two Brothers	William Urquhart	32
1866	G. H. B.	G. H. Bissett	35
1866	Ocean Bell		32
1867	Jenny		24
1867	Julia	Maurice Burke	20
1867	Ajax	Urban/David Sampson, broke up 1903	40
1867	Janie Louise	Henrie Currie	24
1867	Reaper	James R. MacLean Sold to William Boak of Halifax in 1868	25
18??	Whisper	James MacLean Sold to William Burke of Halifax in 1868	27
1867	Siren	Peter Landry	17
1867		K. MacKenzie	20
1870	Angelique	Louis Bouchie	20
1870	Theodore	G.H. Bissett Broke up 1884	20
1870	Eugenie	G.H. Bissett (Lost in Gulf of St. Lawrence Gale of August 24, 1873)	29
1872	Katie B	Peter & Desire Bouchard	35
1875	Neptune	Michael/Charles Boudrot broke up 1906	26
1875	Mary Moulton	Celestin Cordeau & Abraham Fougere Broke up 1894.	27
1875	Lennox	George Edward Bissett	74
1880	C. P. M.	Desire Burke. Burned in Sydney 1914	22
1881	Philomene	Tranquil Digout/Desire Dugas renamed Minnie Pinkey, rebuilt in West Arichat 1905 Abraham LeBlanc, John Pelham Total Loss, 1917	22
1881	Eliza B	Charles Boudrot. Later Charles Ainslie Lost, North Sydney, 1894	42
1883	Lady Fougere	Docite Fougere	11
1883	Lumen Dei	Urban Sampson. Broke up 1910	17

Year	Name	Builder/Owner	Tons
1886	Ellerie	Charles Boudreou	29
	Fanny R C	Peter Boudro	21
1875	Mary Moulton	Célestin Cordeau	26
1883	Lumen Dei	Urbain Sampson	19
1891	Partners	Simon Goyetche	25
	Alpha	Charles Boudreau	41
1892	Alex Fraser	Anselm Sampson	32
	C P M	Alex Bourk	21
1892	Fanny S	Daniel Sampson	28
1893	Stella	A.J. Boyd and F.A. Burke 64'-4′x18'-4"x7'-4"	46
1895	L. Lixie	Charlie Boudreau	56
1896	Lilian Linwood	Charlie Boudreau	66
	Partners	Béni Sampson	25
1899	Annie May	Placide Dugas	11
1903	Tyler	Charlie Bouchie ?? @ Wm. LeVesconte	50 or 60
1905	Minnie A	Anselm Sampson	46
	Quickstep	Isaie Boudreau	12
	Alice May	Béni Sampson	38
1906	Ada Mildred	Abram Bourque (William Levesconte ?	99
1908	Florence	Charles Boudreau	32
	Minnie A	Anselm Sampson	46
1913	Rosie M.B.	Anselm Sampson	75
	Minnie A	A. Landry	46
	Florence B	Charles Boudreau	32
	Mary Jane	Simon Goyetche	33
1900s	Perma	Placide Bouchard (Anthony Landry's grandfather)	
1914	Minnie D	Abraham Bourque	75
1916	Flora M. J.	Charles Boudreau	77
1927	Thora	Wm. LeVesconte 3 H. P. motor, sold	18' -0"

1936 A Cape Islander, built by Charlie Burke and Leo Digout in LeVesconte's workshop, next to the lighthouse. It was 30 feet x 9 feet in dimensions.

1930s Vessel owned by Emile Touesnard. Thomas Clannon cut it in two and added 10 feet to it's length. Work was done at Anselm Sampson's shore.

1935-39 *Sea Sled*. This 18-foot speed boat was built by Leo Digout and Charlie Robertson on the second floor of G.H. Bissett's last standing buildings next, to the Government wharf.

1930s *See You Later* Speed boat built by Jim Bouchie

Acadia Gas and Engine designed and manufactured several types of motors one of which was manufactured specifically for the marine industry. These engines were famous for their reliability and efficiency. **Plate 219** shows a cut-out of such a motor.

Some of the first gasoline-powered boats included the *Thora* owned by William LeVesconte and a boat owned by Joe D. Burke.

The first deisel-powered boat was the *Romana F.* built by Tom Clannon of L'Ardoise and owned by Simon Fougere of Cannes. The boat sank with a load of gravel and was resurfaced by John J. Sampson.

Dredges and Scows

Because of the high vessel traffic prior to the 1920s, it was necessary to maintain clear deep channels to accommodate the deep schooner keels. Steam–operated dredges removed silt and widened the channels particularly in front of frequently used wharves. The excavated material was placed on a barge fitted with openable underside hatches for unloading. Jack LeVesconte frequently watched barges being towed to deep water outside of St. Peter's bay and L'Ardoise. There were two dredges recalled by most older residents, namely the *Quincey* and the *Peppernell.*

The *Quincey*

This dredge remained mired on the mud flat, close by Anselm Sampson's residence in the Lower End, following a Northerly gale. It remained here between 1919–1922 and was the centre of attention because of its great size. Children dove off it and skated around it. Lawrence Sampson recalled hitting his head on the boom. This dredge was equipped with eating and sleeping quarters, it was also infested with rats. In 1927, with the assistance of John J. Sampson, the diver, the vessel was towed to Anselm Sampson and Boyd's wharf for temporary repairs. On it's return to Sydney it sank off Rocky Bay.

The *Peppernell*

Jack LeVesconte recalls this scow vividly as the vessel and its crew remained anchored below his father's house during one winter in the late 1920s. The dredge worked the harbour during the summer. In the fall, the operator dredged a deep hole close by the shore below his father's barn and moored the dredge over it. This location was out of the main channel and protected from heavy Easterly and Southerly gales. In the spring, it was towed to Batiste Burke's workshop on the South Side where repairs were completed.

Abandoned Scow

Many will recall the scow which remained grounded at Pointe à Bouleauo on the South Side for many years. This vessel broke anchor during a heavy Easterly gale and was blown onto the shore where it was left to deteriorate. Peter Landry attempted to purchase the vessel to construct a wharf, however, he was unable to obtain possession of it. (Perhaps because of insurance claims). In the spring of 1973 the remains of the scow were hauled up the shore by John Goyetche of Louisdale and dismantled.

Private Scow

John Sampson, the diver, owned 30 acres of land on the peninsula, known as *The Island*, located directly across the water from his residence. He worked the land with his horse and had a substantial garden and hay field. To gain direct access, he constructed a scow measure 8 feet x 16 feet x 2 feet in depth to transport his horse and farm equipment. He towed the scow by row boat at high tide, when the current was reasonably still. Hay was hauled across the ice by horse and sled. The scow, which was resting on the shore close to Vincent Sampson's, rotted away in the early 1950s.

Appendix 3

MacLean Carding Mill

Hugh MacLean constructed his dam using rocks, timber, earth and a considerable amount of animal and human labour. When filled to capacity, the reservoir measured 50-feet x 300-feet. The mill was built 400-feet downstream to assure an adequate head of water was available during dry spells. Water was carried from the dam to the paddle wheel via a 6-feet x 3-feet deep sluice carved into the bank running parallel to the stream. The last 50-feet of sluice, which was above ground, was constructed of hand–hewn timber and supported by wooden posts.

Water to the overshot wheel was controlled by gates at the dam and at the sluiceway. The wheel measured 10-feet x 5-feet. The drive-shaft entered the building 2-feet below the first floor, turned within large cast iron, babbitt-lined bearings, supported by heavy concrete pillars. Power generated from the wheel was transmitted to the carding equipment by a series of leather belts riding on wooden pulleys and rollers and controlled by a clutch.

Process

Mechanical carding required the use of two machines; a picking machine and a carding machine. When wool arrived at the mill, it was treated with

Lard Oil and soap, to prevent the fibres from breaking, and run through a picking machine which separated the fibres and removed dirt and dust. This machine could also blend different colours of wool. Following this process, wool was fed into the carding machine which pulled the wool onto the carding cylinder by licker-in-rollers. Two iron carding cylinders worked in conjunction with smaller worker and stripper rollers to card the wool. The carding cylinder and rollers were covered with carding cloth, made from strips of leather set with steel teeth. Excess wool built up on the card cloth was removed with hand cards. The last roller on the carding machine was called the dofter. The fleecy web strips that came off the dofter, called cardings or rologs, were ready for spinning. These cardings were approximately 2-feet in length and 1-inch in diameter.

Water Power

A considerable amount of power was required to operate the heavy milling equipment. The large wheel found on the MacLean's mill had the ability to generate a large power output. The following information relating to the Wile Carding Mill in Bridgewater gives one an appreciation of the potential power from a water wheel.

Wheel: 5-1/2 feet wide, 9-feet in diameter

Buckets: 40, 9-inches deep, 6-inches wide at in-take and 4-inches wide at bottom

Flume: 5-feet wide (Capacity 8-inches)

With the flume gates opened at one inch, the wheel turns at approximately 7 revolutions per minute and develops approximately 8/10 h. p. With eight inches of water through the flume, approximately 7 h.p. was developed.

Appendix 4

Outside Employment

During the 1920s and 1930s, there were hard times in the community and jobs were scarce. Fishing was on the decline and the overall economy was in poor condition. Many of the families left for the USA, many landing in New London, Connecticut. Such was the case for the Potties, Burkes, and Dugas. Amable Pottie cooked on dredges, Joseph Amos Bourque, cook, and Amable F. Bourque both worked on the New London. Joseph, Amable's brother, froze when he became separated from the mother ship, while fishing pogie.

Some of our natives lent their skills on projects such as the Windsor-Detroit Tunnel. These included carpenters such as D.A. Sampson, David Sampson, Andrew Boudreau, as foreman on concrete formwork, Austin Burke and James Sampson. The latter individuals poured concrete from a buggy which travelled on a track, delivered concrete, and poured down shoots to the forms for road-beds. Upon completion of the road-bed, concrete was poured around the perimeter of the steel tube and the sections were launched, floated in position, sunk, and joined together to form the tunnel in use today. Cameron Boyd, who was an office worker on the project, was responsible for getting Austin and James their jobs. Others who worked on the famed Welland Canal included: Charles P. Sampson, Eugene Digout, Felix Bona, Jim Bouchie and David Sampson. These men used to board at Elie Boudreau's house, Sam Boudreau's brother.

Within the province but away from home, residents found work at the turn of the century in Marble Mountain, which employed some 750 men, producing dolomite and limestone for the Dominion Steel Company. Mary Emma Digout reported that there were many people working at the mine including her husband Victor. His pay was $1 per day. The Bras d'Or Lime Company was also mining limestone at the same time and several people were working there at the quarry or cutting hardwood for the kilns. At the turn of the century, the Steel Plant in Sydney employed a considerable number of local men.

Employment was found in Cheticamp and Ingonish during the early and dangerous stage of constructing the Cabot Trail. Among these men were David Sampson, my grandfather, who was a master carpenter and skilled at constructing bridges using wood pegs, Jim Bouchie, Walter Bouchie and Charlie Burke. David Touesnard and James A. Sampson, my father, owned dump trucks and worked from Cheticamp in 1936 and 1937. When they were barely teenagers, Charlie Robertson and James A. Sampson worked on the Mount Carmel farm in Antigonish. James delivered milk to St.FX University and Mount St.Bernard in 1925. Father Edward Robitaille, Fr. Peter's brother, was a priest in Antigonish at that time. They travelled to Antigonish on the freight train.

Appendix 5

On the oath of J. Luce Esq.—This Indenture made and entered into this nineteenth day of May in the year of our Lord one thousand eight hundred and thirty, Between, John Peter Landrie, Belony Landrie, John Sampson, Basil Bouchie, Peter Bourque, Simon Landry, Joseph Bourque, Louis Bouchie, Peter Bouchie, John Bourque, Andrew Dougat and Anselm Landrie all of River Bourgeois, in the County of Cape Breton and Province of Nova Scotia, Yeoman of the one part and the Reverend Joseph Narcife Trudel of L'Ardoise in the County and Province aforesaid, clerk and missionary priest of the parish of Saint John Baptiste at the River Bourgoise and Basil Bouchie of the River Bourgoise aforesaid church. Members of the said Parish of Saint John Baptiste for and on behalf of the Holy Roman Catholic Church of the said parish of Saint John Baptiste of the other part.

Witness that for and in consideration of the sum of three pounds of lawful money of the Province of Nova Scotia to them in hand well and truly paid by them the said John Narcife Trudel, John Landrie, John Bourque and Basil Bouchie at hand before the ??? in delivery of those present the receipt whereof is hereby acknowledged they the said (above wardens repeated) have and each of them Hath granted, bargained, sold, conveyed and confirmed and by these present, doth grant bargain, release and convey unto said Joseph Narcife Trudel, John Landrie, John Bourque, Basil Bouchie and their successors in office respectively as Missionary Priest and church wardens of the Roman Catholic Church thereof:

All that certain tract, lot of land, situated, lying and being at River Bourgoise aforesaid, being butted and bounded as follow, that is to say; beginning at a stake and stones at the east side of a small peninsula lying on the South side of the eastern arm of the River Bourgeois aforesaid thence by the magnetic north seventy degrees west one chain and fifteen links, Thence south twenty degrees west eighteen chains more or less to the northern corner boundary of a tract owned by Joseph Bourque, thence south seventy degrees east four chains and ninety links, thence north twenty degrees east twelve chains more or less to the shore at the return of a cove on the South side of the eastern arm of the River Bourgois aforesaid, thence northerly along shore to place of commencement.

The last paragraph of the indenture reads:

I, J. Luce, received on this day of the date of the within written indenture from the therein named Reverend Joseph Narcife Trudel, Missionary Priest of the Parish of Saint John Baptiste and messrs John Landrie, John Bourque and Basil Bouchie, wardens of the same, the sum of three pounds currency being in full consideration, money therein mentioned to be paid to us.

Signatures of wardens, marked by X's
Witness, George E. Bissett, signed J. Luce

Appendix 6

Church Modifications and Alterations

During the period 1903–1909, significant alterations were made to the church to increase its seating capacity. Modifications were made in modules to conform to the original architecture. The following is a summary of the work undertaken during that time, and in the years following.

Exterior

1) The length of the church was increased by 10 feet toward the belfry to its present 88 feet. The width remaining the same at 46 feet. Side wall heights were increased by 48 inches and the roof height at peak by 9 feet, 6 inches.
2) The steeple and belfry were increased in height.
3) Extended the vestry by 12 feet to 38 feet while its width remained unchanged at 26 feet. Ephrem Boudreau suggests this work was done in 1928.
4) New taller window units were installed in the church and the number of glass panes was reduced from 41 to 9 per unit.
5) A new porch was added to the south side of the church to access the crawl space and cistern.
6) Pilasters were added at the exterior of the church between the window sections and at the corners for stability.
7) Gutters and down-spouts were installed to channel water to the cistern.
8) A new chimney was constructed between the church and the vestry.
9) A basement area was excavated under the vestry to accommodate a new steam furnace.

Interior:

1) Installed cathedral ceiling.
2) Installed pulpit, balcony, crescent window above the altar and a circular window over main entrance at the balcony.
3) Constructed side altars and seats for the altar boys.
4) Increased the size of entrance lobby to 4 feet, 6 inches x 12 feet, 6 inches.
5) Redecorated the entire church.
6) Installed new communion rails and steps. (The old communion rails were purchased by William LeVesconte who installed them in his new house between 1903 and 1904.)

1917–1918

Interior renovations by Mr. Marcus from Quebec; Rev. Robitaille's home town.

1938

Refinishing and painting by parishioners.

1951

Sam Burke and Nick McPhee reshingled the church roof. The old wooden shingles were replaced with asphalt shingles. Numerous one-inch thick defective boards were replaced by materials obtained from Allen Touesnard, who had purchased and dismantled buildings at the Mindimar Mine operation in Sterling Mines.

1954

1) Construction of new Rectory.
2) Installed new concrete steps at the entrance of the church.
3) Erected large wooden cross and statues at the highest point of the cemetery, including lighting.
4) Sub-division of vestry, installed altar and confessionals.
5) Installated electric chimes in 1953.

1955

In August, Hurricane Hazel blew off the steeple. It was reinstalled after reducing its height.

1967

1) Installed exterior siding and removed pilasters.

2) Altar modifications and removal of pulpit.

3) Renewed chimney.

4) Extended the vestry at the entrance, installed new concrete foundation and enlarged the basement.

5) Installed a new hot air furnace.

1989

1) Installed new ladders to attic.

2) Replaced 55-inch diameter wheel at bell mechanism (see **Plate 300**) and reinforced the deteriorated bell supports. This work was completed by Anselm Sampson.

1990-1991, Main Church

1) Replaced rubble stone foundations under exterior walls and pilasters with poured concrete.

2) Installed new entrance porch and steps and refurbished storm windows.

3) Erected a new steeple on September 18, 1991.

Vestry

1) Realigned the exterior walls, installated a new roof and ceiling, and relocated washroom to the porch.

2) Constructed a new entrance to the vestry basement measuring 7 feet, 6 inches x 9 feet. This work was completed by Leo Fougere with the assistance of Gordie, John and Andrew Fougere.